Celebrating Forty Years of *Faith in the City*

— EDITED BY —

TERRY DRUMMOND & JOSEPH FORDE

Sacristy Press

Sacristy Press
PO Box 612, Durham, DH1 9HT

www.sacristy.co.uk

First published in 2025 by Sacristy Press, Durham

Copyright © Sacristy Press 2025
The moral rights of the author have been asserted.

All rights reserved, no part of this publication may be reproduced or transmitted in any form or by any means, electronic, mechanical photocopying, documentary, film or in any other format without prior written permission of the publisher.

Scripture quotations, unless otherwise stated, are from the New Revised Standard Version Bible: Anglicized Edition, copyright © 1989, 1995 National Council of the Churches of Christ in the United States of America. Used by permission. All rights reserved worldwide.

Every reasonable effort has been made to trace the copyright holders of material reproduced in this book, but if any have been inadvertently overlooked the publisher would be glad to hear from them.

Sacristy Limited, registered in England & Wales, number 7565667

British Library Cataloguing-in-Publication Data
A catalogue record for the book is available from the British Library

ISBN 978-1-78959-394-5

Contents

Contributors v
Introduction *(Terry Drummond and Joseph Forde)* 1

Part 1. Historical background 5
Chapter 1. *Faith in the City*: Historical background
    (Andrew Bradstock) 7

Part 2. Personal reflections. 27
Chapter 2. *Faith in the City*: Forty years on *(Alan Billings)* 29
Chapter 3. Urban ministry, liberation, and *Faith in the City*
    (Ian K. Duffield) 52
Chapter 4. *Faith in the City*: A Personal Perspective *(David Walker)*. 75

Part 3. Urban mission and ministry 97
Chapter 5. Liverpool: Urban mission and ministry
    (John Perumbalath) 99
Chapter 6. Urban mission and ministry: The challenge for the
    Church of England *(Terry Drummond)* 116
Chapter 7. Paradoxes of the parochial: The urban parish and a
    new, progressive political theology *(Susan Lucas)* 141
Chapter 8. More than bread—More than words: Good news on
    our estates *(Sophie Valentine Cowan)* 164
Chapter 9. "Building a People of Power": Community organizing
    and parish mission in East London
    (Angus Ritchie and Averil Pooten Watan) 181

Part 4. Contemporary challenges 209
Chapter 10. Church, State and welfare in England today
    (Joseph Forde) 211

Chapter 11. Whose side is the Church on? Dialogue with the
    Catholic Social Thought tradition *(Jenny Sinclair)* 234
Chapter 12. Drawing together the themes
    (Terry Drummond and Joseph Forde) 265

Suggestions for further reading............................. 268

Contributors

Alan Billings was the Police and Crime Commissioner for South Yorkshire 2010-24. He has degrees from Cambridge and Leicester universities and a doctorate from the New York Theological Seminary and was also at various times a parish priest in Sheffield; Vice Principal of Ripon College, Cuddesdon, Oxford; Principal of the West Midlands Ministerial Training Course and Acting Principal of the Queen's College, Birmingham; and Director of the Centre for Ethics and Religion, Lancaster University. He is a former Deputy Leader of Sheffield City Council and a board member of the Youth Justice Board for England and Wales and the England Committee of the Big Lottery Fund. He is a former contributor to *Thought for the Day* on BBC Radio 4 and the author of a number of books, including *Secular Lives, Sacred Hearts: The Role of the Church in a Time of No Religion* (London: SPCK, 2004); *God and Community Cohesion: Help or Hindrance?* (London: SPCK, 2009); and *Lost Church: Why We Must Find It Again* (London: SPCK, 2013).

Andrew Bradstock has been researching, teaching and writing about the relationship between faith, politics and social engagement for more than 40 years. After gaining degrees in Theology, Politics and Church History from the universities of Bristol, Kent and Otago, he lectured at colleges of higher education in Southampton and Winchester, and served as national Secretary for Church and Society with the United Reformed Church and Co-Director of the Centre for Faith in Society at the Von Hügel Institute, St Edmund's College, Cambridge. From 2009 to 2013, he was inaugural Howard Paterson Professor of Theology and Public Issues at the University of Otago, where he established New Zealand's first Centre for Theology and Public Issues. He was elected a Fellow of the Royal Historical Society (FRHistS) in 2013, and is an emeritus professor at the University of Winchester. His latest book is the authorized biography of

Bishop David Sheppard, a key driver of the *Faith in the City* report—*David Sheppard: Batting for the Poor* (London: SPCK, 2019).

Sophie Valentine Cowan is from Corby in Northamptonshire. Having trained for ordination at Wycliffe Hall, Oxford, she served her curacy in Desborough (Anglican–Methodist LEP), Dingley, Brampton Ash and Braybrooke in the Peterborough Diocese, and is now a parish priest in Ipswich. Having grown up and lived most of her life on estates, Sophie is aware of the many challenges faced by those living in economically deprived areas, and the prejudices that are often projected on people from such communities. Sophie is a PhD candidate at the University of Wales Trinity St David, researching estate churches and writing from a working-class, feminist perspective.

Terry Drummond was commissioned a Church Army Evangelist by Archbishop Michael Ramsey in 1972. Since then, his ministry has focused on linking the local church to the wider community. It has included work on a housing estate, a ministry with the street homeless, and nine years with lead responsibility for non-residential social work and policy development for the Church Army. While in this post, he gave evidence to the *Faith in the City* commissioners and was responsible for drafting the Church Army's response. This was followed by a 15-month secondment to the government's Inner Cities Unit, working on behalf of the Church of England and arranged as a response to the publication of *Faith in the City*. Subsequently, he spent 15 years working with local churches in the London Borough of Croydon. Between 2005 and 2015, he was bishop's chaplain to the Rt Revd Tom Butler in Southwark, and later bishop's advisor on urban and public policy to the Rt Revd Christopher Chessun in Southwark. In 2016, he was ordained a distinctive deacon by Bishop Christopher. He will shortly be submitting a PhD thesis to the University of Manchester on "Urban Mission and Ministry in the Church of England after the report *Mission-Shaped Church*".

Ian K. Duffield is an Anglican priest who spent most of his 40 years in parish ministry in urban Sheffield, including 17 years on council estates on the Manor and in Southey. In the diocese, he chaired the response to *Faith in the City* and the diocesan Church Urban Fund Panel that considered parish projects and was deputy chair of the Faith in the City Committee. For the last 40 years, since gaining his Doctor of Ministry, Ian has been a member of academic staff at the Urban Theology Unit/Union, running its Urban Ministry course, supervising postgraduate students, editing course materials such as *Contextual Analysis*, and being Director of Research since 1997. He has essays in *Faithfulness in the City*; *Bible and Practice* (British Liberation Theology 5); and *The Servant of God in Practice* (Practice Interpretation 5). Ian contributes sermons for *The Expository Times* and to *Theology*'s "Difficult Texts" series.

Joseph Forde is Honorary Research Fellow in Historical Theology at the Urban Theology Union, Sheffield. After working for 26 years in NHS management, he was awarded a PhD in Theology from the University of Manchester, having previously gained degrees in History from the universities of Lancaster (BA Hons) and Sheffield (MA), and in Human Resource Management (MA) from the University of Huddersfield. He is a Fellow of the Chartered Institute of Personnel and Development. Since taking early retirement in 2014, he has been chair of Sheffield's Church Action on Poverty Group. He researches and writes about welfare and Christianity, and has a particular interest in the contribution that the British churches have made to welfare provision since the middle of the nineteenth century, including their influence on shaping government policy on welfare. He is the author of *Before and Beyond the 'Big Society': John Milbank and the Church of England's Approach to Welfare* (Cambridge: James Clarke & Co., 2022).

Susan Lucas has served in urban parishes in the dioceses of Chelmsford and Liverpool and became the Archdeacon of Southend in February 2025. She was ordained in 2008. Prior to ordination she worked in education and examining, and came to theology from graduate work in philosophy, with her PhD studies focused on the philosophy of Wittgenstein. More recently, she has edited a book on mission in the Catholic tradition of the Church of England, *God's Church in the World: The Gift of Catholic Mission* (Norwich: Canterbury Press, 2020), and contributed a chapter to *Theology Transforming Society: Revisiting Anglican Social Theology*, edited by Stephen Spencer (London: SCM Press, 2017). She has also contributed papers to the Centre for Applied Philosophy and Ethics at the University of Brighton and the Centre for Newman Studies at University College, Dublin, and a "Temple Tract" on William Temple and Hannah Arendt, published online by the William Temple Foundation. She is committed both to supporting those in active ministry at the grassroots, and to reflecting and writing on some of the theoretical and theological issues this raises.

Before retiring in January 2025, the Revd Dr **John Perumbalath** had served as Bishop of Liverpool since 2023. He has a PhD in Hermeneutics from King's College London. He moved to the UK in 2001 and served at Beckenham St George's as Associate Rector, at Rosherville St Mark's as Priest-in-Charge/Team Vicar and at Northfleet All Saints (all in the Diocese of Rochester) as Vicar. He was the chair of North Kent Council for Inter-faith Relations from 2008 to 2013, during which time he was also the Diocese of Rochester's Urban Adviser and Link Officer for the Church Urban Fund. He was collated as Archdeacon of Barking on 15 September 2013 with the oversight of the Anglican churches in the London boroughs of Barking & Dagenham and Havering. During this time, he also served as the chair of the Church of England's Committee for Minority Ethnic Anglican Concerns (CMEAC), chair of the London Churches Refugee Network, and as a member of the Mission and Public Affairs Council of the Church of England.

Angus Ritchie is the founding director of the Centre for Theology and Community (CTC). Ordained in the Church of England in 1998, he has served throughout his ministry in parishes in East London involved in community organizing, currently assisting at St George-in-the-East in Tower Hamlets. These parishes have played a founding role in campaigns for the living wage, affordable housing and legislation to tackle exploitative lending. He is married to Jennifer, and has two sons, Callum and Euan. Angus is the author of a number of books, reports and essays, including *Inclusive Populism: Creating Citizens in the Global Age* (Notre Dame, IN: University of Notre Dame Press, 2019), which was cited by Pope Francis for expressing his vision of "a politics of fraternity, rooted in the life of the people". With David Bunch, he edited *Prayer and Prophecy: A Kenneth Leech Reader* (Boston, MA: Seabury Press, 2009).

Jenny Sinclair is Founder and Director of Together for the Common Good (T4CG), a charity dedicated to spiritual and civic renewal. Drawing on Catholic Social Thought, T4CG resources Christian leaders and churches across all denominations, as well as schools and charities, to read the signs of the times and play their part for the common good. She writes and speaks about the vocation of the Church in society, and is co-host of *Leaving Egypt*, a transatlantic podcast exploring what it means to be God's people in times of unravelling. Among her advisory roles, she serves as a trustee of the Common Good Foundation and on the Caritas Social Action Network Reference Group. Prior to 2011, she was a graphic artist, a charity worker and volunteer, and an ambassador for Liverpool Hope University. Daughter of the late David Sheppard, Anglican Bishop of Liverpool, Jenny was received into the Catholic Church in 1988.

David Walker has been a Church of England bishop since 2000, serving first as suffragan Bishop of Dudley, then, since 2013, as Bishop of Manchester. Until the end of 2023, he was for several years deputy chair of the Board of Governors of the Church Commissioners, and a member of the Strategic Investment Board (later Strategic Mission and Ministry Investment Board) of the Archbishops' Council, overseeing the awarding of major grants to dioceses. He has served as a trustee of the Church Urban Fund, and as chair of a number of housing associations and charities. As a member of the House of Lords, he speaks on issues related to poverty and welfare, as well as human rights, policing and migration. He is currently co-chair of the National Police Ethics Committee and also chair of USPG, one of the oldest Anglican mission agencies. He and his wife Sue are Franciscan tertiaries.

Averil Pooten Watan is a mother, wife and community leader in Waltham Forest, East London. She is one of the churchwardens in St Barnabas and St James, Walthamstow. This enables her to live out her faith in service of others. She is a trustee of the Centre for Theology and Community (CTC) and co-chair of The East London Communities

Organisation (TELCO). Averil is co-chair of Forest Women's Interfaith Network (WIN), actively participating in many interfaith activities, including WIN's annual interfaith walk. She is also a trustee of the Igorot UK charity (an indigenous Filipino grassroots organization), and is passionate about her community and ensuring Filipinos are represented in the mainstream culture. Lastly, she manages a residential care home for adults with long-term mental health conditions. Through this role, she is the borough lead for Care Providers Voice, an independent network of providers supporting providers in social care.

Introduction

Terry Drummond and Joseph Forde

Faith in the City, published in the autumn of 1985, was a landmark publication in the history of Church-State relations in England. It is difficult to think of any publication from within the Church of England that has received the level of intellectual and political hostility that it encountered from some government ministers, including the Prime Minister, Margaret Thatcher. It was a report that had been commissioned by Archbishop Robert Runcie out of a concern—widely held within the clergy—that the economic and social polices being pursued by Mrs Thatcher's government were having a damaging impact on inner-city communities, and had contributed to the cause of the riots that had broken out in several English cities in 1981.

Runcie was keen to get to the bottom of what had been taking place, as well as for the Church of England to be in a position to influence matters in ways that were intellectually—as well as morally—credible, and to be able to contribute on a practical level to improving conditions for those who had been worst affected. For this, he knew that the report would have to be based on an assessment of a wide range of opinions, including from some of those who were living in inner-city areas that were experiencing high levels of social deprivation and poverty. He therefore tasked an 18-member commission, drawn from a variety of backgrounds, to produce an evidence-based report along these lines. The commission spent two years gathering evidence from a range of urban contexts. Its report made a number of recommendations to government on how it could intervene to improve matters in policy areas such as unemployment, policing, housing, education and urban regeneration. It also made a number of recommendations on how the Church of England could contribute to bringing about improvements to the lives of those living in urban contexts.

In this collection of essays, commissioned to celebrate the 40th anniversary of the publication of *Faith in the City*, we shall examine the impact that the report had at the time of its publication; the changes that have taken place in the political landscape in the period since; the changes that have taken place in English society in the period since; and the changes that have taken place in the Church of England in the period since, including in its approach to urban mission, ministry and welfare provision, before reaching some conclusions on the way forward.

The volume begins with a chapter by Andrew Bradstock that covers some of the historical background to the publication of *Faith in the City*. Alan Billings then writes about his personal reflections on his work as one of the commission members. Ian K. Duffield writes about the impact Faith in the City had on developing the new Urban Theology in Sheffield, as well as on shaping his own ministry. David Walker provides a personal perspective on Faith in the City, and how it helped to shape his ministry. John Perumbalath writes about urban mission and ministry in his work as Bishop of Liverpool. Terry Drummond writes on *Faith in the City*'s contribution to shaping urban mission and ministry in the 20 years after it was published, and on the decline in urban mission and ministry in the period since. Susan Lucas writes about local urban ministry in Newham, London, and the impact that neoliberal economic and social policies have had on reshaping the city's landscape in the period since *Faith in the City* was published. Sophie Valentine Cowan writes about estate ministry today and the challenges it poses for the Church of England. Angus Ritchie and Averil Pooten Watan write about community organizing and volunteering and offer a new model for local churches. Joseph Forde writes about Church, State and welfare in England today, by making reference to *Faith in the City*'s approach to welfare, and to what has come after. Jenny Sinclair writes about *Faith in the City* and its dialogue with the Catholic Social Thought tradition, as well as the contribution that Catholic Social Teaching is making to strengthening the bonds of social trust, at all levels and in all sectors.

We are of the view that these essays convey a sense of the considerable impact that *Faith in the City* had on the political and ecclesiastical scene in England at the time of its publication. We believe that the contribution that it made to our understanding of what was happening in inner cities across England at that time—painting as it did a disturbing picture of rising social and economic levels of deprivation in the inner cities—merits revisiting, at a time when we are still seeing high levels of social and economic deprivation in parts of some towns and cities in England today. We hope that these essays convey a sense of how, in the 40 years since *Faith in the City* was published, a considerable amount of good work has been done by the Church of England towards the goal of reducing the levels of economic and social deprivation in our towns and cities and thus advancing the cause of social justice. There is, therefore, much justification for celebrating the 40th anniversary of the publication of *Faith in the City*. However, as we shall see in what follows, there is much work that still needs to be done in this regard. At a time when the Church of England is seeking to halt—if not reverse—the decline in observance and affiliation that it has witnessed since the early 1960s, we are of the view that a refocusing by the Church on the contribution that urban mission and ministry can make towards achieving that end is both necessary and urgent.

PART I
Historical background

1

Faith in the City: Historical background

Andrew Bradstock

In May 1981, *The Times* published an article by its religious affairs correspondent, Clifford Longley, entitled "The prophets of the press confounded".[1] The thrust of Longley's piece was that, while his newspaper had described the Church of England as being "on the brink of crisis" 15 years before, it was now, in fact, in good heart, and "even beginning to pick up a little".

Reading this while overseas, the Archbishop of Canterbury, Robert Runcie, wrote to Canon Eric James requesting him to respond. James had long experience of urban ministry and knew, like Runcie, that whatever else might be true about Longley's assessment, the prophets of the press had been right as far as their Church's witness in the inner cities was concerned.

James duly wrote to *The Times*, citing areas of London where clergy numbers were approaching half of what they were in 1966. There has been a "policy of withdrawal from the inner city", James wrote, which "has been forced upon the leaders of the C of E ... by many and complex factors", including finance, manpower and "the problems of a mainly middle-class and married clergy relating to working class areas". "I should myself like to see the immediate appointment of an Archbishop's Commission ... called the 'Staying There' Commission ... ", James continued. "It would report on the Church's strategy for the inner-city, and would need of course to consider the theology and spirituality of

---

[1] C. Longley, "The prophets of the press confounded", *The Times*, 25 May 1981.

the church in the inner-city, not just finance and manpower."[2] James then persuaded the archbishop to adopt his suggestion, and the process leading to one of the most significant church reports in recent times was underway.

Runcie asked James to draw up "terms of reference" for a commission and suggestions for membership. James thought that the commission:

> must listen more profoundly than a Bible Society Gallup Poll can do to what people have to say in the inner cities. It must try to discover what lies behind the apparent indifference to the Church in such areas. It must identify what would be effective forms of ministry to those in the Urban Priority Areas. It must articulate questions about public policy at the national level of both Church and State. And it must communicate its findings in a way which will speak to the suburban and rural as well as the urban Church: indeed, in a way which will speak to the nation as a whole.[3]

Runcie wanted to involve an informal grouping of urban bishops, and James met with them in June 1982 to make his case. Not all warmed to the idea of a commission, but the following day one of their number, David Sheppard of Liverpool, sent a draft proposal for such a commission around the group.

The remit was even wider than that conceived by James. "The questions which need to be raised are not simply about what happens in Church and society in the Inner City", Sheppard wrote:

> Deprived areas did not create their own deprivation; nor can all the answers be found within the Inner City... The affluent need to see that the deprivation of the poor is the reverse side of their success. Questions will be raised concerning theology, politics

---

[2] Letters, *The Times*, 27 May 1981.
[3] "The C of E's new mission field", newspaper article by Eric James, n/d [July 1983].

and economics, which affect the whole of Church and society in this country...[4]

Runcie himself had also been thinking about the cities and the situation which had prompted the concerns expressed by James and Sheppard. A White Paper in 1977, entitled "Policy for the Inner Cities", had identified the need for action regarding the cities, describing the situation in many as one of "multiple deprivation". But while the Callaghan and Thatcher governments had taken some action in response, data from the 1981 Census showed that the situation had worsened in those four years.

The year 1981 also saw the crisis in some major cities brought starkly to the public's attention, with rioting breaking out in Brixton (London), Toxteth (Liverpool), Handsworth (Birmingham), Chapeltown (Leeds) and Moss Side (Manchester). In response, the government instigated an immediate enquiry under Lord Scarman, whose report—chiefly into the situation in Brixton—concluded that "complex political, social and economic factors" created a "disposition towards violent protest" in the area. Highlighting problems of discrimination based on race, and inner-city decline, Scarman argued that "urgent action" was needed to prevent racial disadvantage becoming an "endemic, ineradicable disease threatening the very survival of our society".

Runcie had learned first-hand of the situation in Brixton from an ecumenical delegation of local church and youth leaders, and from the community work resource unit at the British Council of Churches. During a Lords debate on the troubles in Brixton and Toxteth, he pledged the Church's determination "not to abandon the inner city and retreat to suburbia".[5]

---

[4] D. Sheppard, "Draft proposals concerning an inner city commission", June 1982, David Sheppard papers, Liverpool Central Library, 18.6.
[5] Hansard, Lords, "Brixton Disorders: The Scarman Report", 4 February 1982, cols 1413-15.

The Archbishop's Commission on Urban Priority Areas (ACUPA) was launched on 6 July 1983, with Sir Richard O'Brien, a former chair of the Manpower Services Commission, appointed chair, and—at O'Brien's request—Sheppard vice chair. O'Brien, a lay Anglican and chair of the Engineering Industry Training Board, was determined from the outset that the report the commission produced should be unanimous. Consideration was given to making the commission ecumenical, but the view prevailed that, if it had too broad a base, it might let the Church of England off the hook when there were issues which it must face in detail.

The commission thus included only two non-Anglicans, although in its report it affirmed that it had "paid close attention to the ecumenical dimension of the Church of England's ministry in the cities", and received full co-operation from the Roman Catholic Church, the Free Churches, the British Council of Churches, and from independent Black-led churches.[6] Eleven of the members were lay—experts drawn from the fields of the social sciences, education, social work, management, the trade unions, housing and the voluntary sector—and seven were clergy, including two bishops, Sheppard and Wilfred Wood, the Bishop of Croydon. Two of the clergy also had significant "secular" roles, one as deputy leader of a city council, the other as a borough social development officer. Only three of the 18 members were women.

In addition, some "resource bodies" and "advisers" were appointed. These included Christian Action (represented by its Director, Eric James), the Evangelical Coalition for Urban Mission, the William Temple Foundation, and the Boards and Councils of General Synod. A senior civil servant at the Department of the Environment, John Pearson, was seconded to work full-time as secretary to the commission. The decision to set up an Archbishop's Commission, as opposed to a synodical commission or something wholly unofficial, allowed greater freedom in the choice of membership and terms of reference.[7]

The commission's terms of reference were:

---

[6] *Faith in the City*, p. iii.
[7] See A. Dyson, "Faith in the City: ten years on", <https://www.theway.org.uk/>, accessed 31 January 2025.

> To examine the strengths, insights, problems and needs of the Church's life and mission in Urban Priority Areas and, as a result, to reflect on the challenge which God may be making to Church and Nation: and to make recommendations to appropriate bodies.

The term Urban Priority Area (UPA) was defined as including "large Corporation estates and other areas of social deprivation" in addition to inner-city districts.[8]

The commission met over several weekends, augmented by visits to some 30 cities and towns, and nine inner London boroughs. "We decided at the outset", the commissioners wrote in their introduction:

> that we must spend some time in the UPAs to see for ourselves the human reality behind the official statistics. In the course of a series of visits we saw something of the physical conditions under which people in the UPAs are living, and we listened to their own accounts and experiences at open public meetings and in smaller invited groups.[9]

The commission also met with representatives of local government, the police, social workers, caring agencies and local churches. As one of its advisers, Prebendary John Gladwin, later wrote, it could not have done its job with integrity without gaining first-hand evidence of life in the UPAs. It also needed to test its deliberations, and the evidence submitted to it, in these areas. The visits profoundly influenced the report, Gladwin noted. Seeing the effects of high unemployment levels, of poor and deteriorating housing, and of "strained and crumbling services", upset even those on the commission familiar with UPAs.[10]

---

[8] *Faith in the City*, p. iii.
[9] *Faith in the City*, p. xiv.
[10] J. Gladwin, "Faith in the City", *Crucible* (Jan-Mar 1986), p. 5. Gladwin was an adviser to the commission representing the Church of England Board for Social Responsibility.

That commission members needed to see for themselves "the physical conditions under which people in the UPAs are living" highlights the fact that no resident of a UPA was invited to actually join the commission. While its report was committed to improving the quality of life of people in the inner city, and drew extensively on the input they provided, it was essentially a voice "for" inner-city people rather than "of" them. There is a telling reference early in the report to many UPA residents living in "a wretched condition which none of us would wish to tolerate for ourselves or to see inflicted on others".[11]

—

The commission summarized its observations in the introduction to its report. *Poverty* would be one word to describe what we have seen, they stated. People in Britain were not starving, as in the developing world, but:

> many residents of UPAs are deprived of what the rest of society regard as the essential minimum for a decent life; they live next door to, but have little chance to participate in a relatively affluent society.

Poverty is at the root of *powerlessness*, they continued. Poor people in UPAs lack the means and opportunity of making choices in their lives, being "trapped in housing and environments over which they have little control" and "at the mercy of fragmented and apparently unresponsive public authorities".

These phenomena, the report continued, may be seen "as signs of an evident and apparently increasing *inequality* in our society". "The UPAs lie at the centre of an unequal society, their poverty obscured by the busy shopping precincts of mass consumption, their bare subsistence of dole and supplementary benefit existing alongside material opulence."

Polarization was another way of analysing what the commission had witnessed, with the "impoverished minority" becoming increasingly cut

---

[11] *Faith in the City*, p. xv.

off from mainstream life, and "rich and poor, suburban and inner city, privileged and deprived" becoming more sharply separated from each other.

None of these categories must distract from the plain message of our observations, they concluded. This was that "the nation is confronted by a *grave and fundamental injustice* in the UPAs". The situation "continues to deteriorate and requires urgent action", but "no adequate response is being made by government, nation or Church". The 1977 White Paper contained some good proposals, but there had been no sustained effort by governments to put them into effect.[12]

The report ran to 400 pages and made 61 recommendations, nearly two-thirds of which were addressed to the Church. In a preliminary chapter to the Church, entitled "What Kind of Church?", the commission challenged local churches to be committed to the communities they served, outward-looking, and willing to participate "by *collaborating* with the best expressions of local life and by *contributing* to the transformation of life in UPAs through God's sustaining power and purpose".[13]

A priority for dioceses, the report argued, is "to implement an effective system for identifying and designating UPA parishes" using the "national indicators of deprivation" produced by the Department of the Environment from 1981 Census data. These indicators were: levels of unemployment; overcrowding; households lacking basic amenities; pensioners living alone; ethnic origin; and single-parent households.[14] A particular recommendation for UPA churches was that they adopt a "systematic approach" to developing their life and mission, using an "Audit for the Local Church" resource prepared by the commission and included as an appendix in its report. This should not be viewed as a box-ticking exercise, the report argued, but as:

---

[12] *Faith in the City*, pp. xiv-xv; p. 21 (§1.42); pp. 173-4 (§8.19-20).
[13] *Faith in the City*, pp. 74-7.
[14] *Faith in the City*, pp. 82-3 (§5.2-3).

a means of enabling local Churches to undertake, in a fairly consistent way, an outward-looking review of the needs of their area and the role of the Church in responding to those needs.[15]

Proposals were also included for improving training opportunities for both stipendiary clergy and laypeople in UPA parishes, who often found the educational courses run by the Church to be inappropriate for their particular contexts and even to render them unfit for urban ministry.

Another recommendation to the Church was the establishment of a Church Urban Fund (CUF) "to strengthen the Church's presence and promote the Christian witness" in UPAs. This would be resourced in part with monies made available by the Church Commissioners. Behind this initiative was a concern to see the resources of the Church distributed more evenly, and the commission also recommended that "the historic resources of the Church" be redistributed between dioceses to equalize the amount parishes contributed to clergy and licensed lay minister stipends. Synod had carried a motion calling for this in 1983, as Runcie noted when launching the commission.[16]

A Standing Commission on Black Anglican Concerns was proposed, "to enable the Church to make a more effective response to racial discrimination and disadvantage, and to the alienation experienced by many black people in relation to the Church of England". Dioceses were also encouraged to review their structures "to ensure that black Anglicans have a voice in decision-making or advisory processes, and that a concern for racial discrimination and disadvantage is reflected in policies and practices".[17]

Many of the recommendations to "Government and Nation" specifically called on the government to expand existing programmes, set up enquiries, or shift priorities. The report took issue with the government's strategy of promoting home ownership as a means of opening up choice. For low-income city residents, it argued, promising freedom of choice was a cruel deception. It recommended an independent

---

[15] *Faith in the City*, pp. 91-2 (§5.37).

[16] *Faith in the City*, p. 363 (§25); pp. 162ff.

[17] *Faith in the City*, p. 361 (§8); p. 99 (§5.68).

examination of the whole system of housing finance, including mortgage interest tax relief, arguing that it was unjust to tell people in bad housing that there was no money to do anything for them, while at the same time giving subsidies to those on middle and higher incomes. There should be an expansion to the public housing programme "to ensure a substantial supply of good quality rented accommodation for all who need it". Resources devoted to the Rate Support Grant should be increased in real terms, it argued, "and within the enhanced total a greater bias should be given to the UPAs". Public housing authorities should keep and monitor "ethnic records" as a step towards eliminating discrimination in housing allocation.[18]

Another proposal was that the size of the Urban Programme—under which government provided special financial assistance to designated local authorities—should be raised. Other recommendations called for changes to the Community Programme for people in long-term unemployment, particularly to encourage greater participation by women and unemployed people with families to support; an increase to the level of Child Benefit; improvement for the system of funding recognized voluntary bodies; and greater support for small firms in UPAs.[19]

A chapter on "Theological Priorities" referenced measures in the Old Testament "to impose a number of controls upon society to check the inevitable increase of social and economic inequalities". While the report acknowledged that there was no "generally agreed manifesto for a Christian social order" in Scripture, there was a "fundamental conviction" within Christianity that "even in this fallen world there are possibilities for a better ordering of society".[20]

Rather than offer a predetermined theology of urban mission, the commission felt it should first share the experience of people in UPAs. As one of its members, Canon Anthony Harvey, later explained, the report avoided attempting a comprehensive "theology of the city", believing rather that "any such theology ought to come out of, rather than be

---

[18] *Faith in the City*, p. 366 (§19); p. 257 (§10.98); p. 366 (§16); pp. 364-5 (§2); p. 366 (§15); p. 239 (§10.37).
[19] *Faith in the City*, p. 365 (§3, 9, 12, 5, 6).
[20] *Faith in the City*, pp. 51-2 (§3.11, 3.13).

imposed upon, congregations in UPAs".[21] This decision was informed in part by an engagement with liberation theology, which had emerged in Latin America in the 1970s, and which argued that a "theology of the poor" needed to emerge from poor communities themselves, not be constructed by others on their behalf.

How successful the report proved to be in drawing on grassroots theology has been debated, not least since its approach was to speak *on behalf of* people living with poverty rather than enable them to speak *for themselves*. Perhaps, as Malcolm Brown has put it, it ended up with "not a theology *by* the poor ... rather an imaginative leap into what such a theology might look like".[22] The report also assumed that, when Christians related their standards of human justice to their understanding of the justice of God, as revealed in Scripture, "these standards are for the most part ones which are shared by the majority of their fellow citizens".[23]

—

The week before the report's publication in December 1985, Bishop David Sheppard wrote to the Prime Minister. Mrs Thatcher had initiated a discussion about the work of the commission at a meeting with Sheppard in November the previous year, and Sheppard reminded her of their earlier correspondence and said that its work was now complete. "The report is a very thorough piece of work", he wrote. "There is a great deal of detailed analysis and recommendation for the Church. And we have raised public policy questions about the confusing and interlocking factors, which make urban life what it is." Sheppard hoped

---

[21] A. Harvey, *By What Authority? The Churches and Social Concern* (London: SCM Press, 2001), p. 23. Harvey is credited with dreaming up the title "Faith in the City".

[22] M. Brown, *After the Market: Economics, Moral Agreement and the Churches' Mission* (Bern: Peter Lang, 2004), p. 39.

[23] *Faith in the City*, p. 327 (§14.5.1).

that the government would regard the report as constructive and that it would have lasting value.[24]

He, and other members of the commission, could hardly have been more disappointed. The report had been embargoed until Tuesday 3 December, but the Sunday before a "senior government figure" was quoted in the press saying that parts of it were "pure Marxist theology".[25] *The Sunday Times* report also said the commission had called for an end to mortgage tax relief, which was "certain to anger Mrs Thatcher", whereas in fact it had advocated "phasing it out in favour of a more equitable way of using that huge subsidy"—a recommendation of the 1984 Rowntree inquiry into housing chaired by the Duke of Edinburgh. The media buzzed with the story throughout the day, and it was front-page news on the Monday.

The commission held its press launch as planned on the Tuesday, but the government had already given its work more profile than they could ever have imagined. Ironically, No. 10 had decided a few days before that "no attempt should be made to pre-empt the report this weekend ... a pre-emptive strike could draw more attention to the report than it would otherwise get". "Kill it with kindness", the Prime Minister's private secretary David Norgrove advised her. "A Church-Government row would keep the Report on the front pages."[26] The report would eventually sell 50,000 copies.

Behind the scenes a more considered response was being prepared by the Prime Minister's chief policy adviser, Brian Griffiths, who thought the report tried to avoid a confrontation with the government and was not condemning its policies wholesale. Nevertheless, there was running through it "a deep hostility to government policy and the philosophy

---

[24] D. Sheppard, letter to the Prime Minister, 25 November 1985, Sheppard papers, 29.8.

[25] "Church report is 'Marxist'", *The Sunday Times*, 1 December 1985, p. 1. Norman Tebbit has often been cited as the source of this quote, but he has always denied this.

[26] Memo from Bernard Ingham, 28 November 1985, The National Archives (TNA): PREM 19/1920_2; Charles Moore, *Margaret Thatcher: The Authorized Biography*, vol. 2 (London: Penguin, 2015), p. 446.

on which it is based". Griffiths described the report as "collectivist, determinist and Keynesian". It had nothing to say to the individual family wishing to escape from poverty. A practising Anglican, Griffiths expressed concern that a church which stressed the value and dignity of each person should play down the importance of individual effort. Griffiths thought the report was Marxist in the sense that it emphasized "the *structure* of society being the cause of poverty" rather than individual agency. At Cabinet on 5 December the government agreed to follow Griffiths' line.[27] Margaret Thatcher later expressed her "absolute shock" that the Church had failed to say anything to individuals and families: for her, as she once remarked in an interview with the *Catholic Herald*, poverty was a consequence of either "bad budgeting" or a "personality defect".[28] Mrs Thatcher's commitment to the creed of individual responsibility is at the heart of her address to the General Assembly of the Church of Scotland in Edinburgh in 1988, possibly a response to the *Faith in the City* report.[29]

The government's hostility to the report should be viewed in context. Relations between the church hierarchy and Margaret Thatcher's government had been strained since her first election victory in 1979. The service to mark the end of the Falklands War in 1982 had been an early cause of friction, with the Church wanting to acknowledge the Argentinian dead and avoid a triumphalist note. A 1982 report by the Church entitled *The Church and the Bomb* had been perceived by some to be taking a unilateralist stance. The miners' strike was another source of tension, with several bishops publicly criticizing the government's approach. Some leading bishops regretted Thatcher's decision to end

---

[27] Memo from Brian Griffiths, 3 December 1985, TNA: PREM 19/1920_1. Emphasis in the original. CAB 128_81_35.

[28] H. Young, *One of Us: A Biography of Margaret Thatcher* (London: Macmillan, 1989), p. 417; E. Filby, *God and Mrs Thatcher* (London: Biteback Publishing, 2015), p. 174.

[29] On this see J. Raban, *God, Man & Mrs Thatcher* (London: Chatto & Windus, 1989).

the post-war "Butskellite" consensus in favour of greater freedom for the market. For them, community was an important biblical concept: Bishop Sheppard, for example, often spoke of being "members one of another", a term of St Paul's (Romans 12:5). The Prime Minister, however, put her faith in free-market economics and a scaled-down welfare state. There was little common ground between the bishops and the government: in the House of Lords, 61 per cent of votes cast by bishops during the 1980s were against the government, and just 27 per cent in support.[30]

Against this backdrop, *The Times'* political columnist, Ronald Butt, described *Faith in the City* as "in many ways the high-water mark of systematic criticism of the Government's policies" by the Church of England.[31] With the Labour Party weakened by its election defeat in 1983, and the defection of some of its leading MPs to the Social Democratic Party, the Church of England was almost the *de facto* "loyal opposition"—a term Runcie was to appropriate himself a few years later. The Church's adoption of the term "commission" for its enquiry could also be understood as suggesting it saw itself having a degree of official authority. In response to more general criticism of the Church for involving itself in politics *per se*, bishops argued that they had a right to speak out on public issues on account of having seats in the House of Lords, and the Church's presence in every parish, giving it regular contact with grassroots opinion.

It was a moot point, however, whether the Church's stance was due to a conscious shift to the left by the bishops, or a consequence of the Conservative Party moving in the opposite direction after 1979. Clifford

---

[30] A. Partington, *Church and State: The Contribution of the Church of England Bishops to the House of Lords during the Thatcher Years* (Milton Keynes: Paternoster, 2006), p. 90. Whether the bishops reflected the wider view of the Church is a moot point: surveys during the 1980s suggested that more than 60 per cent of committed Anglican worshippers consistently identified as Conservatives (Liza Filby, "God and Mrs Thatcher: religion and politics in 1980s Britain", PhD thesis, University of Warwick, p. 112).

[31] R. Butt, "The Tension of the 1980s", in Michael Alison and David L. Edwards (eds), *Christianity and Conservatism: Are Christianity and Conservatism Compatible?* (London: Hodder & Stoughton, 1990), p. 41.

Longley has argued that one reason the churches looked increasingly left wing in the 1980s was that the Conservative Party "had started to move steadily to the Right" after 1979. "Without changing its outlook, therefore, the Church leadership in Britain ... gradually found itself in increasing opposition to the major direction of government policy."[32] Another view is that the Church slipped into its oppositional role "almost by accident". As Malcolm Brown and Paul Ballard have written, adhering to a belief in social consensus, and acting as it had always done, the Church was "not only ill-prepared for the emerging creed of Thatcherism but ... almost inadvertently found [itself] articulating the anxieties and bewilderments of a society in turmoil".[33] Eliza Filby thinks the Church of England's role in the formation of the welfare state in part explains its commitment to defending the post-war settlement.[34]

The Times argued that the balance of the commission was "so clearly to the left of centre, the outcome was predictable", a view echoed by cabinet minister Norman Tebbit. Tebbit even requested a dossier on all the members of the commission, from which he concluded that it had been unbalanced and included no one from the political right. Kenneth Baker was another government minister who was publicly critical of the report, and the Prime Minister herself was once heard describing *Faith in the City* as "that *wicked* report". The recent chair of the Conservative Party, John Selwyn Gummer, opined that "[It] is the word of God which the Church of England should be bringing to our God-forsaken inner cities not soggy chunks of stale politics that read as if they have been scavenged from the Socialist Party's dustbin."[35]

Positive references to liberation theology in the "Theological Priorities" chapter, and parallels suggested there between aspects of Marx's teaching and the Old Testament, gave further grist to the mill of those accusing the commission of left-wing bias—as did references in the report to government policies giving "too much emphasis ... to individualism,

---

[32] C. Longley, *The Worlock Archive* (London: Geoffrey Chapman, 2000), p. 317.
[33] M. Brown and P. Ballard, *The Church and Economic Life: A Documentary Study: 1945 to the present* (Peterborough: Epworth, 2006), p. 182.
[34] Filby, *God and Mrs Thatcher*, p. 176.
[35] Filby, *God and Mrs Thatcher*, pp. 174-5.

and not enough to collective obligation", and recommendations that expenditure on public services be increased to create jobs, funded, if required, by "tax increases or higher rates of public borrowing".[36]

Yet the commission had consciously solicited someone from the right to prepare the economics sections, Professor John Pickering of the University of Manchester Institute of Science and Technology, and there were other members who were closely in touch with the CBI and considered to be from the political centre among industrialists.[37] Critics from the left also challenged the extent to which the report actually was "left wing". In an essay marking its tenth anniversary, Hilary Russell noted that, while it:

> was an indictment of the consumer society [it] seemed to assume only that it needed to be given a kinder face, not that its very basis should be questioned ... Its reformist incremental recommendations came as an anti-climax.[38]

Furthermore, despite being designated a "Marxist" report, it could hardly be said to deal adequately with the major structural issues of class and power in society given, as Eliza Filby has put it, its "essentially paternalistic tone", with:

> the 'poor' the subject of the piece rather than the intended audience ... [and] ... little sense that the 'poor' could be initiators of their own emancipation.[39]

Indeed, the purpose of the report was not to provoke action by those on whose behalf it was speaking, but rather, as Filby notes, to stir the consciences of those in "Tory-voting middle-class

---

[36] *Faith in the City*, p. 208 (§9.46); p. 212 (§9.64); p. 213 (§9.67).
[37] Pickering in fact declined a request to write a chapter on economics.
[38] H. Russell, "Reuniting the cities", in Hilary Russell and Graeme Smith, *Keeping Faith with the Cities* (London: Christian Socialist Movement, 1995), p. 5.
[39] Filby, *God and Mrs Thatcher*, p. 174.

constituencies—crucially those areas where the Church still had some influence".[40] This was made explicit by David Sheppard in a letter to the Chief Rabbi, Immanuel Jakobovits, another outspoken critic of the report: much of *Faith in the City*, Sheppard wrote, "is rightly aimed at suburban Christians, who all too easily seem to blame those who have been left behind".[41]

Yet the commission members themselves were clear that they were motivated by moral and theological concerns, rather than political ones. In a telling passage they acknowledge that:

> the Church of England cannot 'solve' the problem of unemployment. It possesses neither the mandate nor the competence to do so. Yet as it is in the position of being the national Church, it has a particular duty to act as the conscience of the nation. It must question all economic philosophies, not least those which, when put into practice, have contributed to the blighting of whole districts, which do not offer the hope of amelioration, and which perpetuate the human misery and despair to which we have referred. The situation requires the Church to question from its own particular standpoint the *morality* of these economic philosophies.[42]

To which critics of the report, including the Prime Minister herself, retorted that, while the Church often seemed concerned about "public morality", it was much more cautious on the issue of *personal* morality.

Not all government ministers were critical of the report, however. The Energy Secretary, Peter Walker, regretted the "absurd outbursts" by his colleagues, who he said had not read the report. "I can only express my own gratitude to you for all you have done in this sphere and only hope it will meet with success", Walker wrote in a personal letter to

---

[40] Filby, *God and Mrs Thatcher*, p. 178.

[41] Letter dated 4 March 1986, Sheppard papers, 29.1. Jakobovits had written a pamphlet critical of *Faith in the City* which was commended by Margaret Thatcher.

[42] *Faith in the City*, p. 208 (§9.41).

Bishop Sheppard.[43] The then Leader of the House, John Biffen, told the Commons the report should be treated as "a serious contribution to studying the problems in our city centres ... We know from the words of the Bishop of Liverpool that it is a substantial and carefully researched report by people who know a good deal about the cities."[44] Douglas Hurd, then Home Secretary, was impressed with the report's conclusions on crime. By the end of the week, the press was reporting a "mood of contrition" among some ministers. One was quoted as saying that the report was "well meant but misguided".[45]

The senior Conservative figure who engaged most positively with *Faith in the City* was Michael Heseltine. Shortly after he resigned as Defence Secretary in January 1986, Heseltine wrote a 19-page response to the report. He later met with six members of the commission. Heseltine disagreed with parts of the report and thought it "ridiculous" to blame the government entirely for the situation. But he agreed with the commission's claim that urban areas were "suffering from economic decline, physical decay and social disintegration". He also agreed that there were deep questions at stake. "Damn the statistics; just go and look!", he wrote. "Of course there are clear moral issues involved in the political challenges we face." Heseltine told Runcie, "Your bishops have got it all wrong. Things are much *worse* than they say!"[46]

—

Faith in the City spawned several initiatives. Synod initially rejected its call for a Commission on Black Anglican Concerns, but a less

---

[43] Letter dated 4 December 1985, Sheppard papers, 30.1; cf. David Sheppard, *Steps Along Hope Street: My Life in Cricket, the Church and the Inner City* (London: Hodder & Stoughton, 2002), p. 251.

[44] Hansard, Commons, 3 December 1985, vol. 88, cols 151–2. Biffen's words might be taken two ways!

[45] D. McKie, "Ministers regret berating Church", *The Guardian*, 7 December 1985, p. 3.

[46] M. Heseltine, "Faith in the City: A Step Forward", 22 March 1986, Sheppard papers, 30.1; Sheppard, *Steps Along Hope Street*, p. 251.

independent Committee for Black Anglican Concerns (CBAC) was created to monitor Synod "with a view to supporting efforts for racial justice" and to assist dioceses "in developing strategies for combating racial bias within the Church".[47] The report's affirmation of church-based community and voluntary work gave fresh impetus to bodies such as The Children's Society and Barnardo's, the latter when it was looking to make its Christian tradition "more tangible" by linking with urban churches. The report aroused interest in the City, prompting the Dean of St Paul's to set up a *Faith in the City* group to organize visits to deprived areas for bankers and businessmen.

The most high-profile outcome of the report was the Church Urban Fund. In its first five years, CUF raised £18 million, with a further £18 million in its next ten years. The brainchild of David Sheppard, the fund made grants to parishes and ecumenical projects that, as Sheppard himself put it, "had never dared hope they might have the money to dream of new ventures" and which, as a result, made them "more outward-looking into the community".[48] The fund's impact was often overshadowed by the political fallout from the report itself.

Most dioceses took on board the recommendation that the resources of the Church be redistributed according to a formula that took into account "potential" giving. This meant that those dioceses which had a "financial cushion" provided by the generosity of past Christians or historical accident, and which therefore contributed less towards clergy stipends than poorer dioceses, now contributed more. This equalizing of the Church's resources, together with the creation of CUF, gave the Church more credibility when pressing government to spend more on its Urban Programme. The Church was now redistributing its resources from rich to poor, a policy it wanted the State to pursue.[49]

---

[47] Bishops' Advisory Group on UPAs, *Staying in the City: Faith in the City ten years on* (London: Church House Publishing, 1995), p. 79. CBAC was later renamed the Committee for Minority Ethnic Anglican Concerns (CMEAC).

[48] Sheppard, *Steps Along Hope Street*, p. 259.

[49] *Faith in the City*, p. 162 (§7.87).

Follow-up activity to *Faith in the City* constituted "a remarkable allocation of ecclesiastical energy", one commentator noted.[50] According to the official progress report, *Living Faith in the City*, four years after its publication every diocese had a "link officer" for UPA matters. Most had debated the report in their synod, and over 30 had co-ordinating committees following it up. Some were employing urban officers. Dioceses were "well on the way" to raising their target of £18 million for the Church Urban Fund. More than £5 million had been allocated towards the funding of over 200 projects to strengthen communities.[51]

"In very many parishes and synods there was a really encouraging response to the report's publication", Prebendary Pat Dearnley recalls:

> The report unquestionably raised the morale of many clergy and alerted suburban congregations (and not infrequently rural ones as well) to the problems facing residents in the inner cities and outer housing estates. I was inundated with requests to visit places, and especially noteworthy were meetings I addressed in solidly "Comfortable Britain".[52]

Dearnley was appointed by Runcie to co-ordinate the Church's response to the report.

Response to the policy recommendations in the report was less encouraging, however. One commission member, Ruth McCurry, estimated that only one of its 23 recommendations to government and nation had been carried out within the first ten years. This contrasted with 15 of its 38 recommendations to the Church.[53] This may be

---

[50] H. Clark, *The Church Under Thatcher* (London: SPCK, 1993), p. 104.

[51] *Living Faith in the City: A progress report by the Archbishop of Canterbury's Advisory Group on Urban Priority Areas* (London: General Synod of the Church of England, 1990), p. viii.

[52] Correspondence with the author.

[53] R. McCurry, "Ten years on", in Peter Sedgwick (ed.), *God in the City: Essays and Reflections from the Archbishop of Canterbury's Urban Theology Group* (London: Mowbray, 1995), p. 4. See also Clark, *The Church Under Thatcher*, p. 107.

unsurprising, given that many recommendations looked to the State to provide solutions. But more important was the extent to which the report inspired the government to tackle the situation in the inner cities more urgently.

Brian Griffiths, an insider at No. 10 at the time, recalls that the report was a huge spur to the government to do more on urban issues. While the policies it adopted to rejuvenate the inner cities were different from those proposed in the report, the government's response to the Church's call for action was wholehearted. *Faith in the City* was the "trigger" for a raft of inner-city reforms in areas such as education, housing and law and order, Griffiths has said. It was not the only catalyst for government action, but in terms of providing a "thrust" to more intensive engagement the report was crucial.[54]

Bishop Tom Butler, who chaired the Archbishop's Advisory Group on UPAs which co-ordinated the follow-up to *Faith in the City*, has noted that, while urban issues were not high on the agenda of any political party at the time the report was published, "its effectiveness can be seen by Margaret Thatcher, after her re-election in 1987 saying, 'We must do something about the inner cities.'"[55] A commitment to tackle "the regeneration of the inner cities" was contained in the Conservative Party manifesto for the 1987 election, along with policies to address housing, jobs, social security and local government. As Eliza Filby has argued, the prominence given to urban poverty in the election manifestos of all parties that year is evidence that *Faith in the City* "fulfilled its aim of alerting both the politicians and public to the plight of the nation's cities".[56]

---

[54] Interview with the author.
[55] Correspondence with the author.
[56] Filby, "God and Mrs Thatcher", PhD thesis, p. 129.

… PART II

Personal reflections

2

Faith in the City: Forty years on

Alan Billings

The Commission—and how I came to be a member of it

The social and economic context

The 1980s were a time of social unrest and economic distress. For anyone who did not live through those years as an adult, it takes a supreme act of the imagination to have a sense of how fraught and dark it sometimes felt, particularly for those who lived in urban priority areas (UPAs).

The catalyst for the commission was the urban riots in 1981. These were racial, principally involving Afro-Caribbean young men and white police officers. Even before that, there had been times of tension and fears about community cohesion, especially in the inner cities where Commonwealth immigration was significantly changing the ethnic make-up.[1] In 1968, Enoch Powell, the Urdu-speaking Conservative MP for Wolverhampton South West, and an Anglican, gave a speech in Birmingham to the West Midlands Conservative Political Centre. He warned about the dangers, as he saw them, of unchecked immigration. One of his biographers, Robert Shepherd, believed that what Powell feared was the "communalism" he had witnessed when on active service in India during the war.[2] He had

---

[1] The term "community cohesion" was to become a key concept of the report commissioned by David Blunkett, Home Secretary, following the 2001 disturbances. Ted Cantle, *Community Cohesion: A Report of the Independent Review Team Chaired by Ted Cantle* (London: Home Office, 2001).

[2] R. Shepherd, "The real tributaries of Enoch's 'river of blood'", *Spectator*, 1 March 2008. Powell had opposed Indian independence on the grounds that

29

seen sectarian conflict and feared something similar would happen here if immigrant groups failed to integrate. But Powell was provocative and used lurid language. Quoting from Virgil's *Aeneid*—he was a classical scholar—he spoke of the poet's foreboding, seeing "the River Tiber foaming with much blood". The Rivers of Blood speech, as it became known, inflamed rather than illuminated. It divided the country. A *Times* editorial said it was "evil". But a Gallup poll revealed that 74 per cent of people agreed with him and 83 per cent thought immigration was too high.[3] The tragedy was that he was making a serious point that should have been debated; but the speech had the effect of shutting down debate; any attempt to discuss the issues raised by mass immigration after that was portrayed as racism.

This was also a time when the Church of England was beginning to feel the effects of growing secularization and marginalization, not least in working-class parishes. Church attendance, which was never great, was falling and congregations and their clergy struggled financially, often feeling neglected by their dioceses. In many inner-city areas, the white, working-class population was being substantially replaced by families not only of other ethnicities but also other faiths, principally Muslim and Hindu. In 1960, there were 50,000 Muslims in the country and within five decades that number would reach two and a half million.[4] As Anglican congregations reduced year on year, Muslim congregations increased, growing in confidence, gradually replacing the older re-purposed buildings in which they had been gathering with purpose-built mosques. The urban skyline began to be bisected with minarets as well as spires.

When riots broke out in some of those parishes in 1981, Anglican priests working there and some senior clergy became alarmed and raised their anxieties within the Church. Archbishop Robert Runcie responded by inviting a diverse group of concerned people with relevant experience or expertise to embark on a fact-finding mission and produce a report. The Commission began its work in 1983, and I was asked to join as

---

communalism would make the country ungovernable.

[3] A. Marwick, *British Society Since 1945* (London: Penguin, 1990), p. 165.

[4] J. Morris, *A People's Church: A History of the Church of England* (London: Profile Books Ltd, 2023), p. 355.

an inner-city parish priest who was also an elected member of a large metropolitan local authority. The recommendations in the report were to be for both Church and Nation.

Ministerial and political experience
I had been vicar of Broomhall, Sheffield, a UPA parish, since 1973, moving later to another inner area parish, Walkley, in 1981. In 1980, I was elected Deputy Leader of the city council by the Labour Group, with responsibility for finance and the budget. David Blunkett, who would go on to become MP for Sheffield Brightside and eventually Home Secretary, was elected Leader. Throughout this time, I was seeking to make sense of what was happening to my parish and city, looking to my theological tradition and training to help me shape a meaningful parish ministry.

I had been brought up in an Anglo-Catholic church in Leicester—St Stephen's, East Park Road. But when I was an older teenager, we moved out of the terraced streets of the inner city and attended a church on a post-war council estate to which many had been moved as a result of slum clearance. St Luke Stocking Farm was part of the Parish and People movement which sought to reinvigorate parish ministry, making the parish communion the principal act of worship on Sundays.[5]

My formal training as a priest probably did little to prepare me for a working-class parish. I read Theology at Cambridge, which gave me some resources to draw on, and I was there when members of the divinity faculty gave a series of open lectures about the challenges Christian faith faced in modern Britain. *Objections to Christian Belief* set out the moral and intellectual struggles of those who, as Alec Vidler wrote in the introduction, had been living with "one foot in Christian belief and the other resolutely planted in the radical unbelief of the contemporary world".[6]

My theological college was next to Lincoln Cathedral and my curacy in a middle-class Leicester suburb. While St Mary Knighton was a long

---

[5] See E. W. Southcott, *The Parish Comes Alive* (New York: Morehouse-Graham Co., 1956).

[6] D. M. Mackinnon, H. A. Williams, A. R. Vidler, J. S. Bezzant, *Objections to Christian Belief* (London: Constable, 1963), p. 8.

way from the inner city or a council estate, I was for three years an elected member of Leicester City Council (1970-3) at a time when Idi Amin sought to expel Uganda's Indian population with his "Africanization" policy—expropriating their businesses and transferring them to black Africans. The Indians were given 90 days to leave the country and many who had British passports—a legacy of empire—headed for Leicester. The city became a target for the National Front (NF). The council adopted policies that sought to prevent the Ugandans, who were largely Hindus, settling in the city—on the grounds that the city was "full up".[7] The proposals were supported by all parties and overt racism was a daily fact of life. I was one of nine Labour councillors, two of whom were Anglican clergy, who defied the whip and opposed the policies. My family and I became targets for the NF, causing me eventually to seek my first incumbency in Sheffield Diocese.

The Anglo-Catholic tradition, in which I had been brought up, gave me, in the tradition of the slum priests of the nineteenth and early twentieth century, some models of what urban ministry might look like. Like them, I was committed to a pastoral ministry anchored in the Eucharist and with the same concern for social issues. I was inspired by the words of Frank Weston, Bishop of Zanzibar, at the second Anglo-Catholic Congress in 1923. He told a packed Albert Hall:

> You cannot claim to worship Jesus in the tabernacle if you do not pity Jesus in the slum... You have your Mass, you have your altars, you have begun to get your tabernacles. Now go out into the highways and hedges, and look for Jesus in the ragged and the naked, in the oppressed and the sweated, in those who have lost hope, and in those who are struggling to make good. Look for Jesus in them; and, when you have found Him, gird yourself with His towel of fellowship and wash His feet in the person of His brethren.[8]

---

[7] "Whitehall Told: No More—Leicester Is Full Up", headline in the *Leicester Mercury*, 31 August 1972.

[8] H. Maynard Smith, *Frank, Bishop of Zanzibar: Life of Frank Weston DD, 1871-1924* (London: SPCK, 1926), p. 302.

But this was a very clerical, patronizing model of what it was to be a vicar. It was already outdated in a society where there was a welfare state and increasing numbers of people would be going to college or university rather than into factories and mills. It was something; but there was nothing in my initial training or anything subsequently that gave me any insight into how parish ministry must change, other than what I gleaned from Parish and People clergy. I had to work things out for myself and with my congregations.

When I moved to Sheffield, I was very fortunate in finding theological support and challenge outside Anglican structures. The Urban Theology Unit (UTU) was established in the city in the 1970s by the Revd Dr John Vincent, a Methodist minister. At UTU I found congenial colleagues from a range of denominations and different parts of the country on courses and at conferences who wanted to have serious discussions about the changing nature of urban ministry. We became avid readers in theology and in those disciplines which we thought could help us understand what was happening in the country to create UPAs. John Vincent also introduced us to the more radical liberation theology that was coming from Latin and South America, where theology came from below, in the base communities, rather than from above, from academics and theologians. The debates we held at UTU provided me with a continuing theological underpinning and challenge to my work in urban ministry and local politics for as long as I lived and worked in Sheffield. When the bishop offered me a curate, members of my congregation persuaded me to ask for the stipend to be used for a community development worker instead—a sign of how we were beginning to forge a changing understanding of parish mission.

Time of unrest
Then came the riots. Between April and July 1981, the year after David Blunkett and I became Leader and Deputy Leader of Sheffield Council, there were serious disturbances in a number of English towns and cities, including Brixton and Southall (London), Handsworth (Birmingham), Toxteth (Liverpool), Moss Side (Manchester) and Chapeltown (Leeds). There were no disturbances of any significance in Sheffield and that was

something that we on Sheffield City Council noted and thought deeply about, and I will return to this.

The riots had a racial dimension with mainly black men protesting at their treatment by a mainly white police force. For many at the time, this was primarily what the disturbances were about—disaffected and lawless black youths taking on the police. For those who thought like this, the answer lay in more effective law enforcement. Perhaps it was not surprising, therefore, that the police wanted greater powers and capability. When the cabinet papers for 1981 were made public in 2011 (released under the 30-year rule), we discovered just how much Sir David McNee, the Metropolitan Police Commissioner, wanted: a new riot act, shields, water cannon, rubber bullets, armoured vehicles, CS gas and a mobile surveillance helicopter. In the event, they received 1,500 NATO riot helmets, more baton rounds from army stock and six water cannons (though they were never used). (Much of this was probably as decisive in suppressing the miners' strike in 1984-5 as the building up of coal stocks.)

While racial discrimination by the police was the spark, others believed the reasons for the disaffection of young people went much deeper. Their origins were in poverty and the alienation and sense of hopelessness that follows from that. (Previously, Enoch Powell had seen this differently. Non-white people were alienated because they were alien; they made no effort to fit in. The issue was integration not deprivation.) Much of the poverty was the direct result of fundamental changes to the economy, in particular the collapse of almost all the traditional industries of the first industrial revolution. This industrial decline affected white as well as black, old as well as young. In my own multi-racial parish in Sheffield, I watched all the local employers in cutlery, steel and heavy engineering gradually fail. Proud working-class families found themselves with no jobs and no prospects. One of my churchwardens, who had worked all his life in the steel industry, was made redundant in his early sixties and was so ashamed that he could not bring himself to tell his wife. For several weeks, he continued to go out each morning with his snap and return each evening as if he had been to work. He spent the day in parks on the other side of the city where he was eventually seen by a neighbour and had to admit the truth—to himself as much as others.

These were also years of rising inflation and bold new attempts to tackle it. Margaret Thatcher had become Prime Minister in 1979, and her government sought to deal with inflation by deflating demand, in line with monetarist theory. Cash limits were placed on public spending and the rate support grant to local authorities was reduced year on year. Councils had to cut services in order to prevent excessive rate increases and if they failed to do so, they were subject to further financial penalties. As I looked at the medium-term revenue forecast for the council with the City Treasurer in May 1983, I became alarmed at the implications for local services. I expressed my concern in a letter to the Prime Minister on 2 June 1983. On 9 June Mrs Thatcher replied:

> We made it clear when we took office in 1979 that the country's economic situation required substantial and sustained reductions in the overall level of local government spending, and that has been our consistent policy throughout our term of office. . . . Householders and businesses in Sheffield will get genuine, lasting relief from the burden of high rates only when the level of local authority spending in the City is reduced.[9]

That was clear and unambiguous: the size of the local state had to be reduced and there could be no special pleading. The date is significant: the letter was signed on the day of Mrs Thatcher's second and landslide election victory. (The Prime Minister's popularity had soared after the Falklands War in 1982.) By the time *Faith in the City* was published (3 December 1985), therefore, we could be in no doubt that some of our recommendations were unlikely to find favour with any government led by this prime minister. But we knew there were other cabinet ministers who thought differently, and we wanted to appeal to that alternative view in the hope that at some point in the future it might prevail. (We could not know that Margaret Thatcher would remain Prime Minister until 1990!) Michael Heseltine, for instance, whom I went to see twice when he was Secretary of State for the Environment to plead the cause for increased local financing, told the Conservative Party Conference in

---

[9] I retain the letter.

1981 that more should be given to the inner cities. However, at the same conference, Norman Tebbit, Secretary of State for Employment, said that the unemployed should emulate his father: in the 1930s, he got on his bicycle and looked for work elsewhere; he didn't riot. Both speeches were applauded. And this reflected the tension that remained at the heart of government.

It was, however, only after the release of cabinet papers 30 years later that the extent of the disagreement in the government became clear: Michael Heseltine argued for intervention in the areas of urban deprivation, whereas the Chancellor, Sir Geoffrey Howe, wanted to "manage" their decline. The same debate was to occur again in the Conservative Party in the 2000s. George Osborne, as Chancellor, proposed the idea of a Northern Powerhouse in 2014 and then, at the 2019 election, the Prime Minister, Boris Johnson, committed to "levelling up"—a policy of intervention in blighted areas, in part through the devolution of both powers and funding. (However, devolving some funding while continuing to cut support for existing services did seem a little perverse, not least to those Conservative council leaders who had to manage growing social care budgets.)

Then in 1984-5 we had the miners' strike and found ourselves in South Yorkshire at its epicentre. The headquarters of the National Union of Mineworkers had just relocated from Barnsley to Sheffield and the most violent confrontation between striking miners and the police during the strike took place in June 1984 at Orgreave on the Rotherham-Sheffield boundary. This was probably the nearest we came to having a state-directed police force in my lifetime, and was very frightening. After the collapse of the strike, the closure of pits continued at an accelerated pace with further dismal consequences for young people across the country's coalfields.

During the miners' strike, many clergy and their congregations were active in organizing food parcels for miners' families. Councils too sought to help those made redundant in other industries as far as the law allowed. This included giving financial support to those attempting to start their own businesses. In Sheffield I took the first cheque to a small group of men who had set up on their own in part of an abandoned mill after being made redundant. They were skilled in producing bespoke steel products from sand moulds. But they were half a dozen workers from a factory that had once employed several thousand. And in every part of the country jobs in other manufacturing industries were being shed: textiles, boot and shoe, automobiles, shipbuilding. New jobs in financial services or IT had smaller workforces and could locate anywhere in the country. They did not need a river or a seam of coal or an iron ore deposit nearby. It was hardly surprising that, by 1981, unemployment stood at 3 million. This seemed to many of us working and living in the UPAs to be the more likely underlying cause of the riots.

In Sheffield, where there were no disturbances, we were persuaded that a large contributory factor was the determination of the city council not to allow vital local services to be eroded as a result of government failure to increase revenue support grant in line with inflation. In 1981, I had proposed to the council a rate increase of over 40 per cent in an attempt to save services. This was not an easy decision, not least because at that time business as well as household rates were set by the council. The rates were a cost business could not directly control and, as a result, one way increases might be off-set was by further redundancies, as the Chamber of Commerce reminded me each year at budget-making time. At the same time, however, I required the council to undertake "base budgeting" exercises and make savings, scrutinizing every area of expenditure; though this was never going to be enough to make up for cuts in government support.[10] It was not a sustainable strategy in the long run.

This was the experience as a parish priest and an elected member that I brought to the work of the commission. I thought we might have something to say both to the Church of England and other churches about how we might support churches in UPAs and also how the country as a whole might respond better to economic change, primarily through its government. We said the report was a Call for Action by Church and Nation.

---

[10] The prevailing practice in the local authority was to take the previous year's budget as the basis for the coming year, adding for growth and inflation, subtracting for any identified savings. By asking for "base budgeting", I required each department to build its budget from scratch, from the base, justifying existing jobs and commitments and not just new ones.

Reflections on the impact of the report

I don't think any of us could have anticipated the degree of interest shown in the report by organizations and individuals beyond church circles, including the secular and specialist media. This was in part due to the way the government chose to receive it, but also to the methodology we used and our approach to social theology.

The social theology of the report

There are two theologies in *Faith in the City*. One runs through the whole of the report and the other is found in the chapter headed "Theological Priorities".[11]

The report's methodology was in the classic tradition of Anglican social theology that we associate with the war-time Archbishop of Canterbury, William Temple. We had the same approach to social issues: over two years we gathered empirical evidence and consulted those with relevant expertise. This took us to almost every major industrial city, where we met civic, trade union and business leaders, UPA clergy, their congregations and parishioners. We spent a good deal of time on the ground in the UPAs meeting people and listening to them. We held many public meetings, and they were always lively and very well attended. People could be very frank. One person stood up at a packed gathering in Knowsley, on Merseyside, and said his community had seen every government initiative since the Second World War—he gave a roll call of them—and they had all failed: "Why do you think you can make any difference?" At a gathering of clergy in the North-West, a suburban priest said the Church of England was a middle-class church and we should be careful not to alienate them. Nevertheless, the general tenor of this and all the meetings was encouraging. Many came up afterwards and

---

[11] This is noted in Joseph Forde, *Before and Beyond the 'Big Society': John Milbank and the Church of England's Approach to Welfare* (Cambridge: James Clarke & Co., 2022), p. 186. It was not fully recognized in Malcolm Brown, "The Case for Anglican Social Theology Today", in M. Brown et al. (eds), *Anglican Social Theology: Renewing the Vision Today* (London: Church House Publishing, 2014), p. 10.

thanked us for coming. In addition to what we gained through these engagements, we also received papers by academics and others with specialist knowledge, in the Temple tradition.

Capturing "lived experience"—not a phrase that was used then—made our report different from many others of the time. We regarded meeting people and listening to them in their context as valid empirical evidence and as significant as any statistics. It gave the report an authenticity and sense of urgency. (It is a way of proceeding that is often followed now in public enquiries, and perhaps this was an unintended and enduring spin-off of our work. But its importance needs emphasizing in a technocratic age where increasing store is placed on statistics unleavened by human experience.) In meetings I went to after publication, UPA residents and clergy frequently said they felt they had been heard and their voices captured. Several clergy told me that they had been given fresh confidence to persist in their ministry. In later years, other clergy told me they had sought ordination or urban ministries because of *Faith in the City*.

The report also carried weight because it sought to look at the issues comprehensively. Part III addressed the Nation and covered Urban Policy; Poverty, Employment and Work; Housing; Health; Social Care and Community Work; Education and Young People; Order and Law.

We laid out the evidence, qualitative and quantitative, reached conclusions and made recommendations that we could all support. We represented a range of political and theological positions. We believed that if we could find a consensus among our diverse selves, there was a greater chance of politicians listening. The chair, Sir Richard O'Brien, an experienced former industrialist and senior civil servant, made clear to us that the report had to be unanimous if Church and Nation were going to take it seriously.[12] This too was very much in the Temple tradition.

I re-read William Temple's book *Christianity and Social Order* (1942) when travelling to meetings of the commission.[13] I thought our report could be as influential in shaping public policy towards the UPAs for the

---

[12] The address to the Archbishop, printed as the Preface, ends with the words, "Our Report is unanimous."

[13] W. Temple, *Christianity and Social Order* (London: Penguin, 1942).

1980s and beyond as Temple's book was in stimulating thinking around the creation of the post-war welfare state. In our plenary discussions, we knew instinctively that in order to do that, we had to make our recommendations general, drawing on (Christian) principles of justice and morality, rather than commending specific policies, following Temple's approach in the main text of *Christianity and Social Order*. His generation of social theologians had called these "middle axioms". In the event, because of what we heard directly from the UPAs, we were emboldened to be more specific in policy terms, especially in relation to employment and housing.[14] But the aim was to appeal across a broad political spectrum.

However, there was one theological/political perspective that was not fully represented on the commission and not seriously debated as a result, and that was a mistake. It was articulated quite soon after we reported by the Chief Rabbi, Immanuel Jakobovits, and was closer to the politics of the Prime Minister. In a short report, *From Doom to Hope*, he emphasized the need for the cultural and moral renewal of communities from within and the need to build self-respect through a tough work ethic: cheap labour was always more dignified than a free dole.[15]

For the commission, the key Christian doctrine, which had been the central doctrine for nineteenth- and earlier twentieth-century Christian socialists, was Incarnation: God so loved the world that he became human in Jesus Christ and knew the human condition, therefore, from the inside of a human skin. In the days of his flesh, he revealed in his own life the Father's compassion for the poor and vulnerable, teaching us in turn to love our neighbour in need. Moreover, in serving them, we would be serving him.[16] But we were also drawing, perhaps less consciously

---

[14] This approach created issues for the Industrial Mission which was under pressure from some church groups to move away from its "neutral" political stance. P. Cope and M. West, *Engaging Mission: The Lasting Value of Industrial Mission for Today* (Guildford: Grosvenor House Publishing Ltd, 2011), p. 13.

[15] I. Jakobovits, *From Doom to Hope: A Jewish View on 'Faith in the City'* (London: Michaelson Ltd for the Office of the Chief Rabbi, 1986).

[16] Matthew 25:31–46.

or explicitly, on the work of Reinhold Niebuhr: in complex, modern societies, the way we loved our neighbour, who might be at a distance from us, was through politics—securing social justice—which was how love of neighbour operated at a distance, albeit imperfectly.[17] In other words, we believed there was a role for the State, as well as the individual and the voluntary sector, and the kind of interventions that required action by government. On the whole, neither we, nor the people we met, doubted the ability of politicians to make a difference for good in the lives of those living in the UPAs. There was not the cynicism about politics which is prevalent today. We just needed the political will to get things done. This was one reason why we could have faith in the city.

We could have produced a theological chapter solely along these lines, because this was essentially how we had worked and debated. But other social theologies played some part, especially liberation theologies coming from Latin and South America where theological reflection, leading to action, took place in base communities. Here people were encouraged to reflect on their own lives and experiences in the light of the gospel. One of the leading commissioners, David Sheppard, Bishop of Liverpool, had published a book, *Bias to the Poor*, which picked up on these themes and so they found their way into the chapter on "Theological Priorities".[18] As noted above, I had already encountered a British version of liberation theology at the Urban Theology Unit in Sheffield. We wanted to see UPA churches working at their own theological understanding of what was happening in their communities and how they could work with others for the common good.

In courses at UTU, staff used a parish/neighbourhood audit to help UPA clergy and congregations understand the demographics, economic and social relations, and so forth, of their localities, and I commended this to the commission. A version was placed in an appendix. Many parishes were to use these audits as a way of raising the understanding of their congregations and stimulating discussion and action.

---

[17] R. Niebuhr, *Moral Man and Immoral Society: A Study in Ethics and Politics* (New York and London: Charles Scribner's Sons, 1934).

[18] D. Sheppard, *Bias to the Poor* (London: Hodder & Stoughton, 1983).

But while the Temple methodology commended the report to the Nation, it was the reaction of the government that ensured it received publicity and made it seem interesting and relevant.

The government's reaction

The report was embargoed until Tuesday 3 December 1985. My copy still has the sticker on it that makes this clear. We were invited by the Archbishop to a launch and press conference in London; but over the weekend before, we were to be given a harsh lesson in politics. The embargo was broken by cabinet ministers who had been sent a copy in advance. They could have received the report politely, even if through gritted teeth, and had they done so, after some initial coverage, it is entirely possible it may have gone the way of many reports and gathered dust. In the event, they decided to make pre-emptive statements to some of the Sunday papers and put their spin on it before we could present it. So it was framed as a piece of "Marxist theology" and was seen in that light from publication. On the Sunday evening, shortly after I returned to the vicarage from evensong, I was confronted by a journalist and a photographer from a national newspaper and realized that the story of Marxist theology rather than the findings of the report itself was likely to prevail. On the BBC television news that evening I was described by a minister as the "Marxist deputy leader of a city council". (My stock rose in the Labour Group on the council, where I was generally regarded as on the right of the party.) The government saw this as a way of discrediting the report and burying its recommendations; but it was to have the opposite effect.

In the months following publication, commissioners received many invitations to speak. We were not surprised by those from church organizations, but we were taken aback by the number and range of secular ones. They were often groups that would not normally ask Christians to come and speak about a Church report. I accepted as many as I could. In a very short period of time I had spoken to the northern CBI, chambers of commerce, several constituency Labour parties, a number of trade union branches and graduate students on a course in urban planning at Oxford Brookes University. The discussions ranged widely over all the topics covered by the report, and it was pleasing that the plight of the UPAs was being given such prominence in people's thinking. Margaret Thatcher acknowledged something of this when she won her third general election in 1987. Speaking to her supporters from the window of Conservative Central Office, she said: "Tomorrow morning we must do something about the inner cities."

What made it possible for the report to carry weight was the fact that the national establishment of the Church was supported by a local establishment: the Church of England was organized on a territorial basis with clergy in parishes across the country and, while church attendance might have been low in UPAs, the ministry of the clergy was nevertheless understood and on the whole valued. We were often astonished at how much local knowledge the clergy had and how well known they were to the organizations and businesses in their parishes. The culture beyond the Church was not wholly secularized and not hostile to Christianity. Looking back, this may have been the high-water mark of parish ministry and therefore of that local establishment.

The training of the clergy and the Church Urban Fund
We did not offer a theology of the city. On the contrary, we were clear that UPA congregations had to work at this for themselves. We noted that an overemphasis on a certain type of academic theology might deter UPA Christians from doing this and we wanted clergy who might minister in such congregations to receive appropriate training.

There was an urgent need to prepare ordinands better for working as priests in UPA parishes, but there was no way this could be mandated centrally. Theological colleges were run by independent trusts, and each had its own particular theological emphases. Courses and colleges responded to the dioceses that sent students and the dioceses themselves were, to all intents and purposes, semi-autonomous. Nevertheless, in different ways, many colleges and courses did respond.

The year after publication I joined the staff of Ripon College, Cuddesdon, a liberal catholic Oxford theological college. (Archbishop Runcie had once been the principal.) The majority of students were from suburban or rural parishes and a good number had been educated in private schools. Almost all had a degree. For many, the UPA parish was as alien as a foreign posting would have been to a nineteenth-century missionary.

The principal, John Garton, who had been an inner-city parish priest in Coventry, talked about the possibility of moving the college to a northern city, which would have been a very bold move. I was sent to explore possible sites, such as a former teacher training college in Manchester where there was a theology faculty in the university. The Professor of Social and Pastoral Theology, Anthony Dyson, was a former principal of Ripon Hall theological college and would have been supportive in developing academic courses for ordinands. In the event, this was a step too far: college governors and others argued that a regular supply of Cuddesdon students was essential for maintaining the viability of the Oxford divinity faculty.

I was then asked to make links with my former diocese of Sheffield and Sheffield City Council. We identified the Manor parish as a suitable place for training. The vicar, the Revd John Packer, afterwards Bishop of Ripon and Leeds, was very supportive. Ordinands who already had a theology degree would be resident on the council estate near to St Swithun's church. The Revd Richard Atkinson was appointed as the training priest. We formed a local support group chaired by an Anglican lay woman, Veronica Hardstaff, who had been a city councillor and went on to be a Member of the European Parliament.

Students who went to the Manor parish were introduced to the parish audit and to the idea of the pastoral cycle from liberation theology. The latter is a way of understanding a social context through a process of analysis—economic, political, demographic—and theological reflection leading to action.

At Ripon College, Cuddesdon, we also sent students on placements to John Garton's former Coventry parish, where they lived for a while with non-white families. Groups of us visited worship centres of other faiths—a temple, a gurdwara and a mosque—but in ways that made it clear that interfaith dialogue was not going to be easy. The mosque was very challenging. A Muslim scholar, who was acquainted with the Christian scriptures, gave the students a hard time, speaking about Tawhid and how monotheism and the Trinity were irreconcilable. The Sikhs wanted to know where the ordinands stood on Khalistan and Sikh separatism. Several found the visits disturbing; but if they were going to have a serious ministry in a multi-faith parish, they would need to rid themselves of any vestige of a patronizing Anglicanism.

But better-trained clergy would need resources. One of the crucial recommendations for the Church in the report was the establishment of a Church Urban Fund (CUF). This happened in 1988 and raised some £55 million for projects, including adaptations to church buildings to make them more useable and sustainable. The establishment of the CUF was critical: it indicated that the Church as a whole was prepared to put its money where its mouth was and support the UPA parishes.

In the final analysis, I think the fact that the report was commissioned at all may have been at least as important as any recommendations in it. It gave fresh energy to urban mission and to those who were working in the UPA parishes. Prior to that, they had often felt forgotten by their dioceses, and often were.

Final reflections after 40 years

It is dispiriting to realize that many of the places we visited 40 years ago are still places of poverty and deprivation, and there are new ones: we would need to add coastal towns to the list. There has been some regeneration and gentrification, especially in urban centres where there are canals and waterways. But there is an even more pronounced geographical aspect to poverty now, with the north suffering disproportionately—though foodbanks are ubiquitous.

What we failed to notice

There were also issues that we did not address. Chief among these was the danger of communalism that Enoch Powell had first raised in 1968. This related directly to the riots and went to the heart of how a country that was becoming increasingly plural could nevertheless be socially cohesive, something I have sought to address in my own subsequent writing. Commissioners were liberal-minded people who assumed that a cohesive society would follow if different cultures and faiths were respected and discrimination was made unlawful. This was necessary, but it underestimated the potential for inter-community tensions when ethnic minorities were concentrated in particular parts of a town or city. This was happening as growing numbers of Pakistani Muslim families in particular settled near their extended families and the same mosques and halal butchers.

We also had too benign a view of religion and failed to see how it could be destabilizing, not necessarily contributing to social cohesion. This was borne out quite soon after *Faith in the City* was published, when Salman Rushdie's novel, *The Satanic Verses*, appeared in 1988. The title was a reference to some Quranic texts which Rushdie interpreted to mean that, on one occasion, the Prophet Muhammad had been tempted to speak favourably about three local female deities in order to win over the people of Mecca. Muslims were outraged in this country and worldwide, idolatry being the greatest of sins. Ayatollah Ruhollah Khomeini, the Supreme Leader of Iran, a Shia, issued a fatwa that proclaimed the killing of Rushdie a religious duty. Sunni Muslims burnt copies of the book on the streets of Bradford. Questions began to be asked about how far the settled Pakistani Muslim community was embracing British values. This eventually led to a national debate about what those values might be.

Then in 2001, there were summer disturbances over several nights in northern English towns and cities—Bradford, Oldham and Burnley. Buildings and cars were set alight and the police attacked; but this time the men who took to the streets were Asian (largely Pakistani) rather than black. Especially troubling was the fact that many of those convicted and imprisoned, though not all, were in employment, married and with supportive families. Whatever was happening, it could not simply be about poverty and deprivation.

A report was produced for the government by Ted Cantle in which he suggested that the principal issue was not poverty, but a lack of community cohesion brought about by different ethnic groups living "parallel lives" in the same town—together yet apart. In the inner cities in particular, "white flight" had contributed to enclaves of Asian families in streets that had once been either totally white or more mixed.

The government accepted the Cantle report and "community cohesion" now became central to all public policies.[19] A Home Office Community Cohesion Panel was set up to take forward the recommendations with Professor Cantle as chair. I was asked to co-chair the Faith group, looking specifically at what the faith communities could contribute. We found a great deal of goodwill on the part of the different faith groups, with the more liberal mosque leaders, as far as they could, modelling something like the traditional ministry of Anglican parish churches. They encouraged their members to be involved in wider community events, to help with foodbanks, set up boxing clubs, become councillors, volunteer as chaplains to the blue light services, invite people into the mosque for iftars,[20] and so on. I found it curious that just as the mosques were gaining confidence and looking out into the community, the Church of England was turning its attention away from traditional parish ministry and pursuing a different model of mission and ministry.

But this reaching out was not true of all mosques and, in too many towns and cities, communities of largely Asian Muslim families and largely white, nominally Christian families lived parallel lives with little interaction. As the years have passed, the community cohesion agenda has begun to appear inadequate to deal with the issues posed by enclavization.[21] This became clearer at the general election in 2024 when some Muslims, who in the past would have supported Labour, Conservative or Liberal Democrat candidates, stood as independents, some being elected. What should cause alarm was not that they opposed the support of mainstream parties for Israel's policy in Gaza (some in those parties did the same), but the appearance of a faith-based or sectarian politics. Some of those canvassing for support were openly saying that Muslims should only ever vote for fellow Muslims, though even then only those who were sound on such issues as Gaza and Israel. In many towns and cities where there are large Muslim populations, we

---

[19] T. Cantle, *Community Cohesion: A New Framework for Race and Diversity* (Basingstoke: Palgrave Macmillan, 2005); A. Billings, *God and Community Cohesion: Help or Hindrance?* (London: SPCK, 2009), pp. 115-22.

[20] The iftar is the evening meal that breaks the fast during Ramadan.

[21] See Alan Billings, *God and Community Cohesion*.

may see more of this in the future, in local as well as national politics, with little idea of what the consequences might be. There is still faith in the city; but it begs the question: is there also the beginnings of the communalism that Powell feared in 1968?

The riots of 2024
Forty years after *Faith in the City*, we had further urban riots, though this time the rioters were white, protesting against "immigration" and its consequences. Many were also racist and Islamophobic, attacking mosques as well as hotels where asylum seekers were housed. The new Labour government reacted swiftly to ensure that rioters were identified, arrested and convicted. Many commentators saw the riots as the result of right-wing extremism, and some indeed were politically motivated; but there was no obvious directing mind. Most of the disturbances seemed spontaneous, even if fuelled by social media, the response of some very angry people whose grievances could all be focused on "immigrants" and ethnic minorities. Whatever those discontents might be, if a form of sectarian politics does develop among ethnic minorities, it is likely to find an echo among the disaffected white communities who feel let down by the failed promises of such policies as Brexit and Levelling Up. This will make integration and cohesion all the harder.

The erosion of parish ministry
But the contemporary Church of England is scarcely able to comment on what is happening in the more deprived parts of the country today in the way it could 40 years ago. In 1983, the local churches understood themselves to be "parish" churches as opposed to "associational" or "gathered" congregations.[22] Associational congregations come together because of shared commitments and beliefs; they attract individual consumers of religion and could meet anywhere. The congregations of parish churches and their clergy think of themselves as part of a national church, organized territorially, having a responsibility before God for

---

[22] See Alan Billings, "The parish church", in Martyn Percy (ed.), *The Study of Ministry: A Comprehensive Survey of Theory and Best Practice* (London: SPCK, 2019), pp. 388-402.

all who live or work in their parishes. This is why parish boundaries matter: they ensure that every part of the country is the prayerful and pastoral concern of a local congregation and its clergy. Members of parish churches join or support local organizations and in so doing contribute towards building social capital in their neighbourhoods, which is crucial for community resilience. This is why, as we travelled about the country, we found UPA clergy and congregations that were rooted in their communities and able to speak knowledgeably about local issues. This gave the report much of its authority and authenticity: it was the local establishment on which the national establishment of the Church depends.

But this understanding of the parish church, reflected in the Book of Common Prayer and accepted at one time by evangelicals and catholics alike, is fading in many dioceses. This is only partly because declining numbers make it harder to resource the parishes. It is also because the Church has failed to grasp the significant contribution that parish churches made to cohesive communities. As a result, many dioceses have abandoned the traditional concept of parish ministry and have adopted a different set of assumptions. One northern diocese has this as its defining mission:

> The Diocese of ... is called to grow a sustainable network of Christ-like, lively and diverse Christian communities in every place which are effective in making disciples and in seeking to transform our society and God's world.

This is not a call to renew the parish churches but to create alongside them or instead of them gathered assemblies meeting or planted in a variety of venues whose primary objective is "growing disciples" rather than the traditional concerns of parish and pastoral ministry. As a result, the Church attempts to support two operating models simultaneously—the "mixed ecology" of parish churches and gathered congregations—while lacking the human and financial resources to do both. It sets itself up to fail and fatally weakens its place in the local community and, ultimately, nationally.

The driver of this is fear—fear that traditional parishes are incapable of growing and the Church will wither and die as a result. But this failure of nerve is leading to a profound re-fashioning of the Anglican mind and imagination and its role in building community. It is hardly surprising that the traditional parishes struggle, especially those in UPAs, and the mind of the parish church is lost in those gathered, mainly evangelical, congregations. There is little evidence that these new "communities" are any more successful in drawing in the people of the UPAs, and as well as attracting they also repel, something that is often overlooked. The doors of the traditional parish church were always open, literally as well as metaphorically. The modern congregation—whether a Fresh Expression or a plant—is more like a private club.

In 2020, Covid presented a severe test and many parish clergy were dismayed that the bishops ordered churches to be closed when, arguably, places of worship could have been places of sanctuary and consolation. It was even more depressing when clergy were prevented from visiting their flock. The Book of Common Prayer envisaged the clergy taking the sacrament to the sick in a pandemic even if to no one else.[23] Times have changed; along, it seems, with job descriptions.

As a result of this parish ministry over generations, clergy retained with the public a measure of trust, sometimes even affection. The "vicar" or "rector" is a role that means something to people outside as well as within the Church of England: it has social value. This often enables a priest to play a part in the community at critical moments of celebration or grieving—as we saw in 2024 when local churches opened their doors to a shocked community in Southport after three young girls were murdered there at a dance class. (This sparked the 2024 riots because social media had identified the killer as an immigrant and asylum seeker—which was not true.) The Christian culture is much weaker than when *Faith in the City* was written; though it is far from non-existent. However, the waning of the traditional Anglican mind means that there are far fewer congregations deeply rooted in their localities, especially those that we once called UPAs.

---

[23] Final rubric for The Communion of the Sick in the Book of Common Prayer.

Is there still faith in the city?

The common Christian culture might be weaker, but we should not underestimate the salience of religion more generally, as the appearance of more sectarian Muslim politics has shown. In the decades since *Faith in the City* was written, Britain has become both more secular and more religiously plural and that poses questions about the place of the Church of England in such a society. It is not impossible for the Church to retain the local role which was crucial in enabling us to write *Faith in the City* and which justifies its national role as the established church; but only if it is prepared to support again wholeheartedly the idea of the local parish church and parish ministry embedded in particular places and communities. We would still find "faith in the city",[24] but there would be more ambiguity in that phrase than when we first coined it 40 years ago.

---

[24] The last sentence of the report is: "We have found faith in the city".

3

Urban ministry, liberation, and *Faith in the City*

Ian K. Duffield

My relationship to *Faith in the City* has gone through four phases that track my life and ministry: an anticipatory pre-phase, an exciting dominant phase, a disappointing post-phase, and a life-after phase. A pre-phase may sound rather odd, so let me explain.

Pre-phase

As a teenager, I first felt a call to be ordained and then a call to be a theologian and was ordained by Robert Runcie, as Bishop of St Albans, in 1973, before he became the archbishop who initiated the commission that produced *Faith in the City*. In the late 1970s, I found myself in charge of a district church in one of the wealthiest (least deprived) parishes in the country; and it was there (precisely there) that I felt a call. What that was I could not easily determine, although, as someone interested in systematic theology from university days, I had begun to read Latin American liberation theology, in particular *Marx and the Bible* (ET 1977) by the Mexican theologian José Porfirio Miranda, which I found both exciting and challenging, particularly in its reading of Scripture. After exploring various options, I felt a vocation to urban ministry. Knowing that I would need training for that, I discovered the Urban Theology Unit in Sheffield (UTU) and signed up for its Urban Ministry course; at the same time UTU's energetic founder, John Vincent, persuaded me to do the Doctor of Ministry programme (DMin) that was run in conjunction with the New York Theological Seminary, which I readily embraced as part of my vocation to be a theologian, albeit outside the academy. I consulted Canon Eric James, the diocesan missioner, who supported me in this move, not knowing that he would be an instigator, through a letter to a national newspaper, of what became Runcie's commission.

When I accepted the call to study at UTU, I explained to John Vincent that there was a problem: my ministerial context was not urban. John said there were plenty of jobs in Sheffield, so why not apply for one. So it was that I went for an interview for an urban parish in Sheffield. Frankly, Bishop David Lunn told me that I probably wouldn't get the job, and if so to contact him straightaway, as he had another post he'd like me to look at. Bishop David was right, and I immediately went to view a vacancy in a large team ministry on the well-known (that's a euphemism) Manor estate that they'd been unable to fill. Once I got on the estate, I knew this was where I was called to be and managed to persuade my family when I got home that this was an exciting venture. So, in 1981, I moved with my wife and two young children to the Manor estate, at the time regarded as one of the most deprived parishes in the diocese, and the primary school to which our children went was described by a national newspaper as the worst school in the country (disclaimer: it wasn't true), where I became a governor. By 1985, I had completed the Urban Ministry course and my doctorate, which included a project in ministry on my deprived council estate with a small congregation whose church had been demolished and not replaced. At the same time, the DMin developed my knowledge of, and interest in, liberation theology and its methodology and practice. We read and discussed, for example, *Frontiers of Theology in Latin America* (ET 1980), edited by Rosino Gibellini, with essays by luminaries such as Rubem Alves, Leonardo Boff, José Miguez Bonino, José Comblin and Gustavo Gutiérrez, and Juan Segundo's challenging *Liberation of Theology* (ET 1976); also, I discovered Ernesto Cardenal's remarkable record of exchanges between Nicaraguans discussing Scripture: *The Gospel in Solentiname*, e.g. *Love in Practice* (ET 1976/7). Along the way, I was invited by John Vincent to join UTU's core staff as a volunteer to help run the Urban Ministry course and supervise postgraduate students. This all happened before the publication of *Faith in the City*.

Dominant phase

I call this the dominant phase because when *Faith in the City* was published, I found it an affirmation and confirmation and clarification of what I was already doing. For many people, of course, it was more of a revelation. Despite reservations in some quarters, the report was not put on a shelf, as is often the case—there was a real positive reaction. Clergy posts in urban areas became sought after; courses and conferences were sponsored; theological colleges set up urban placements. All in all, doing urban ministry became the "flavour of the month", or even the decade.

Significantly, UTU's Urban Ministry course—which was personally an induction into a way of operating—always began with what John Vincent called "Situation Analysis". This was a comprehensive investigation of local realities, both ecclesial and secular, that was then supplemented by "Gospel Analysis". Out of these investigations and the dynamic between them participants were encouraged to frame and engage in a Gospel Project that related to their context. In this way, analysis and thought and Bible were in service to action. At UTU, we used "Situation Analysis" with students at all levels, and the document went through various editions over the years. The latest version, which I edited, called "Contextual Analysis" (2018), deliberately included a section on Analysis and Action, because it is not analysis for the sake of analysis, but as a prelude, as it were, to action and to inform decision-making. But interpreting facts is hardly ever straightforward and discernment is required. Also, there are various responses to the facts, which can include non-action and reaction, whereas, following liberation theology, we are interested in action towards transformation and liberation.

By the beginning of the century, we had started to talk about contextual theology, of which the urban theology that Vincent had pioneered was a particular form, which, in its turn, was also related to liberation theology. I found myself writing on the inter-relationship between these overlapping types of theology, years later: in *Crucibles: Creating Theology at UTU* (2000), pp. 20ff., which I wrote with Christine Jones and John Vincent; and, again, in John Vincent (ed.), *Faithfulness in the City* (2003), pp. 273ff. The relationship with liberation theology had become more explicit when Chris Rowland (Professor of NT Theology at Oxford) and John Vincent began editing a series of volumes, published by UTU, on *British Liberation Theology* back in 1995, to which I also contributed, as we sought to see how liberation theology from a totally different social context in another part of the world had implications and ramifications for us in the UK. In some sense, this was a taking up of the baton presented by a chapter in *Faith in the City* on liberation theology (see below), although UTU's interest and involvement pre-dated that publication. In this way, I was finding my feet as an urban practitioner and contextual theologian, with my feet in the city, in the urban, on the streets.

And, so, the dominant phase took shape. I can't remember quite when the Urban Mission Training Association began, but we started holding annual conferences that were well subscribed. Neville Black from Liverpool, Michael Eastman from London, Derek Purnell from Manchester, and representatives from organizations such as EUTP and Salford Mission came together to consult, to share and to support each other in offering training in urban ministry and mission. There was a real sense that *Faith in the City* had changed the conversation and that what we were doing in different urban areas across the country was suddenly validated and taken seriously.

Sheffield Diocese started responding and taking initiatives. It was very exciting. Bishop David invited me to chair a small diocesan group to produce a report to provide a local response to *Faith in the City*. This took up a lot of my time and attention, on top of my work running a parish, and along the way I moved to an urban village in Sheffield. UTU's "Situation Analysis" had taught me the importance of understanding the facts on the ground, so I found myself playing a very small part nationally in the designation of what came to be called UPAs, i.e. "urban priority area" parishes. Thanks to John Chilcott, I attended national consultations on how this might work in the dioceses. Taking up a government term (urban priority area) and applying it to parishes was a significant task. First the parishes had to be mapped carefully to enumeration districts (the basic unit of data collection), which I undertook (with help) for the whole of the diocese. As I look back, it was a massive task, but I realized at the time it was a fundamental exercise to obtain empirical data. In this someone working for South Yorkshire County Council (which no longer exists) was immensely helpful, perhaps delighted that someone in the Church was interested in his statistical expertise. The results were a revelation to some in the diocese, as it challenged some parishes' perception of their population size or whether they were as deprived as they thought they were. I also got involved in things like Z-scores, which was a sophisticated, statistical way of combining various deprivation factors such as unemployment into a single score. Once again, I was delighted that someone from Hallam University (thanks to the local Methodist minister) seemed only too willing to explain to me the statistical methodology being used. In the end, we were able to list the UPAs in the Diocese of Sheffield and provide parishes with percentages for a range of deprivation factors. A few years down the line, a new system came in and it all had to be done again, as a way of trying to be as accurate as possible, with the added complication that they decided to change the statistical method, so back to the drawing board in trying to understand the selected system.

At the same time, the small group which I chaired had to come up with a strategy for the diocese. The result of this was two particular moves that were distinctive to Sheffield, although other dioceses did similar things, but not, I think, with the solidity of our approach:

1. The formation of a *Faith in the City* committee, as a new part of the diocesan structure, that was comprised of people from UPAs and met not at diocesan headquarters but moved around the UPA parishes.
2. The employment of a full-time *Faith in the City* development worker based in a UPA (most dioceses added this task to an existing task, e.g. social responsibility officer, thus reducing capacity) to support and advise UPA parishes and their projects.

This structural rooting of the diocese's response was designed to embed it into the system to ensure its continual validity and effectiveness.

Our report, *Partnership for Action* (1987), foregrounded the poor and the powerless as "high priority" for all the diocese's plans, policies and prayers. It encouraged parishes to be bold and to follow *Faith in the City*'s threefold advice to be: (1) truly "local" by being committed "to the local people and to the places where they live, work and associate" (*Faith in the City* 4:7), (2) "outward looking" by taking "seriously the local realities of life as an integral part of its mission to UPAs and the whole of society" (*Faith in the City* 4:13), and (3) "participating" by "collaborating with the best expressions of local life and by contributing to the transformation of life in UPAs" (*Faith in the City* 4:20). It was assumed that this entailed engagement in local projects to the benefit of local people, not just the church.

At the same time, nationally, the Church Urban Fund (CUF) was set up to fund local projects in parishes. Again, Bishop David, who was utterly committed to following through with *Faith in the City*, and sat on the *Faith in the City* committee as a member, invited me to chair a diocesan CUF panel to review applications for funding along with a few others from the committee, including the *Faith in the City* development worker: a Methodist, Ian McCollough, whom I'd met previously when he was running a Community Programme scheme. My UTU experience really paid off on the panel, because I was totally familiar with the whole business of local projects and making them robust and effective. As I've said, we would intentionally try to meet in the UPA parish itself that was requesting funding. We deliberately met on *their* turf to discuss *their* project in *their* locality. We were keen that projects would be successful and were able to fund many such local projects over a period of time; and in many cases to suggest revision of their plans to be more outward-looking and effective. Unfortunately, our promotion of credit unions was not accepted nationally.

So, as you can see, there was a dominant *Faith in the City* phase for me that validated the report and its significance, not least at the local level. But inevitably, I suppose, this couldn't last for ever, and the energy and focus started to slip, which brings me to the disappointing post-phase.

Post-phase

I can't quite remember when it started, but the original excitement and energy associated with *Faith in the City* began to dissipate. It links in my life to two particular experiences. One was the decision by the diocese to end the *Faith in the City* committee and merge it with Social Responsibility. Through argument and discussion, the new committee was given a new name: it was called Faith and Justice, as a way of not merely being subsumed under Social Responsibility, that I had perceived to be the original danger, which is why we argued initially for a separate committee. However, now *Faith in the City* became merely an item on a much larger socially liberal agenda, i.e. it became downgraded, and the membership was much broader, neutering UPA voices on the committee. After a while, in 2005, I no longer thought it right to stay on the committee.

The second experience was related to the Church Urban Fund. There was a change in the way funding was organized, which meant that the national fund was targeting dioceses rather than parishes and looking for bigger projects, but ones not necessarily rooted and grounded in local communities. Again, I felt that something was being lost and found myself unable to continue. Although both changes could probably be justified in terms of efficiency, I thought that both constituted a shift towards the diocese rather than the parish and to an agenda that was more oriented towards social responsibility rather than *Faith in the City*. Others disagreed with me (although, much later, the social responsibility officer told me he thought I had been right). Whatever, the end result was a reduction of energy, in myself at least. The dominant phase of energizing activity prompted by *Faith in the City* that had lasted for a good season had seemed to come to the end of a cycle: I discerned that urban ministry was no longer the "flavour of the month".

This was emphasized for me by the relative neglect of the publication *Faithful Cities: A Call for Celebration, Vision and Justice* (2006), an attempt 20 years on to reboot *Faith in the City*. The commission members were well chosen, and its format more interesting than the original. It contemplated "what makes a good city?" as it sought to re-stimulate the *Faith in the City* agenda. In particular it contained the interesting notion of "faithful capital", on which I can remember Rob Furbey, from Sheffield, discoursing well. This was an extension of the valuable idea of "social capital", which is crucial to sustaining and building up communities, to the religious sphere. In the end, the report was probably not in the right key to get a good listening, despite being produced in a friendlier (and shorter) format than the original report. In fact, although the endeavour after 20 years to not only mark the occasion but also to try and re-stimulate energy was worthy, it was overtaken by events. As Terry Drummond makes clear in his thesis, the publication of *Mission-Shaped Church* in 2004 trumped it and signalled a change of direction for the Church of England that had been underway for some time. Here was the latest "flavour of the month", and the important theological critiques of it by John Hull and especially Andrew Davison and Alison Milbank (*For the Parish: A Critique of Fresh Expressions* [2010]) had little effect. Talk of mission and fresh expressions to counteract the decline in people attending church services began to dominate Church of England discourse. Its success in changing the narrative and the direction, of which the effective sidelining of *Faith in the City* was perhaps an inevitable side-effect, became even clearer with the fusillade of reports from the Archbishops' Council ten years later. The Reform and Renewal agenda or, as it became known, Renewal and Reform, has dominated the Church of England discourse and energy to this day. This is leading to a downplaying of parishes, evidenced by the emergence of a Save the Parish campaign (in which Alison Milbank is prominent) to counteract its influence, which is detrimental to ordinary parish churches and their functioning and, consequently, what we used to call UPA parishes.

As I've already said, I was drawn to liberation theology in the late 1970s and had drunk from its wells in the early 1980s; so, I was pleased to see that *Faith in the City* had a theological chapter devoted to it. This was written by A. E. Harvey, my former theological college principal. Of course, Harvey was an excellent writer who had written valuable books on the New Testament and various aspects of biblical ethics. But he was not a liberation theologian. Moreover, the chapter, as Alan Billings has pointed out in conversation, was a stand-alone and didn't really influence the report, which was based more on a William Temple model of doing theology: the gathering together of experts and theologians to produce reports that presented facts and promulgated Christian perspectives in relation to current issues. Although, insofar as it produced recommendations to the government as well as to the Church, perhaps it had taken up a more directly political edge for a Church of England report. However that may be, it seems as though this way of producing church reports has now virtually died out. In the past, there have been many reports, whether on abortion or euthanasia or welfare, etc., that have been produced in this way, but these seem to have come to an end. At the same time, there has recently been much more politically engaged interventions by bishops. Of course, some will welcome this activist approach, but it has not been distinctive of the Church of England, and it risks the Church being seen as party political rather than being able to offer a judicious moral perspective on policy from time to time, rather than a running commentary, which had seemed to somewhat characterize the forays of the former Archbishop Justin Welby.

Since then, we've seen the end of the classic phase of Latin American liberation theology as the political realities changed in El Salvador and Argentina, etc., with the ending (largely) of dictatorial rule. Moreover, the latest phase of liberation theology appears to have departed from its roots, with emphasis now placed upon socio-political analysis with almost no place for biblical engagement (see *The Future of Liberation Theology* [2004] by Ivan Petrella). In other words, it has become much more ideological. The classic See–Judge–Act procedure (which actually pre-dates liberation theology) has morphed into a See–Act procedure, as if the facts or analysis already determines the action. This is why there is no need for Scripture; the judging is already in the seeing and present in the acting; and the acting is now seen in a much more explicitly political way with little sense that there are any difficulties in assessing the facts or knowing how to respond to them. In other words, the Bible has ceased to be a discrete phase in a process that appears more ideological. This, for me, undermines the use of that latest iteration of liberation theology today for the Church, whereas the classic liberation theology canon can still inspire and provide resources for the discerning.

John Vincent's response after nearly two decades of *Faith in the City*, which pre-dated *Faithful Cities*, was to produce a book of essays through the annual gathering at St Deiniol's Library of the Urban Theology Collective that John had begun with the support of Peter Francis, the library's warden. The volume attempted to ensure that urban ministry and theology did not fade from the Church's agenda and was entitled *Faithfulness in the City* (2003). This hardly had any impact even though it had a number of weighty contributors: Greg Smith, Ann Morisy, Colin Marchant, Chris Baker and Michael Northcott. However, the resolute implication that the faithfulness of local Christian communities was what mattered was apposite, and I imagine that something similar could be attempted all these years later. This volume flagged up that what was needed in needy communities was faithful Christians, faithful to the Church and faithful to their local community, to their city. As *Faith in the City* might have put it: being truly local, and faithful in being outward-looking, and participatory.

Nevertheless, sadly, *Faith in the City* has run its course, and *Faithful Cities* (let alone *Faithfulness in the City*) did not produce a resurgence, and nothing since has either, as Renewal and Reform continues to cast its shadow over the Church, and other shadows—such as safeguarding scandals and Living in Love and Faith disagreements—continue to dominate church affairs and sap its energy. Although this may cause dismay or depression or dissolution, this is not an appropriate attitude. Those of us who have been inspired by what *Faith in the City* unleashed and who believe in urban ministry need to have a more positive view of the future.

So, the post-phase has been disappointing. Of course there are shafts of light. Although I'm not up to date on its work, the Estates Network still brings people together to share, to think, to plan; and over ten years ago I and two colleagues wrote a piece on Lament from the Sheffield chapter (see Ali Dorey, Ian K. Duffield, Julie Upton, "Rediscovering Lament as a Practice of the Church—Especially on Poor Housing Estates", *Theology and Ministry* 1 [2012]). Also, community organizing still exists, with a former director of UTU, Keith Hebden, keeping the flame burning. And there is the Asset-Based approach to community, which I worked with others to introduce into Sheffield Diocese, just before I retired, when I was working on another council estate in north Sheffield. This approach starts not from need or deprivation but asks what assets a community (however deprived) has and then works from that base. This *positive* approach helps to provide a healthy realism that is not overwhelmed by the problems and seems more likely to be a way to go in the future. It's also a good way for viewing a congregation and helping it move forward. Church Action on Poverty continues to have branches in major cities, and I contributed to a reflective commentary for its Urban Pilgrimage in Sheffield in 2024, which emphasized the spiritual and theological dynamics of such pilgrimages (see Joseph Forde and Ian K. Duffield, "Urban Poverty Pilgrimage: Towards a Theological Practice" on its website).

A life-after phase: Reasons to be cheerful

Looking back 40 years must not be separated from looking forward, even though the current scene does not appear propitious. As I look back and look forward in retirement, I think there are grounds, solid theological grounds, for not despairing, even though the season of *Faith in the City* has ended. There are three reasons, in particular, to be cheerful, as Ian Dury once sang.

1. God hears the cries of the poor: this is what the Scriptures affirm and what liberation theology has taught us. Because God has a preferential option for the poor, then it will not be surprising, although we may not be ready for it, if God raises up witnesses among the poor and to the poor in the years ahead. This is something we should expect, if we cannot anticipate it or predict it.
2. Although we live in the time after, *Faith in the City* remains: it now stands as an historic marker in Church of England history to which people may look for inspiration and encouragement. It has become part of the tradition. So many church reports just sit on the shelf and nothing happens. *Faith in the City* testifies that this is not always true. For nearly two decades, *Faith in the City* informed and featured strongly in the life of the Church of England. Although its influence has waned and been replaced by

other concerns, *Faith in the City* stands tall as an exemplification and crystallization of the importance of the poor within the life of the Church. As such it (a) points backwards to those other signs that God loves the poor, in, for example, the slum priests of the nineteenth century, (b) points to those who today continue its emphases; and (c) points forwards to new ventures by the Church that will give priority to the poor. *Faith in the City* constitutes a boundary marker for the Church of England; and, as Scripture says, cursed are those who move their neighbour's boundary marker.

3. Most people active today in ministry probably can't remember the heady days of *Faith in the City*, because those who were at their prime when *Faith in the City* emerged are now in retirement or have gone on before us. However, we must not imagine that there will not be some, if only a few, who will be guided by the Spirit into urban ministry among the poor and will remind others that God loves the poor; after all it's in our Scriptures and central to Jesus' ministry. The same might be said about liberation theology. Its classic period has passed, but just as there were witnesses before to God's bias to the poor, as David Sheppard put it (*Bias to the Poor* [1983]), there will be witnesses in the future too, although we do not yet know their names.

What is going to be important in the future is continuing to focus on context. Reading the context from the streets, engaging with the realities of urban life, will inevitably lead some to gospel projects among the poor. We can see this in the present day. I, for one, do not look askance at foodbanks, as if they shouldn't exist. After all, Canada has had them for years. (For a positive perspective see, for example, the article in the *Church Times*, 17 January 2025, about the initiatives of one foodbank in London.) Also, soup kitchens, and friendly warm spaces, retain a role, if primarily in winter. And in the past, we had jumble sales which recycled clothes and shoes and so much else, cheaply. It's only natural for the Church to engage in such local projects: meeting need where it needs to be met, responding to local people in really helpful and practical ways. Not talking about the poor abstractly or imagining reality idealistically or proposing utopian projects, as if we can stand above it all, but rather engaging with people where they are and helping them to help themselves, as liberation theology has also taught us.

And if people engage with realities on the ground, then it will give them protection from presumption and arrogance and elitism. People will be less likely to be seduced by rhetorical gestures such as "Make Poverty History", as if that was a realistic proposal. After all, because we're talking about relative poverty in this country, then poverty will always continue because there will always be people, statistically, below the average—that's a consequence of what an average is! More on this in the next section. In other words, we must try to avoid those peddling resentment and grand political programmes and grand economic analyses that over-focus on measures of inequality measured by the Gini coefficient. What this means, for me, is best expressed, dialectically:

- Yes: to Church Action on Poverty. No: to the illusion that we can completely eliminate poverty rather than ameliorate or reduce its effects.
- Yes: to befriending the poor and working alongside them. No: to imagining that we can stand above it all and come up with foolproof schemes to eradicate poverty, as if it was a disease that needed the right treatment.
- Yes: to analysing what's going on and why people are poor. No: to presuming that we can solve a problem that has been endemic throughout history for all sorts (so many sorts) of reasons.
- Yes: to the Church placing itself among the poor and accepting that the poor are naturally part of the Church. No: to the Church preferring the rich (see the Epistle of James) or ignoring the poor or failing to listen and learn from them.

Perspective 2025

Finally, I want to offer some critical reflections, to challenge and stimulate our thinking about poverty and society in the future.

We could be forgiven for thinking, in recent years, that it's all hopeless, as we're continuously told we live in a grossly unequal society, plagued by social injustice: by inequity, racism, misogyny, transphobia, Islamophobia, with rampant consumerism within an exploitative capitalist system. This narrative, or some version of it, is dominant in 2025; I come across it all the time. It makes it seem as though life today is more difficult than in the 1980s, as if we've gone backwards rather than forwards. But that doesn't seem right, because it's viewing reality through a skewed lens. Of course, real problems remain and life in Britain has got difficult since the financial crash and Covid, with our current economic fortunes as a country not looking good. But then again, we do not live in a perfect world and our society in many ways is inevitably immoral, to some degree, as Reinhold Niebuhr taught us (*Moral Man and Immoral Society* [1932]). Yet, most of us—black and white and brown—are, generally (in the aggregate, over time), privileged to be living in the twenty-first century (for all its faults and stresses), even though we may not acknowledge it. In short, we are continuously presented with many reasons to be depressed or anxious about society and urban life in particular that we find many reasons not to be cheerful. But this kind of narrative depends upon a crude and simplistic view of what is going on, where everything is seen in binary terms and where suspicion lurks at every corner. Of course, those of us brought up on liberation theology know that it is sometimes necessary to adopt a hermeneutic of suspicion; but many social activists adopt a systematic and ideologically relentless suspicion today that takes no prisoners. So, men (all men) become misogynists, and white folk (all whites) are racists/supremacists, and Westerners (all of them) are viewed as unforgiveable imperialists. This is not based upon a careful adjudication of the evidence but is a blanket moralistic judgement that we are right to be suspicious about.

The data in *Faith in the City* may be out of date, 40 years on, but hopefully the careful marshalling of evidence, as indicated by *Faith in the City*, is still an important task. But how often, today, are statements made and policies developed without a careful reading of the facts, which are often hard to interpret well. This certainly applies to language about people being rich or poor (see below). One of the things I think I've learnt in recent years is that we need to avoid any simplistic rhetoric about such important matters. So—with regret or resignation, if not resentment—folk say: "the rich get richer and the poor get poorer". Although we hear this all the time, and we may say it ourselves, it's at best misleading, because even though it might have been true in the past, in the modern era it's truer to say: "the rich get richer, and so, too, do the poor" (generally, even if you can always find someone who stands outside it). For most of history, life (including biblical times) has been a *zero-sum game*: with a limited-sized pie, so that if some got more of the pie, then others inevitably got less. However, in modern times, the pie has been increasing to such a degree that all of us are better off than we were.

When I think of my childhood in the early 1950s, we weren't poor but we had no TV, no telephone, no fridge, no central heating, no car, no computer—all things that many now regard as essential, yet back then were the stuff of dreams—and when we were married, we didn't get central heating until the late 1970s, and a small colour TV until the 1980s. In this new century, most people have these things; indeed, most people have smartphones, giving access to information at the click of a button (or is it a swipe of a key?), along with laptops and streaming services at their fingertips. When our family first got a TV, there was only one channel in black and white; now there are a staggering number of channels and streaming options—too many to watch. Choice has ballooned beyond imagination; and it's not only the rich or privileged who have access.

As it happens, Gordon Brown, the former Chancellor and Prime Minister, in an interview on Radio 4 (19 January 2025), as I was finalizing this section, claimed that children were as poor now as they were back then in his home town of Kirkcaldy; I doubt it, but when you compare now with the 1950s, 1960s, 1970s, when you were a child, what do you think? Part of the problem is that the Joseph Rowntree Foundation (JRF), which does stalwart work on compiling data on "poverty", is actually talking about *relative* poverty, relative to a calculated norm for our society (see its *UK Poverty 2024: The essential guide to understanding poverty in the UK*). This does not enable an understanding of how people are now generally better off, whatever their subjective impressions. Using a measure of absolute poverty would provide that.

In fact, all those things I mentioned above (which are often included in calculations by the JRF about what is necessary to participate in our society) were not on the horizon back in the early 1950s. However, the fact that they are now available to the majority indicates a fundamental move forward within society, which we have all witnessed and participated in. Over time, there has been the "Great Enrichment"—as the great Anglican transgender economist and historian, Deirdre Nansen McCloskey, terms it in the final volume of her monumental trilogy, *Bourgeois Equality* (2016). The Great Enrichment, since 1800, is ongoing, in lifting people out of subsistence living. The world is better: worldwide, in the aggregate, people are healthier and live longer, with better incomes which can buy more (and at better quality) than they used to be able to. From a long-term historical perspective, "betterment" (another McCloskey term) has happened, and this widespread betterment is a tremendous achievement, with millions of people being lifted out of absolute poverty, and most people having a higher standard of living. However, people continue to think we still live in a zero-sum world. A reason to be cheerful: we don't.

There is a contemporary variant on the "rich get richer" proverb, which is just as common. When an Anglican theologian—Alison Milbank, *The Once and Future Parish* (2023)—went to her local market one Saturday and asked people what they were bothered about, among other things they said: "the gap between rich and poor is *widening*". This kind of statement is so common, and we often hear concern in the Church, as elsewhere, about the widening (and its implied inequity and, therefore, iniquitousness); but, once again, it is misleading. In the past there were a few rich people who comprised a static group and the poor were almost everyone else, whereas now who is rich and who is poor, and all those in between, is in flux (think J. K. Rowling and Ed Sheeran; see the discussion in Deirdre Nansen McCloskey, *Bourgeois Dignity* [2011]: Ch. 8). Furthermore, although on some measures the gap is wider at some points in time, we have to balance the fact that life, on the whole, is better for everyone (in the aggregate). Even if the cohort of the rich at a particular moment are better off, it does not mean everyone else is not better off than they were, even though it may not feel like it; and, of course, it doesn't feel like it when we spend our energy noticing how well others are doing. Of course, the destitute, roofless and starving among us are not doing well: and they are the poorest of the poor. But that's not where most people are; although even the middle class in many places can feel that they're not doing well when they look at how the conspicuous elite are doing (cf. my sermon in the *Expository Times*, August 2024, which discusses these common proverbs in relation to Proverbs 22 and James 2).

Another cause of resentment is the feeling that things are not equal (especially in the sense that there is no "equity", which has become a kind of contemporary moral touchstone: a shibboleth): the sense that there are injustices being done, that discrimination is rife. Of course, there are so many disparities we can point to in life that offend our moral instincts. Why are some people so much better off than others? However, unless you adopt a moralistic approach, it's really difficult to answer the question about a perceived widening gap. Merit, luck and hard work all have their place, just as natural advantages (such as aptitude and temperament) and good fortune play a part. The problem is that the more you stress the gap and bemoan it, the unhappier you become—it is spiritually dangerous. Differences and disparities do not mean discrimination or injustice, as the great black American economist Thomas Sowell points out: *Discrimination and Disparities* (2019). It's an ethical fallacy to think that any disparity, of whatever kind, must be the result of discrimination or injustice. Of course, discrimination exists, and people can be dealt with unjustly, but "it's not fair" is an inadequate yardstick. One woman I know told me their family motto is that life is not fair. If you realize this, you save yourself and others a whole lot of agony. However, it becomes vital to discern where discrimination is actually operating or unjust dealing is being done. Claims that it's "structural" or "institutional" are often a shorthand for claiming the high ground and for not doing any empirical research, and sometimes for trying to railroad others. There is, of course, such a thing as "structural" or "institutional" sin, but not just because things are not fair within a system. And, of course, any system will have weaknesses that need addressing and reforms that need making to keep it operating as well as possible. Infamous cases where particular systems are failing or corrupt do not give us any privileged insight into other institutions. What we do know is that systems are not perfect and often require reformation or correction, especially as circumstances change or complacency or corruption sets in. In other words, it's part of the human condition that we cannot produce faultless or completely fair systems. Whenever any law or arrangement or protocol or deal is put in place, some people will be on one side of the line and others on the other side. The larger the system the more this is true. This is not a counsel of despair, simply an observation and acknowledgement of reality to which we have to attend. In other words, we must be realistic in what we imagine can be changed, and to what degree, to make things better. After all, we will all have noticed how, unintentionally, changes can sometimes make matters worse than if we had left things alone. However rational we imagine ourselves to be, it does not make us immune to short-sightedness or seeking short-term gain, not realizing it may be at the expense of the long term.

So, by 2025, we should be aware that poverty in this country is relative and that the Great Enrichment has happened. Over decades and continuing into this century, there has been an increase in general wealth, an increase in facilities and options, an increase in the quality of goods, an increase in the availability of new products, an increase in medical treatments and medicines, an increase in entertainment options, an increase in educational opportunities. Of course, downsides remain, but we do not think straight if we do not acknowledge the upsides and talk as if we were still living back in the 1980s, let alone the 1880s.

Of course, there are disparities of wealth, but to focus on that is to miss the big picture and to nurture resentment, which is counterproductive to social cohesion and the common good. As we've seen, it's not true, as the frequently quoted saying goes, that "the rich get richer and the poor get poorer". That is to play the zero-sum game which, although it has been operative for most of human social existence, is no longer operative. It is not true that if someone gets rich, I must, inevitably, get poorer. That is only true when the sum total of goods is static; but when goods are expanding in both quality and quantity, it is not true, and has not been true for many a year. When I think back to the Manor estate in the 1980s where houses had to be propped up because the wall-ties were corroding and making them unstable and people struggled to live in a place stigmatized by others, this bears so little resemblance to now, as it probably bore little resemblance to those living in the Sheffield slums in the 1930s where houses didn't have bathrooms and the shared toilets were at the back of the yard. When people left the slums, they were only too glad to move to the new council houses on Manor and to have an internal bathroom, even though rumour had it that some put the coal in the bath. That was progress, but 50 years later in the 1980s . . .

However poor people are today, it is of a different order from previous times, thank God. This is not to say that people don't struggle or that some folk don't have a tough time or that there aren't needs to be met. But these needs keep shifting. As Jesus once said, the poor are always with you, and so it is, and so it will be, and so the Church will always have to respond in different ways in different circumstances; again, as Jesus also said, there are always occasions when we can help the poor, or perhaps better, help them to help themselves to have a better and more fulfilling life. It is certainly the case that having money helps, but having money does not guarantee happiness or family solidarity or personal fulfilment or productivity or self-discipline or creative endeavour. To fixate on the amount of money that anyone has is not the way to address the needs of anyone who is in need and needs to be taken to a place of rest, or needs a cup of water or a friendly word. Where injustices occur they must be faced and action taken to right them, however long it takes (think Mr Bates and the Post Office). Where someone has been defrauded or cheated or physically abused or illegally treated, then support and advocacy are needed and Christians will, if their track record is anything to go by, set up groups and organizations to tackle the needs of the poorest and most vulnerable (think Alcoholics Anonymous and Samaritans). Human creativity in response to human need is amazing and we should never underestimate it and the way it can empower ordinary people to do extraordinary things. This is perhaps the main reason we have reasons to be cheerful: God will always raise people up to act, as individuals, in associations, in churches, in groups: all the little platoons that Edmund Burke saw as the bedrock of society. The Church needs to look to this sector for its prime activity and not be seduced by the profile of higher politics into public grandstanding or virtue signalling or political complaining or asserting our moral superiority over others. Such human self-assertion may make us feel better or superior, but it will not necessarily help the poor and it will beget sin. Better to stand with, or sit alongside, the poor in humble, sharing, mutually supportive ways. That has always been the main Christian, ministerial option, and it remains so. In fact, we didn't need *Faith in the City* or liberation theology to know this, although they have taught us and inspired us in so many ways, and God has used them to teach us or, better, to remind us.

The more I have reflected on these matters in this new century, the more I've come to realize that there are more fundamental questions than "what makes a good city?" They are: "what makes a functioning society?", "what makes an effective state?", "what makes a successful civilization like ours, which has developed democratic institutions?" If Plato (philosophically) and Augustine (theologically) help us answer the question about the city, who helps us to answer these more fundamental questions? These have become existential questions for societies like ours and for the civilization that we are a part of, as is made clear by the threats to it. Recent books by Douglas Murray (*The War on the West* [2022]) and Frank Furedi (*The War against the Past* [2024]) describe those threats, many of which are internal. But when it comes to understanding how our civilization has developed over time to where we are now, other thinkers help us to understand something of the process that that has entailed, for example, Getrude Himmelfarb (*The Roads to Modernity* [2004]), Rodney Stark (*How the West Won* [2014]) and Thomas Sowell (*Conquests and Cultures* [1998]); but the most comprehensive attempt has been made by the Japanese-American political scientist Francis Fukuyama in his two-volume magnum opus that examines how political order has been established historically, and the various factors that are essential to good governance: *The Origins of Political Order: From Prehuman Times to the French Revolution* (2011) and *Political Order and Political Decay: From the Industrial Revolution to the Globalization of Democracy* (2014). These books show that states are vulnerable and that certain factors must be in place for good, stable government to emerge, and that for most of history they have not come together, but, by fortuitous historical events over time, the requisite combination has been achieved in Western democratic societies, for all their differences.

But this achievement cannot be taken for granted. Even more so, we would be naive to think that there can be no regression on the Great Enrichment that has happened over the last few centuries. All this puts in a wider perspective our concerns about Britain and our cities and urban localities. So, naked, generalized attacks on our government or institutions or culture are to be eschewed as incompatible with mature debate and attention to evidence. The neo-Marxist goal to overthrow the West is not dead. The post-modern desire to destabilize society continues. The anarchistic impulse to disrupt order is often present among some young people and their adult mentors. To have faith in "the city" means to turn our back on such attempts to undermine our cities and our political order, flawed as it might be. So, we also need to have faith in "our society", and faith in "our civilization", despite our misgivings or any lingering unrealistic, idealist conceptions. At the end of the day, we must eschew utopian thinking, imagining that we can have perfection now or can establish faultless systems and find incorruptible leaders. So, we need to steer not only away from dystopian projections but also from utopian dreams: the twin temptations of the morally aware and the concerned conscience. Furthermore, as McCloskey argues—*The Bourgeois Virtues* (2006)—we need more than one virtue at a time. It's no good trumpeting "justice" if we do not also proclaim "mercy" that tempers it and prevents it becoming dictatorial. It's no good proclaiming "freedom" unless we also adhere to "order", which ensures that liberty does not lead to licence or chaos. It's no good advocating "courage" to change if we do not also encourage "prudence" to ensure that we do not change what doesn't need to change or lose something profound because we were not paying close enough attention. It's no good advocating "equality" (especially equity) if it ends up restricting "freedom", because the only way you can have absolute equality (equality of outcome) is by dictatorial measures that diminish liberty until it is non-existent. So it is that zeal for a single virtue leads to vice. The good when taken to the extreme becomes evil. This is why zealots of all kinds remain a problem for a mature, ordered society seeking the welfare of all its citizens.

It's been common to use a text from Jeremiah 29 when discussing urban ministry and mission and its practice: "seek the welfare [shalom] of the city" (v. 7). In the light of the discussion above, this pregnant phrase invites extension through various sectors and dimensions, where subsidiarity suggests we should privilege the lowest level possible: seek the welfare of (a) the local community/neighbourhood, (b) the city, (c) the society, (d) the country/state, and even (e) the civilization in which we are embedded, especially as Judaeo-Christian values lie behind its development over time (see Tom Holland, *Dominion: The Making of the Western Mind* [2019] and Rodney Stark, *The Victory of Reason: How Christianity Led to Freedom, Capitalism, and Western Success* [2005], and compare Melanie Phillips, *The Builder's Stone* [2025], which emphasizes Jewish values as foundational). So, what does it mean to seek the welfare, the shalom, at all these different levels? It certainly doesn't mean defending the indefensible or avoiding critique or complacently going along with things so as not to cause any fuss. However, it does mean being constructive, working with whoever and whenever we can to make things better: Christians playing our part in being part of a local community or society. It does mean avoiding joining forces with those who seek to dismantle the West or overturn capitalism or anarchically upset order at the neighbourhood or state level. Seeking the welfare (especially in the sense of shalom) does not mean overturning the political order unless one finds oneself in an utterly exceptional, existential situation, as the great reformed theological ethicist Helmut Thielicke argues in *Theological Ethics* II (1969 [1958/9]). Even then one is compromised, ethically and religiously, as the great Lutheran pastor-theologian, Dietrich Bonhoeffer, acknowledged in Hitler's Germany.

So, finally, I come back to almost where I began. For it seems to me that the "Situation Analysis" that I first learnt at UTU remains an essential prelude to effective urban ministry: looking at the facts in the eye, whether they accord with our presumptions or not. Then acting in response in the light of the Gospel of Liberation, taking on board local dynamics and interests and possibilities: finding a liberational angle that will help transform people and their situation, most notably through their own agency. Mark R. Gornik and Maria Liu Wong (*Stay in the City: How Christian Faith is Flourishing in an Urban World* [2017]) tell us to "Begin with What Is in Front of You" (p. 59). That's wise advice, but there is little recognition in the volume of the fragmentary and transitory nature of urban life, of the rage, apathy and failure that attend ministry at the bottom of society. This is because they have eschewed urban ministry being about those in greatest need (p. 27). Their view of urban ministry is about what happens in any and every urban setting, but a focus on the poor and powerless is essential to what I regard as urban ministry. That's part of the reason we look back to *Faith in the City*, because it made that focus clear at a particular time in our country. It's the focus, too, of John Vincent's Urban Theology and of classic liberation theology. It's a focus we must not lose as we debate what poverty means and its causes and remedies. It's a focus that the Church of England is once again in danger of losing as it is deflected by other concerns and issues. It's a focus of which the Church of England, and whoever the new Archbishop of Canterbury will be, needs reminding.

4

Faith in the City: A Personal Perspective

David Walker

One of the privileges of my current position is serving as a member of the UK House of Lords. My first four years encompassed four different Prime Ministers. As the ruling Conservative Party fought within itself, it was a time characterized by instability and a lack of obvious direction. Yet, while at times the Church faced criticism from some Conservative members for taking a strong public stance opposed to government on issues such as asylum seekers, for the vast majority of my time, the contributions of bishops have been much appreciated. As I reflect on that, I am convinced that the credibility of bishops in Parliament is grounded not primarily in our theological erudition, political acumen or oratorical skills, but in that we stand on the work being done on the ground, by local church communities in our dioceses. Building on the stories of social action projects, I am able to offer credible reflections, and to reflect theologically, on the role that faith, including the diverse faiths I work with in the Manchester area, plays in public life and discourse. It is work that in many places still, 40 years on, owes much to the impetus *Faith in the City* provided.

Faith in the City has been at the forefront of how I have sought to offer leadership in mission and ministry as a bishop over the last 24 years. It has occupied that place not simply because it made theological sense to me, but as a result of it having been the inspiration for much of the practical focus of my ministry in the 17 years I spent as a parish clergyman and industrial chaplain, prior to my being ordained bishop. When I moved to Dudley as suffragan bishop in 2000, one of the few essential requirements in the person specification had been that the new bishop would arrive fresh from parish ministry. My task would be to lead and encourage as bishop, the things I had long been practising as priest. Hence, while in this chapter I will be seeking to reflect from my experience as a bishop, my earlier years, ministering in the light of *Faith in the City*'s publication, form an essential part of my story.

The Church of England published its seminal report in the year after I was ordained priest in the Diocese of Sheffield. My sending diocese had been Ely—I was researching in Pure Mathematics at King's College, Cambridge when God's call became too urgent to put off any longer. Leaving Cambridge, I'd chosen to train for ordination in Birmingham, drawn by the urban context and ecumenical nature of Queen's College. The principal had kindly allowed me to spend my final year almost full-time in an inner-city, multi-ethnic and religiously diverse parish. I loved it. The church was deeply embedded in its community. It lived out God's love in lots of practical ways, from a sheltered housing scheme, via youth work among black teenage boys, to a daily lunch club for the elderly. I read as much as I could find about mission in such places. Bishop David Sheppard's *Bias to the Poor* chimed deeply with me;[1] Fr Kenneth Leech's writings, with their combination of incarnational theology, catholic spirituality and radical political action, all set in the East End of London, bowled me over.[2] Yet the writings of such inspirational clergy seemed a long way from a Church of England which, at an official level, appeared content to look the other way while the dominant political ethos of the Thatcher years wielded its axe over the communities dependent on traditional male manual work, in sectors such as mining, steel working and heavy engineering.

Unlike some, I can't point to a particular moment of conversion when I became a Christian. My faith had come alive over a period of some months around the time I was leaving school and beginning university. What I can look back and see quite clearly is the impact my new, or newly recovered, faith had on the way I looked at the world around me.

---

[1] D. Sheppard, *Bias to the Poor* (London: Hodder & Stoughton, 1983).

[2] A useful collection of some of Kenneth Leech's writings can be found in A. Ritchie (ed.), *Prayer and Prophecy: The Essential Kenneth Leech* (New York: Seabury Press, 2009).

Suddenly, people mattered, because they mattered to God. Indeed, they were made in God's image. I'd never been interested in politics, but now it began to matter because the political choices we made affected the lives of those I was beginning to be drawn to care about, especially the poor and marginalized. I joined the political party that seemed to have the closest affinity to the issues and people I wanted to see get a better deal. I even toyed with whether I might work my way up the political ladder to becoming a Member of Parliament. But politics never felt like the whole answer. Instead, as my call to ordination became more urgent, and through my training, I began to see how the work of a priest might be more effective in improving human lives than that of a politician. In my time at theological college, especially in that inner-city-based final year, everything came together.

I'd known early on that my calling was to return to the industrial North of England, where I had been born and brought up. And so, by the time *Faith in the City* was published, I was into the second half of my curacy, combining all the traditional elements of 1980s parish ministry with helping host a government-funded programme offering short retraining opportunities for adults whose previous occupations were fast disappearing. Both the publication of the book itself and the fact that it was an official Church of England report, endorsed by the General Synod, despite senior government figures denouncing it as Marxist, took me from having thought of myself as somewhere on the edge of the institutional Church to feeling part of an exciting movement of God's Holy Spirit.

I would have struggled, even then, to list in detail the recommendations the report set out. For me, it has never been about the specifics. Three things have always mattered: that the Church, through whose structures I was seeking to follow Christ, showed it cared about the kind of communities to which I felt called; that it was prepared to be bold enough to address its recommendations both to Church and State; and that it was committing itself to raise a significant pot of money which could be used to part-fund projects in the kinds of parishes in which I saw myself serving. It also delighted me that news of the report cut through well beyond church circles. Would any cabinet minister today feel a church report with which they disagreed merited a sustained public attack rather than simply ignoring it?

By the end of the following year, I had moved to be team vicar and industrial chaplain in the South Yorkshire mining town of Maltby. Its colliery had survived the massive culls which had accompanied the recent year-long strike, but the huge redundancy programme across the coalfield meant that any jobs which became available were filled by miners relocating from closing pits. Unemployment, especially among young men, was rising rapidly; meanwhile many families were struggling to recover from severe debts accrued during the strike. Tony, my predecessor, had set up an ecumenical group with a remit to respond to the problems of the post-strike period. One of my first tasks was to turn it into a company, then a charity. The wide scope we sought for it was reflected in the name we chose, Maltby Rainbow Projects. But its inaugural project, a retraining scheme similar to that in my previous parish, built on familiar ground.

Over the next few years, *Faith in the City* served both as a backdrop against which we scrutinized our progress and, through its most tangible legacy, the Church Urban Fund, a key catalyst for new work. Sheffield, like many dioceses, had appointed a Faith in the City officer, along with a structure for assessing bids for funds. Then, and throughout my parish ministry, his advice was crucial to our formulating workable plans. Equally valuable was that CUF sought to be an early funder. The impact of that was summed up for me during a meeting with a senior cabinet member of Rotherham Borough Council and his chief officer. I was pitching for support for a new project and had gone into the room with £30,000 of CUF money promised. When I shared this figure, the response was instant: if the Church is prepared to allocate money for work to alleviate problems in our borough, then how can the council itself not support the scheme? Half an hour later we had a further £100,000, enough to ensure that the project would run. It wasn't just public money which that early Church commitment leveraged. Other strands of work benefitted in turn from support from secular charities, housing associations, a nearby university and Comic Relief.

Some projects were relatively simple. Our Good Neighbour Scheme linked volunteers, largely but not exclusively drawn from the congregations of the town's churches, to offer their services, such as driving elderly residents to medical appointments, or light gardening. A small fund allowed the local job centre to direct people to us who needed money for transport to attend an employment interview. Others, such as the training scheme, were copying practice already well established in neighbouring areas. But we also found ourselves at the cutting edge, piloting projects not yet widespread in England, such as a town credit union.

Faith in the City gave us, particularly the Anglicans among us, the necessary backing when we faced challenges that this was the Church meddling in things that were none of its business. Why were we focusing our efforts on the physical and mental wellbeing of the people of our town when there were souls to be saved for Jesus? Why was the weekly giving of church members elsewhere in the diocese being spent on paying me to do work that didn't have a clear route to putting bottoms on pews on Sundays? It was only as a bishop, some years later, that I came across a comment by Archbishop William Temple, himself a former Bishop of Manchester, that were we forced to choose between saving souls and improving social conditions we would have to choose the former, but in fact no such forced choice is needed; the two go hand in hand.

There's a certain logic to the pattern of church engagement with an issue which says that you do all the theology first and then work out how to put it into practice. Notoriously, Church of England reports begin with a theological chapter, even if it is obvious to the reader that it has almost certainly been written last. Logical, but I've never found it either practical or compelling. As we sought to put *Faith in the City* into action in our specific context, we found that we were doing our theology along the way. The notion of theological reflective practice was relatively new and rare at the time, though it appeared to more closely model how Jesus and his disciples had done their theology than the more formal methods prevalent in church documents. One theme that, at least for me, began to dominate, and has stayed central to my practice as priest and bishop ever since, was that of prophetic action.

It emerged first in the work we were doing to retrain people for new jobs, along with the three dozen or so small starter office/workshop spaces we had worked with the local council to set up. The latter emerged because we began to discover people who wanted to try their hands at self-employment but who needed a supported environment in which to begin their ventures. Someone had challenged us that, despite our efforts over several years, we had not eradicated unemployment in the town. What was the point? Part of the answer was familiar, that to us and God every human individual matters. We were making significant, positive differences in the lives of a good number of those with whom we engaged. But a deeper answer was that, even if only in a small way, we were making statements about what the world is like when the laws of God's Kingdom are being followed. That's how I define prophetic action for today. In the Kingdom that Jesus heralds, everyone has gifts to offer. We are called to create space in which those whose skills and experience are rejected in the world around us can develop fresh talents and share them. At one point we arranged an art and craft exhibition in the main parish church of the borough; the only requirement was that all the work on display had to have been produced by people who were classed as unemployed. It was only when we had begun to recognize the prophetic in what we were doing that we felt confident to turn direct to the Scriptures and see whether we could lift a prophecy straight from the pages and enact it in our community.

As the 1980s drew to a close, we had become increasingly concerned at the growing housing problem in the town. British Coal, formerly a major landlord in mining towns, had sold off its stock, firstly to those existing occupants who could gain a mortgage, and then to private landlords. At the same time, the government's Right to Buy scheme had radically reduced the capacity of council housing to meet the needs of young adults, both singles and couples, seeking to set up home independently. Moreover, this was precisely the generation who were finding it hardest to secure employment at a level of remuneration sufficient to enable them to rent privately or to buy.

Maltby Self Build was easily our most ambitious venture, and it came directly from our attention being drawn to Isaiah 65:21-2:

> They shall build houses and inhabit them;
> they shall plant vineyards and eat their fruit.
> They shall not build and another inhabit;
> they shall not plant and another eat;
> for like the days of a tree shall the days of my people be,
> and my chosen shall long enjoy the work of their hands.

Planting vineyards in South Yorkshire might not have been practical, but could we make the rest of that prophecy come true?

The council gave us a parcel of land. A Yorkshire-based housing association agreed to fund the building and to own the properties, which were to be permanently available to rent. Our own training organization would take on the self-builders and provide them with such skills as it could. We would focus the scheme on young adults, aged 18 to 30, especially those with the least qualifications, who would find it hardest to gain jobs. The builders themselves would be their own legal entity, employing supervisors and craftspeople to deliver parts of the project that required specialist qualifications they could not gain in the time available. At the end of the project, the cash saved by self-building compared with employing conventional constructors would be handed over to the participants to share equally between them. As well as the qualifications they had achieved, and being able to put something pretty amazing on their CVs, they would, in line with Isaiah's prophecy, have the right to be the first tenants in the homes they had built. The money being shared out would come just at the right moment for them to furnish their new homes.

In Isaiah's vision, everyone can build their own home. That was way beyond our scope, but what we could and did do, with very few participants withdrawing once the work on the homes had properly begun, was to show that being able to organize a group, both to build and to manage the building of nine homes, was not restricted to the better-off groups within society who had more commonly undertaken self-build projects. To fulfil a sign of God's Kingdom, even in one small place and at one moment in time, is to act out prophecy. *Faith in the City* and the Church Urban Fund had, between them, given us the wherewithal to do so.

The credibility the Church had won through *Faith in the City* opened doors for me and others. At one point in the mid-1990s, I had brought together three different departments of the same local authority to partner with a company the churches in my latest parish had set up. Our challenge was to enable young people on benefits to access the private rented housing sector, and then to sustain a tenancy within it. Bond Guarantee Schemes were largely unheard of in the UK at that time, but we had caught wind of them through someone on a national committee I was part of, who had seen them in Australia. We thought it could work here too. Six months or so into the operation, and again with huge early support from CUF, I asked why it had needed the churches to set up something that the local authority departments could have done, had they been so minded, without us. I've never forgotten the answer one of their senior staff gave. "The problem is", he said, "we don't trust each other, but we all trust you and the Church." That trustworthiness owed much to the track record of partnership and action that *Faith in the City* had inspired. We were now able to approach potential partners with the confidence that came both from knowing that we had our Church behind us and from having been seen to deliver on previous tasks we had set ourselves.

In the years after its publication, *Faith in the City* helped set the tone for ministry in much of the Church of England, if not beyond. It inspired gifted clergy to want to work in inner cities and outer estates; there was a kudos to being at the cutting edge. Good work in one place sparked replication elsewhere. Dioceses were keen to access the resources. In many parts of the country, various European funding initiatives channelled additional support to those parts of the UK which, prior to the eastward expansion of the EU after the fall of the Berlin Wall, counted as among some of the poorest parts of the Union. In South Yorkshire, we had employed a team of four staff largely to help churches of all denominations write high-quality bids for public funds. The results were deeply gratifying. Inner-city ministry could be exhausting, for clergy, lay staff and volunteers, but it was richly rewarding too. Research into burnout, including among clergy, repeatedly shows that human beings can cope well with quite high and persistent levels of stress, as long as there is a balancing factor of things which provide high levels of satisfaction.

The Church Urban Fund had been set up with a simple financial model. It had £20 million in endowment, a mixture of donations from individuals, parishes and dioceses, combined with a substantial sum gifted from the Church Commissioners. The plan was to spend this out over a 20-year period and then wind up. By the time that original deadline was drawing close, in my early years as a bishop, I had moved from being a supplicant at the fund's door to serving as one of its trustees. We were caught between two stools; the money was, as planned, running out. Ongoing fundraising during the intervening years had been minimal, as that had never been the intention, but we had not eliminated the problems besetting urban Britain which *Faith in the City* had so clearly documented two decades before. If anything, they had got worse. It would have been a brave, and perhaps foolhardy, charity that would have gone ahead with the original plans to wind up in such circumstances. Instead, we took the decision to carry on. We recognized that we would be a smaller grant-maker than before, and would have to tailor the work we could fund in dioceses and parishes to projects for which we could generate income from other sources, be they private charities or government bodies. Pivoting from the original methodology proved to be far from straightforward. Not least, it required a very different skill set among the staff team.

This was also a period when *Faith in the City* seemed a long time ago. The Church faced pressures from other priorities, especially those that had come much more recently to the fore. Some of this came from rural dioceses, who understandably felt that the focus on urban areas ignored the significant problems of rural poverty. Indeed, I soon found as Bishop of Dudley, in a diocese that also contained the county of Worcestershire, that being poor in a rural area, especially when surrounded by predominantly affluent towns and villages, brought a level of isolation and deprivation that was not, as in more urban areas, offset by the provision of services directed towards the needs of the less well off. To be poor in an area with limited, if any, public transport, where shops price their wares for the wealthy, and where social provision is negligible, is arguably significantly worse than being poor in a predominantly poor town. Other pressure came from a growing awareness that, with ever-falling church attendance, energy needed to be put into addressing the decline more directly than by relying wholly on Temple's dictum that an engaged and credible Christian witness through social action would, of itself, convert significant numbers of people into being regular church attendees and generous givers. The highly influential volume *Mission-Shaped Church* was published not long into my episcopate.[3] It brought fresh insight and impetus to a more church-centred mission. It described a model of church that took careful note of the way in which many people now lived their lives, more network than neighbourhood, and advocated models of church which went with that grain. In my view, it was admirably suited to the predominantly suburban, or city centre, settings where lives were indeed network-based. But inner-city, and outer-estate, parishes with poor populations, along with their rural counterparts, still lived lives much more centred on local community, and indeed do so today. Seeking to push such places into adopting forms of ministry birthed in and befitted for a very different context felt like a project destined to fail.

Outside of CUF, one place where *Faith in the City* thinking still lingered was in a group called the Urban Bishops Forum. Chaired by the energetic Stephen Lowe, Bishop of Hulme, who at some point was formally seconded from Manchester Diocese to hold the title of Bishop for Urban Life and Faith, it became a key reference group for a project to issue a new report, 20 years on from *Faith in the City*, which we hoped might go some way to reigniting the fires. As a piece of writing, *Faithful Cities* has much to recommend it,[4] though I found having to explain the multiple meanings of the word "faithful" in the title an interesting challenge when faced, a few months later, with having to introduce the report to the massed ranks of the National Assembly of the German Protestant Church. Many of our inner urban parishes were indeed places that were full of faith, and where the Church had remained faithfully

---

[3] G. Cray (ed.), *Mission-Shaped Church: Church Planting and Fresh Expressions of Church in a Changing Context* (London: Church House Publishing, 2004).

[4] Commission for Urban Life and Faith, *Faithful Cities: A Call for Celebration, Vision and Justice* (London: Church House Publishing and Peterborough: Methodist Publishing House, 2006).

present even while many other bodies had either collapsed or withdrawn to the suburbs and town centres. We had told ourselves that we were not intending it to be a *Faith in the City* Volume 2, a work to provoke response from across the whole of society. Yet I have to confess that within a few months of its publication it had, like many church reports before and since, vanished onto the dustier bookshelves of vicarage studies, leaving little evidence of its having been written.

Where a new report failed to make a clear impact, the legacy of *Faith in the City* was instead taken forward by the new partnerships that a more entrepreneurial and income-seeking Church Urban Fund was able to forge.

The first of these arrived with the incoming Conservative and Liberal Democrat coalition government in 2010. This quickly spawned the Near Neighbours partnership, drawing on the experience and credibility of the Church in bridging the space between different world faiths living in the same geographical area. At times of heightened tension, locally or nationally, warm relationships between the various worshipping communities can make a major difference. Yet such links cannot be forged instantly, in response to problems; they have to be built slowly and sustainably, over long periods of growing trust.

Generous support from a private donor over several years enabled the setting up of a second initiative, a series of local "Together" projects, joint ventures between CUF and individual dioceses. In Manchester, as elsewhere, many of these projects continue to do impressive work, having made the transition away from being dependent on core funding from CUF. They have proved adept at co-ordinating responses to issues such as rough sleeping, across churches and beyond. Because they are governed through their own local boards, they are able to respond to the specific needs of their own region, rather than being local offices mandated to deliver a national programme.

Understanding the challenge of the city in the 2020s

Faith in the City took seriously its analysis of urban life in the mid-1980s. Any attempt to do the same today must take a similar fresh look, both at the context of our cities and at their churches.

Social changes over the last four decades have, I would argue, made the challenge of offering Christian-based responses to tackle the problems of poorer urban neighbourhoods harder. In my experience, the issue is not the increased presence and activity of other world faiths in our inner cities; indeed, as Near Neighbours has shown, they are often our most committed allies and partners. The problem lies more with what has happened to white working-class identity over the last 40 years.

The collapse, which peaked in the 1980s, of well-paid male manual work has had far more than simply an economic impact. In many of the areas with which *Faith in the City* concerned itself, it sparked a collapse in belonging and identity which has only become fully visible in more recent times. Nor is it a problem confined to Britain alone. Its most visible symptom is, in my view, the rise across much of Europe, during the last decade or so, of far-right populist political movements. Hot summer evenings and some isolated spark events have, perhaps on average once a decade, brought a few nights of civil unrest to the streets of British towns. Yet the cohort of those arrested in July/August 2024 looks somewhat different from previous occasions. Violent disorder this time was not predominately teenage and young adult men taking an opportunity to loot consumer goods. While those convicted of violent disorder remain largely male, their demographic range covers everything up to and beyond pension age. Their anger is directed not against some perceived immediate injustice committed by police or a rival group; their targets are symbols of the diversity of modern UK society, and particularly those who they feel do not belong in Britain.

Many long-term inhabitants of inner-city and outer urban estates now see themselves as living in a society that has successively taken away their worthwhile jobs, given the homes they aspired to live in to "foreigners" and, perhaps most recently, added insult to injury by replacing the stories of a glorious past, when the British Empire led and civilized the world, with a shameful narrative of how our ancestors abused, enslaved and exploited the people of the lands they conquered. When they protest, they find themselves directly pitted against one of the few remaining professions disproportionately populated by white working-class men like themselves: the front-line officers of UK police.

Part of the lost belonging that this disaffected group seeks to appropriate is a sense of being Christian. Some far-right leaders have made claims about being defenders of Britain's Christian identity. However, this is very much a churchless form of Christianity, a cultural belonging rather than one that requires positive commitment. It appears to be more about being over against other world faiths, who are caricatured as alien and unwanted. Hence it cannot easily be drawn upon as a motivation for living out *Faith in the City* ideals.

One key asset when it came to responding to the problems of the mid-1980s was that the high unemployment, consequent on rapid contraction of traditional industries, had created a large cohort within the population of fit and active adults not seeking paid work. Many had accepted fairly generous severance terms plus early pensions, and had taken retirement, often in their early fifties; with lower longevity, their parents' generation had largely died. Mostly, they lived in or close to the places they had been born and brought up in, and to which they had a strong sense of belonging. By contrast, most of today's retirees are well into their late sixties. A couple in that age bracket are likely to have between them at least one elderly parent requiring time and attention, often, due to increasing population mobility, living a considerable distance away. Increased geographical mobility across all sectors of society means they are also, even in inner-city parishes and on outer estates, less likely to have developed a strong sense of belonging to their neighbourhood.

Today, poor, older, fewer in number, and less naturally committed, the present generation of retirees provide less fertile ground for producing the key volunteers to run church-based projects. Meanwhile, those among them who attend churches face constant pressure to take on internally facing roles as church officers, not least as the 80-plus generation, still holding many such positions, seek to lay down their burdens.

One further challenge comes from the greater degree of polarization found nowadays, not only in society but also between traditions within the Church of England itself.

For much of my ministry, I have felt that while there were many Christians who might not share my view as to what issues matter most, they left people like me to get on with them while they themselves remained disengaged. However, in recent years I am finding more direct opposition within the Church. There are those for whom matters that I see as basic justice are actually at deep variance with their particular church tradition or theology. This is especially visible in the field of what is often called identity politics (that is, politics that are based on a particular identity such as race, gender or social class), but it is also sometimes present in attitudes towards climate change. I deeply respect Christians who take their Bibles as seriously as I do myself, and yet find in them conclusions that are almost directly opposite to my own. Moreover, as a bishop, it is incumbent on me to make space for diverse views to be held and to flourish in my diocese, even where those views are opposed to my own.

Responding to the city in faith and hope

Notwithstanding the challenges noted above, the ethos of *Faith in the City* would have us seek to engage and to provide better narratives of belonging and self-worth. I believe there are a number of distinct signs of hope, both within and beyond the Church.

Recently, Britain has, for only the third time in my 40-plus years of ordained ministry, seen a significant change of government. Both previous occasions brought with them a fresh energy and a willingness to engage with the Church as a partner. In 1997, I had the privilege of serving on a Government Policy Action Team as part of the newly formed Social Exclusion Unit. In 2010, it had been Near Neighbours, and a promising but short-lived attempt to focus ideas around the concept of a "Big Society". In that early period, I had helped initiate a series of informal conversations at Lambeth Palace between bishops and senior government ministers and their teams. By contrast, it seems to be a symptom of governments in their latter years, when they are running out of steam, that they become less inclined to be open to external voices and influence. That gives me hope that the next few years may be ripe for further co-operation, as long as two conditions can be met. Firstly, the Church needs to find a similar motivation and capacity to that which *Faith in the City* earlier provided, to rise to the opportunity, and secondly, we need to find ways by which urban society as it now is will accept responses grounded, even if not always explicitly, in Christian faith.

Since the late 2010s, in Manchester we have worked at setting up small cell-like churches on some of the most deprived of our predominantly white working-class estates. These deliberately don't seek to replicate the patterns of church life seen in the suburbs. Recognizing that, in such communities, people are more drawn to relational models of belonging than those based on shared interests, they are deliberately intended to remain small. Should they be blessed with growth above a certain threshold, then they would be encouraged to divide in two and build again. We recognize that lifestyles can be unsettled in these communities, but it is the strong relationships that can be forged which provide a degree of stability, especially when those relationships are marked by Christian virtues such as forgiveness and unearned love. As the work has matured, we have seen potential leaders emerge, and now have a number in training for ordination, including as stipendiary priests. This has not always been easy. People who have had periods of chaotic living, perhaps marked by crime or drugs, do not readily satisfy the requirements around safeguarding that are, in another change from the early days of *Faith in the City*, now demanded of those engaging with children or vulnerable adults. But I am impressed at the number of leaders who are emerging. Quite deliberately, the work on deprived white estates is one half of a wider project which also includes cell churches focused on the very inner-city minorities who attract the anger and resentment of the far right. Relationships are being built across the two strands. We are not naive about the limited impact small worshipping communities can have in places where deprivation feeds resentment. However, they are, in my view, another example of small prophetic statements. These are modest groups, who live the love of Jesus in overt ways, untouched by the reserve and embarrassment over having faith, and sharing it, which impairs the mission of many of our more middle-class congregations.

Much of the parish-based work I did, post-*Faith in the City*, was ecumenical. In the 1980s, that typically meant Anglicans, Catholics, traditional nonconformist denominations such as Methodists and URC and, though less often, Baptists. Pentecostal churches, both white and black majority, were largely disengaged, as were independent evangelicals. If anything, they gave the impression that social action was a distraction from true gospel work. Over more recent times I have seen an increasing willingness among a good number of such congregations, especially the larger ones, to engage in such areas. Some of it may reflect a confidence born of numerical growth, some reflects the increasingly high level of theological education among the leaders of such churches, who are equipped and motivated to move beyond inherited patterns of ministry. With this increased confidence they feel more able to partner with traditional denominations without losing their distinctiveness.

Partnership is increasingly not only between different Christian churches, but also at a multi-faith level. As in other countries across Europe, the Commonwealth, the Americas and beyond, the relationship between faith and public life is often longstanding, and was forged in the more specific relationship between the dominant forms of religion at the time when the state emerged into the shape it now holds. The laïcité of France is very different from the separation of Church and State in the USA. Closer links, whether formalized by constitution, as with Pakistan or Israel, or more through custom and practice, as in the Nordic lands, are again diverse. The kinds of things that religious communities across a wide spectrum see as forming a proper part of their activities in England owe much to the particular Anglican model of pastoral care, liturgical performance and social action. As more recent communities settle and establish themselves, my observation is that they imbibe this model from the surrounding culture, and their practices adapt accordingly. Meanwhile, they also begin to exert influence on the existing religious culture. As most communities settling in the UK come without substantial resources, they tend to find their first homes in poorer urban areas, where housing is cheapest. There they are surrounded by a model of social action which owes much to the legacy of *Faith in the City*. It is not surprising, then, that some begin to develop similar programmes, or to partner in multi-faith ventures. As they do so, they also strengthen the bonds between different faiths in their neighbourhood.

Alongside this, churches in my diocese and elsewhere, in what *Faith in the City* would have designated as Urban Priority Areas, have begun to show clear signs of growth, growing numerically and growing younger at the same time. Three factors appear to lie behind this. First is the influx of Anglicans from other parts of the world, especially Africa. Unlike the Windrush generation, when they turn up in a parish these are not usually being shunned or advised to find a black-led church elsewhere; rather they are welcomed, integrated, and encouraged to move into leadership roles. That they can see people who look like them already in leadership, both locally and elsewhere, gives further encouragement to them. Secondly, there are those who convert to Christianity from other world religions. Again, they are able to see and connect with lay and ordained leaders who speak their own mother tongue. Finally, the clear decision taken by the major grant-making body of the National Church Institutions shortly before the Covid lockdown to prioritize applications focused on poorer and more ethnically diverse communities means that those who do find the Church of England from less traditional backgrounds find a better range of resources to support them. It might appear strange that the Church should take such a decision now, when business sense might say the best route to sustainability is to pour resources into the suburban parishes that account for the great majority of numerical decline. Yet perhaps one of the legacies of *Faith in the City* is that, at least for a little while longer, those of us who, as young adults, were most inspired by its vision remain well represented among the senior leadership echelons of the Church.

I am also encouraged by new ways of thinking about how we find volunteers. It used to be said, in South Yorkshire, that if you wanted a fast bowler, you whistled down the shaft of a coal mine and one would emerge. By the same token if, as a young priest, I wanted a volunteer to work on some scheme or project, I put out a notice at the Sunday morning Eucharist. My operating model was that people came to faith, attended church weekly, grew in faith, and then began to act out their faith in practical forms of discipleship. It was while researching for what would become my PhD in the late 2000s that I became convinced I'd got the model wrong. Observing how churches worked with their local communities, I began to see almost the reverse formation. A non-churchgoer would join in on some one-off piece of work, perhaps an environmental initiative, or helping lead a pre-school group, initially just committing themselves for one day. Some would then move on to taking part on further occasions. As they got to know Christians better, and saw how their faith equipped and resourced them for the work, they felt drawn to explore their own faith. From that might come a fresh commitment to Christ, which might, though not always, lead to church attendance. Where previously I had seen non-churchgoers as the objects of the Anglican Five Marks of Mission, I now began to consider how, on the final three of those marks—environmental concern, caring for human needs, and combating injustice—they were my fellow agents of mission.

Faith in the global city

Faith in the City was a specifically English document, written for the Church of England and the nation it seeks to live in and serve. It was certainly read beyond England, not least in the other parts of the British Isles, but it was not directly aimed at their contexts. Nevertheless, I do believe it says something authentically Anglican in a wider context. Perhaps it is no coincidence that the Five Marks of Mission, so widely endorsed and promoted across the whole Communion, were put together very shortly after its publication, with the meeting of human need and the struggle for justice at the heart of them.

It was in the summer of 2000, when I was preparing to be ordained bishop, that Archbishop George Carey told me that in future years the Anglican Communion would become ever more important. He said that it would be vital that the younger bishops, such as myself, were prepared to commit time and energy to travelling around it, to strengthen the bonds of affection holding us together. Given the challenges the Communion has faced in the current century, he was very wise in his words. Imagining *Faith in the City* for the 2020s and beyond inevitably means imagining it in a global context.

Five years after my episcopal ordination, I found myself heading for Peru, to spend a sabbatical in Worcester's link diocese. The Peruvian Church was fascinating because its Anglicanism was not based on the English language—only one congregation in the entire diocese worshipped in English, and that was at the cathedral. Nor was it a child of empire—Peru had never been a British colony or territory. By 2005, it was still a small church, seeking to find its proper place. On one side of it lay a Catholicism which had been pulled back by Pope John Paul II from the liberation theology that had inspired a previous generation. On the other lay a plethora of Pentecostal churches, largely subsidized from the USA. The Anglican bishop had set out a simple aim. The churches of his diocese were to reflect the liturgical good order of the Catholics, along with the vibrancy of worship of the Pentecostals. However, there was to be a vital third element. No congregation could become a parish until it could demonstrate what practical work it was doing to tackle the material needs of its parishioners, and not just those who came to worship. I met some amazing projects, delivering clean water to emerging townships, teaching women how to cook in a more economical way, or giving them practical craft skills so they could produce marketable goods. To see a whole diocese place such a premium on the kinds of work *Faith in the City* advocated was deeply moving. As I have travelled further and more frequently across the Communion in recent years, I have continued to be impressed by the practical outpourings of Christian love I have seen, from advocacy in Angola to schools in Sarawak.

Most recently, my attention has been turned not to an emerging justice issue but to one whose origins lie centuries back, yet where the consequences remain very present today: the legacy of the transatlantic slave trade, and, more specifically, the part that agencies linked to the Church of England played in profiting from and sustaining one of the greatest injustices of all time, the widespread exploitation of fellow human beings as chattels. Having been brought up to believe in the inherent goodness of the British Empire, and to see my Church and nation as having been at the forefront of abolishing a slavery whose origins and industrialization were never explained, it has been a rude awakening. Descendants of those enslaved, transported across the ocean, and worked, often to death, on British- (including Church-) owned plantations not only comprise a significant proportion of the populations of those places today, but are also present in large numbers in Britain, and particularly concentrated in the very areas to which *Faith in the City* directed our attention. Any 2020s version of the report would have to explore how the Church relates to those who still bear the scars, through poorer life chances, worse educational attainment and lifelong micro-aggressions, of a system of exploitation which required them to be designated as lesser beings in order to justify their systematic abuse.

Working with the Church Commissioners as they developed their £100-million commitment opened my eyes both to the sheer scale of the problem and to how we might look to a different and better future, one where relationships are repaired and restored, even where we cannot ever hope to compensate for sins so grievous and so prolonged.

My latest role, as chair of the Anglican mission agency United Society Partners in the Gospel (USPG), has taken me yet further down that road. In the early eighteenth century, the society received a legacy of the Codrington sugar plantation on the island of Barbados, with a stipulation that its profits be used to create a theological training institution for Anglican clergy. The society ran the plantation on enslaved labour for well over a century, right until the UK government abolished slavery, at which point the society received compensation for the loss of its assets. Those who had been enslaved got nothing. I am now working with others on a £7-million project to address the abiding legacy of enslavement in the Codrington area, almost two centuries on. We will seek to find and mark the graves of those who died enslaved; to improve educational chances for local children; to turn qualifying tenants who have lived on the estate and may be descended from those held in slavery into landowners; to build spirituality and theology at the college that reflect the experiences of the area; to research deeper so that as much of the story of the slavery years can be told and made available in a dedicated centre. In short, in penitence of our predecessors' sins, we are seeking to play a part in building a better future. To me, the work of USPG, the Church Commissioners and their partners, in addressing the legacy of slavery, is a clear example of what a present-day *Faith in the City* would advocate.

Methodologies of engagement

As I have worked in the places and on the themes identified in *Faith in the City*, I've come across two distinct main modes of engagement; one builds a coalition and then looks for issues, the other finds an issue and then recruits a coalition.

The community organizing model originated with the work of Saul Alinsky, a Roman Catholic priest in the USA. It seeks to build large coalitions of local bodies, including churches, secular charities and others, who then use their combined strength to confront authority and power structures, such as local councils or significant employers, challenging them with very specific demands. Alinsky himself famously put on large-scale events, disrupting airports or similar, demanding changes from those in charge of them. In the form in which it first arrived in the UK, not long after *Faith in the City*, it struggled, apart from in the East End of London, to take hold. I initially supported it and encouraged church members in my Rotherham parishes to consider getting involved. However, in operation, the model seemed to soak up the energy and enthusiasm of volunteers with a lot of process engagement, sending them back to their host organizations with little left to give. What I wanted in any larger coalition was something that would energize my people, enthusing them for more effective mission and ministry, not something that would weary them with relatively unproductive demands on their time and skills. I was also concerned that the level of confrontation inherent in the model was less well suited to the political and social structures of the UK than it was on the other side of the ocean.

By contrast, I found that building constructive relationships with local power structures, especially in the public and not-for-profit sectors, was bringing results in areas like the self-build housing scheme I described earlier, where a more confrontational approach would have been likely to meet with rebuff. In addition, I found it more productive to begin by identifying an issue and then seek to build a coalition of interested individuals and parties to address it. This seemed a more natural way than to try to build a very generic coalition of diverse bodies, who would then need to be marshalled into agreeing that a particular issue, paramount to at most a minority of them, would be their central priority.

In practice, both methods have their strengths. I suspect the success of community organizing in East London reflected that, in a large city, local groups felt very powerless and ignored. In the mid-sized towns where I have worked most of my life, and even in a city region such as Manchester, many of the leaders in different bodies, including the Church, know and tend to trust each other. Moreover, the distance from the average citizen with a concern on their mind to the key individuals and institutions who might be able to change things for the better is shorter. In these places, the Alinsky model was, and probably remains, less suited.

One of my key influences was, and has always been, Archbishop Desmond Tutu, though it was only when I became a bishop that I discovered a saying of his which I had unconsciously been following for many years. I had always operated by beginning at the pastoral level. Having trained as a mathematician to look for patterns, I naturally identified where the stories of the individuals I met showed similarities. Gradually a picture would emerge, of problems over housing, or poverty, that required more than just holding a person's hand and praying with them. Tutu puts it beautifully and succinctly: "When you've pulled enough bodies out of the river", he wrote, "You take a walk upstream to see who's throwing them in."[5] His analogy fits more readily with my preference for finding the issues first before then creating the partnership to tackle them. Moreover, it is starting at the pastoral level, rather than plunging direct into the political, which makes this a methodology specifically suited to Christian mission and ministry. That move, from the individual to the societal, from the pastoral to the political, encapsulates what began for me when I first read *Faith in the City*, and what, as priest then bishop, I have sought to do ever since.

---

[5] Cited in "20 Famous Desmond Tutu Quotes", *The Standard*, <https://www.standardmedia.co.ke/world/article/2001432840/20-famous-desmond-tutu-quotes>, accessed 3 February 2025.

PART III

Urban mission and ministry

5

Liverpool: Urban mission and ministry

John Perumbalath

It was following the widespread riots of 1981 that Archbishop Robert Runcie set up the Archbishop of Canterbury's Commission on Urban Priority Areas (ACUPA) in July 1983. I write this chapter in the aftermath of riots across England and Northern Ireland in 2024. There is much to make me think that we haven't travelled very far in these 40 years, both as Church and as a nation. The fact that the recent riots started in parts of Liverpool Diocese makes me ask questions which are local alongside the wider issues that are national and beyond.

Today's context: A bird's eye view

Liverpool is the third most deprived local authority in England, with 63 per cent of residents living in areas ranked among the most deprived in England, and three in ten children living in poverty. Ranked by income, it is the fourth most deprived local authority in the country, and employment-wise it is the fifth most deprived. In terms of health deprivation and disability we are also ranked third nationally. Since 1985, massive regeneration has taken place with the result of change in land use and a rise in land values. Inequality has grown, and increased deprivation is experienced in peripheral estates and smaller towns too.

When it comes to the Church of England, Liverpool remains arguably the poorest diocese in the country, as there is no sign of addressing the unfair distribution of historic reserves between the dioceses. Even though the people in our pews give more generously than in many of our richer dioceses, most of our local congregations struggle to sustain their community engagement works for lack of resources, especially after they have paid their parish share. It is by no means justifiable that parishes in a poorer diocese need to raise more money than their counterparts in richer dioceses to make sure that a stipendiary priest is placed in their midst. Twenty-three of our parishes are in the most deprived 100 parishes in the country, 32 are in the most deprived 200, and 50 are in the most deprived 500.

Despite all the noise made around *Faith in the City*, the Church of England as such hasn't changed much. To a greater extent it remains a "one-class" and "one-culture" church that John Vincent spoke about,[1] although it has got used to "accommodating" others slightly better. It is not unusual these days to see celebrations of church growth in certain UPA church plants, often funded specifically by Church Commissioners' money, where people are drawn from middle-class backgrounds and often from outside the parish boundaries. Many of those "flourishing" congregations do not engage with the people of the parish living in economic and social deprivation. A Church Urban Fund review in 2000 concluded that the Church often reinforced the oppressions and divisions in the wider society.[2] The more recent Vision and Strategy of the Church of England, and the funding mechanisms of the Archbishops' Council, also do not pay particular attention to the missional challenges raised in *Faith in the City*.

It is not that the Church of England did not revisit the questions or review the progress in these 40 years. It was noted in 1995 that the general situation was discouraging, although the response in dioceses and parishes was encouraging.[3] Twenty years on, the next report also focused more on the local interventions and engagements and failed to

---

[1] John Vincent, "Signs for Mission", in *Into the City* (London: Epworth Press, 1982), pp. 109-15.

[2] *The Church Urban Fund Review 2000*, a report commissioned by the Archbishops' Council, London.

[3] *Staying in the City: Faith in the City ten years on*, a report by the Bishops' Advisory Group on Urban Priority Areas (London: Church House Publishing, 1995).

review the economy and policies.[4] We seem to have settled there for a mixed economy as the best way forward, with markets contributing to social justice without any systemic change.

Liverpool at the time of *Faith in the City*

Liverpool played a significant part in the conception of *Faith in the City*. David Sheppard, the then Bishop of Liverpool, played a prominent role in the commission. Sheppard had been Bishop of Liverpool for ten years by the time the report was published. He was an active advocate on the subjects of poverty and social reform in the inner cities and a vocal opponent to apartheid. His book *Bias to the Poor* articulated powerfully the need for the Church to serve the people where they are, and generated discussions that led to the new report.[5]

The Liverpool that Sheppard came to minister to was a city on the brink.[6] Between 1971 and 1985, employment in Liverpool had fallen by 33 per cent while the national figure was 63 per cent. The city had experienced a loss of 40,000 jobs between 1966 and 1977 because of business closures. The port also continued its decline during this period—its share of imports and exports was almost halved, and the workforce reduced to 3,000 from 25,000 in 1945. Sheppard also noticed that most of the locally controlled firms had collapsed, and almost all the big businesses were owned and controlled by those who had no particular interest in Liverpool or commitment to its people.[7] Building partnerships that brought people together with a commitment to the local community was Sheppard's task.

---

[4] *Faithful Cities: A Call for Celebration, Vision and Justice* (London: Church House Publishing and Peterborough: Methodist Publishing, 2006).

[5] David Sheppard, *Bias to the Poor* (London: Hodder & Stoughton, 1982).

[6] Michael Parkinson, *Liverpool on the Brink* (Hermitage, Berks: Policy Journals, 1985).

[7] David Sheppard and Derek Worlock, *Better Together: Christian Partnership in a Hurt City* (London: Hodder & Stoughton, 1988), p. 52.

In the late 1970s and early 1980s, Sheppard worked with Derek Worlock, the then Archbishop of Liverpool, in bringing the Anglican and Roman Catholic cathedrals and communities together. They established a new partnership that enabled communities to move from confrontation to co-operation in this city known for sectarian divisions and violence. They together served a city that was polarized, and they spoke about the "tale of two cities",[8] recognizing the wealth and riches on one side and the poverty and deprivation on the other. And they warned that the disparities between the "two cities" were widening.

Many of the recommendations of *Faith in the City* were based on Sheppard's own experience in Liverpool, and what he had already begun to implement since his arrival in the city. In fact, the term "Urban Priority Areas" (UPAs), used to describe urban areas of social deprivation, goes back to Sheppard.[9]

Liverpool beyond *Faith in the City*

Sheppard took a personal interest in following up *Faith in the City* in Liverpool. Apart from forming groups within the diocese and in the ecumenical context to respond to the report, he arranged meetings in each of the district council areas with a cross-section of the community, including council members, attending. The Church partnered with the local authority and initiated social projects to serve the community.

Liverpool has witnessed considerable changes in these last 40 years which are visible both in the Church and in the city. Yet the question remains whether those changes have led to the Church being better equipped to serve the city and its communities, and whether the recommendations produced in 1985 have been taken seriously by both the Church and the nation. We shall look at some of the areas that figured prominently in the recommendations.

---

[8] David Sheppard and Derek Worlock, *With Hope in Our Hands* (London: Hodder & Stoughton, 1994), pp. 41-58.

[9] David Sheppard, *Built as a City* (London: Hodder & Stoughton, 1974), pp. 229, 330.

The diocese beyond *Faith in the City*

In this section we look at the Diocese of Liverpool in the 40 years since 1985 in the light of some of the recommendations made in the report; specifically, those pertaining to the Church of England.

Ministry provided within the diocese
One of the recommendations for the Church was about adjustment of internal distribution of clergy by the dioceses to ensure that UPA parishes receive a fair share. This also meant paying particular attention in this respect to parishes on large outer estates. Liverpool Diocese, like many other dioceses, found it difficult to implement this recommendation, as the way parish-level ministry was funded changed dramatically in the period since the 1990s. As we were forced to reduce the overall number of clergy in the diocese, the UPAs had to face their fair share of clergy reduction too.

At the time of *Faith in the City*, we had around 300 stipendiary posts in the diocese and national church grants covered over 40 per cent of those costs, while also having national funds cover all pension costs and clergy national insurance costs. National funding began to reduce in real terms, clergy costs began increasing and dioceses needed to take on the responsibility for pensions and national insurance costs. Today, the national Church contribution, which comes in the form of Low-Income Community (LInC) funding, covers about 17 per cent of equivalent costs, while the number of stipendiary posts has almost halved.

Our national grant in 1993 was £1.89 million (nearly £4 million in today's money) while our current LInC grant is £1.75 million. This sets the context for how and why things have changed in resourcing within the diocese over the years since then, and the many difficult choices the diocese has had to grapple with during those years. This also resulted in underinvestment in parsonage properties, leading to the less satisfactory clergy housing stock that we have. By the time LInC came along, the contraction of resources had already happened, and it was a significant contraction at that.

Our accounts for 1985 state that "the debate on historic resources continues". Not much has changed in that regard! Many other dioceses were able to fall back on their substantial historic assets and investments to meet their ministry costs, but Liverpool Diocese needed to find that money from the pews. The reality is that an authentic church in areas of multiple deprivation will not be able to afford expensive buildings and the living of a priest. The historic injustice in wealth distribution in the Church of England has restrained the diocese in fulfilling its ambitions in line with the recommendations.

The report identified this problem in the form of another recommendation: the historic resources of the Church should be redistributed between dioceses to equalize the capital and income resources behind each stipendiary minister. Redistribution is not an easy task given the systems and structures that we have as the Church of England, but there was always an option for the Church Commissioners and Archbishops' Council to devise a funding system that would take into account the historic resources of the dioceses. The Church has miserably failed to take care of its own poor, making some dioceses like Liverpool more deprived of resources than they used to be in 1985.

Leadership development in UPAs, as recommended in the report, became a priority in Liverpool. The Group for Urban Ministry and Leadership (GUML) was established under the leadership of Neville Black. GUML helped establish leadership teams in UPA parishes and produced new vocations, especially many locally ordained ministers.[10] Twenty years later, Neville spoke about a regained ascendancy of conventional educational process, and the fact that we did not fully grasp the insights from GUML experience and impact.

Church Urban Fund (CUF) and Liverpool

Following the recommendation that a Church Urban Fund should be established to strengthen the Church's presence and promote Christian witness in the UPAs, CUF was launched in 1987. The financial provision was to be an annual contribution of £1 million from the Church Commissioners and income from a fund raised through a national appeal. By 1989, £12 million was raised as the capital. The expectation

---

[10] Neville Black, *40 Years of Ministry in Liverpool* (Liverpool: 2023), pp. 96-9.

was that CUF would have at least £2 million every year to support projects and work in UPAs.

Among the first projects given a grant was Churches Anti-Racist Enterprise in the Diocese of Liverpool. Its race relations officer was fully funded by CUF. In 2002, CUF funding was made available to the project pioneered by St Andrew's Clubmoor to support local people who struggle with debt or because of living on benefits. This project has developed over the years in partnership with other churches and organizations to what is now the St Andrew's Community Network. The network's current work includes debt and stress counselling and the North Liverpool Foodbank.

The context has changed again. CUF does not have as much money as it used to have for disbursal. The Church of England's annual contribution is £200,000, despite the expectation way back in 1985, which was £1 million. It survives mainly on government and private grants to support programmes. Despite its constraints, CUF remains a credible agency and partner in UPA contexts. In partnership with CUF's Together Network, Together Liverpool was established in 2013. One could only wonder what bigger impact CUF might have had if the Church of England's new Vision and Strategy had recognized CUF's work as missional, and had included significant financial support to promote Christian witness through social engagement.

Together Liverpool

In 2013, Together Liverpool was established as an independently registered charity equipping faith and community groups across the Diocese of Liverpool to take their next step in social action. The report had recommended that the dioceses should support the community work through their Boards of Social Responsibility, but by this time many dioceses had done away with those boards, and some did not have any alternative arrangement for co-ordinating and supporting the community work. Together Liverpool became the diocesan arm in Liverpool for equipping churches and organizations in community engagement.

In April 2021, Together Liverpool launched its Network of Kindness initiative, funded by the National Lottery, to support the growth of inclusive activities serving all members of the community, particularly the most socially vulnerable. Workshops, training events, networking opportunities, resources and grant funding are offered to support the development of projects tackling poverty and injustice. The areas of work covered include food and financial security, modern slavery, displaced people, children and young people, housing and land, environmental causes, mental health and social isolation.

This work reaches communities across the Diocese of Liverpool, not just the city and UPAs, as what used to be urban issues have now become part of human life outside urban areas. Although the charity is Anglican, it has become an inclusive body, welcoming diverse organizations of all faiths and none for the benefit of all people living in the diocese. The network of partner bodies has grown too, and among its recent partners are Clewer Initiative, Just Finance Foundation, Meals & More, Kids Matter, Your Local Pantry, Community Led Housing, Liverpool Dementia Alliance, Compassion Acts, Archdiocese of Liverpool, Zarach Trust and Micah Liverpool.

Racial justice

In response to the recommendation that the Church of England should make a more effective response to racial discrimination and disadvantage, the Church formed the Committee for Black Anglican Concerns (CBAC). The work on racial inclusion was very slow in Liverpool, probably because the city was not considered as culturally diverse as most other British cities. But it has one of the old Chinese settlements, and one of the oldest and most well-established resident black and mixed race communities in Britain.

The diocesan initiatives in the immediate aftermath of the report were in working with marginalized groups that included support for Liverpool Somali Sports Programme, an initiative to increase access to sport and support the confidence and wellbeing of Somali women and girls. Many Somali families moved to the city in the 1980s in response to the civil war. Work with asylum seekers was the main way of reaching out to the people of various racial backgrounds. The Asylum Link Merseyside, with the help of the Church, supported people seeking asylum from 74 different countries, helping them to navigate the immigration system, supporting with housing, transportation, access to education and healthcare. Asylum

Link continues to support those seeking asylum, with its casework team supporting over 900 people in 2024.

Since 2008 the diocese has worked with the interfaith network group, Liverpool Community Spirit, to build community connections with the recently arrived Ethiopian and Eritrean community and the longstanding black British communities in Toxteth, through hospitality events. That work strengthened the partnership between the Ethiopian community and St Agnes and St Pancras church, Toxteth, leading to the establishment of regular worship in the Ethiopian Orthodox tradition.

In 2017, a diocesan social justice strategy was agreed. Collaborating with Together Liverpool, the diocese would encourage and support parishes to engage in social action in new, innovative ways. These interventions included work with displaced people, championing diversity and campaigning for an end to modern slavery and human trafficking. Liverpool Diocese was one of the pilot dioceses that joined the Clewer Initiative in 2016, creating opportunities to highlight modern slavery abuses in church communities. In 2018, Liverpool Diocese invested in a new role, the Dean for Women and Diversity. This role supported clergy through the delivery of training and awareness-raising events, providing opportunities to learn about racial injustice and its impact across the diocese. Our vocations events, Lifecall, focus on celebrating and promoting representative leadership across the diocese and increasing the participation of UK Minority Ethnic (UKME) people in every area of church leadership. This is supported by the UKME Vocations Champion providing additional support through relational networks.

Responding to the report *From Lament to Action*, in 2022 Liverpool Diocese invested once more in racial justice by employing a racial justice officer. Building on the long history of racial justice work in the diocese, a new strategy, From Repentance to Repair, was approved in 2023. This strategy focused on engaging new audiences with the existing good work that had been taking place with displaced people, modern slavery and human trafficking and the Triangle of Hope. It looks to extend the internal work of diversity, equity and inclusion, with a focus on increasing representation in vocations and recruitment and supporting churches and schools to deliver educational interventions, focusing on the impacts of the legacy of African enslavement and racism within church and society.

Triangle of Hope

The legacy of the slave trade cannot be ignored when we speak about the city of Liverpool. We cannot talk about racial justice or economic justice today without addressing the oppressive systems of the past, which were supported by the Church of England. The diocese recognized this need as part of its vison for justice and inclusion. Consequently, the Triangle of Hope was established through dialogue between the Diocese of Liverpool, the Diocese of Kumasi in Ghana and the Diocese of Virginia, USA, tracing the triangular route of the transatlantic slave trade. The first pilgrimage of young people took place in 2013. In 2017, the Bishops of Liverpool, Kumasi and Virginia made a covenantal agreement dedicated to transforming the long history, ongoing effects and continuing presence of slavery and racism in our world through repentance, reconciliation and mission. The work of the Triangle of Hope continues to bring together young people to listen and learn together and create active change for racial justice in their home communities.

There are two main programmes that form the activities of Triangle of Hope: a youth pilgrimage and Tsedaqah community. The participants in the youth pilgrimage prepare together through worship, prayer, study and retreats, then travel together as pilgrims to one of the three partner dioceses each summer for three summers. It is desired that participants journey together for all three years so they may travel to each of the three dioceses in the Triangle. They follow the route of the old "triangle of despair" followed by the slave ships of the transatlantic slave trade, but journey today to learn from the history of the slave trade and about the tragedy that is modern slavery.[11]

Tsedaqah is a missional community based in Liverpool Cathedral, made up of young people from around the Triangle of Hope, living together in community for a year. The community members work in a variety of social justice projects across the Liverpool City Region, in

---

[11] K. Pye, *Two Triangles: Liverpool, Slavery and the Church* (Liverpool: Diocese of Liverpool, 2019), p. 11.

conjunction with the Diocese of Liverpool and Liverpool Cathedral. Every September, members from each point of the Triangle of Hope come to live and work in Liverpool to give a year of their life in service to God. Their communal living includes prayer, study and hospitality and their outreach will take them to a variety of projects and ministries across the city.

This international reconciliation project continues to transform the lives of young participants and the adults who accompany them, and builds the diocese's partnership with many local organizations in responding to the continuing effect of the slave trade, discrimination and racial injustice.

Ecumenical collaboration beyond Faith in the City

The report acknowledged the need for denominations to work together. In the late 1970s, Sheppard and Worlock had worked hard to bring together the churches in Merseyside. In 1976, a church leaders' group was formally established and an ecumenical officer was appointed. The Methodist Church, United Reformed Church, Baptist Union and Salvation Army joined together with the Anglicans and Roman Catholics, as partners in the mission of God to this city and region. Catholic and Anglican relationship reached a high point in 1982 when Pope John Paul II visited the city. Sheppard had made the Queen's visit in 1978 ecumenical, and Worlock decided that the Pope should visit both the cathedrals. These historic events testified to the fact that the city was overcoming sectarianism.

These churches began to address the issues facing the city, with a commitment to work with and for the whole community. In 1984, Churches in Merseyside had created the Merseyside Churches Unemployment Committee (MCUC), which monitored the effects of government policies and surveyed the Church's role in job creation in Merseyside.[12] Churches in Liverpool had been working together on issues related to unemployment since 1977, and in 1979 churches had even

---

[12] A. Bradstock, *David Sheppard: Batting for the Poor* (London: SPCK, 2019), pp. 192-3.

taken part in the protest march by workers at a Dunlop factory, against the closure of the site and the redundancies that would ensue.

The church leaders in Liverpool continued to serve the city together. After the Heysel Stadium disaster of 1985 and the Hillsborough disaster in 1989, the Church was expected to act, and it did so unitedly under the leadership of Worlock, Sheppard and John Newton, the Methodist District Chair. These ecumenical relationships have grown further over the last 40 years, and Churches Together in Merseyside Region (CTMR) is one among the well-established regional ecumenical bodies. CMTR is a founding member of Support for Asylum Seekers (SAS), a partnership organization funded ecumenically by churches across the region. SAS raises funds to support delivery of asylum and refugee interventions through local organizations, including Asylum Link Merseyside and Refugee Women Connect, which provide emergency support and advocacy for people caught in the immigration system.

The influence of the Church and its leaders in public life and society is less apparent today in Liverpool, a bit like everywhere else in the country, yet the bishop enjoys a respectable convening role in the public square and among the faith communities. The church leaders, including the regional/diocesan and the local clergy, did play a significant role in the regeneration of the city. Many organizations and charities that serve the most vulnerable in the city had come into existence with church support, and the partnerships continue. The Liverpool model of ecumenical collaboration inspired the formation of Together for Common Good in 2011 by Jenny Sinclair, Sheppard's daughter. T4CG became a national charity in 2017.

Two of the ecumenical organizations that continue Christian witness in the city need mentioning here.

Micah Liverpool

Micah Liverpool is a social justice charity, registered in 2016, set up by Liverpool Cathedral, Liverpool Metropolitan Cathedral and St Bride's church to relieve Liverpool residents from social injustice and poverty. Among its objectives are: to provide food and other household items through foodbanks or community markets, to provide advice and support to overcome financial problems and maximize their income, to raise public awareness of issues relating to poverty, both generally and in relation to social exclusion, to signpost relevant information and advisory services, and to help preserve and protect good physical and mental health of individuals, families and the wider community of the area of benefit, including the development of employability programmes to assist individuals to contribute productively to society.

Micah provides food for up to 500 people each week through two foodbanks and two community food markets. Foodbank users can receive emergency food provision four times within a 12-week period and receive three days of emergency food aid for each person. They have been able to support approximately 6,500 guests in the last 12 months, including over 1,400 children. They provided an average of 350 food parcels each week and over 18,000 food parcels in 2023. The Community Market is a food membership scheme that provides 15 items of food or household goods for £2 per week. The food and household items are deemed to be surplus to requirement by supermarkets. The main aim of the Community Market is to support people who may be on the brink of using foodbanks. This early intervention will hopefully take the strain off local foodbanks, as well as giving residents the opportunity to come together as part of the membership and sit, chat and have a cup of tea.

Micah's Recruitability Programme is an initiative based at Liverpool Cathedral working with long-term and newly unemployed adults, supporting them for ten weeks to improve their skills, confidence and readiness for work. Each Recruitability participant engages in a work experience placement, which runs concurrently with skills training. A variety of work placements are offered in Liverpool Cathedral and within Micah Liverpool and other partner organizations. Alongside the work experience placement, there is practical training and learning opportunities to help candidates search for, and secure, the right job for them. The training days also include a vocational course, provided by external trainers to strengthen CVs and job applications. The programme also offers one-to-one support from one of the co-ordinators to help participants create CVs and prepare for interviews.

Micah Liverpool is also a partnership hub for Zarach, a charity working to end child bed poverty. Zarach delivers beds to children through a school referral system. The volunteer-led team has delivered over 400 beds to children in Liverpool since the charity launched in July 2023. Micah has a small staff team and large volunteer team and is an excellent example of churches working together to serve the community with relatively small overhead expenses but making a big impact.

Feeding Liverpool
Feeding Liverpool was established in 2015 through Churches Together in the Merseyside Region and is led by an ecumenical group working with people of all faiths and none. It started as a local pilot of Feeding Britain, the independent charity that was established following the All-Party Parliamentary Inquiry into Hunger in the United Kingdom in 2014. The local organization has brought together those concerned with hunger and food insecurity in Liverpool.

Through a partnership with Together Liverpool in 2019, Feeding Liverpool has been able to grow and develop. It played a key role in procurement and distribution of food supplies during the Covid-19 pandemic as part of the Covid Response Project, sustaining the work of emergency food providers in Liverpool. It became part of the city's Food Insecurity Taskforce, responding to the pandemic and working towards the initial stages of Good Food Plan in Liverpool. Good Food Plan focuses on both immediate relief of hunger and addressing the root causes of food insecurity. While making information and best practice accessible to all, it aims to unlock the power of people and enable their voices to be heard.

The Queen of Greens bus takes affordable vegetables and fresh fruit to communities across Liverpool and Knowsley, Monday through to Friday. Each day, the bus takes a different route and is at each stop for half an hour, when people can make purchases using cash, card or approved vouchers. The stops include health and community centres and schools, giving people better opportunities to procure nutritious food nearer their home or workplace. The bus route takes in the communities hit hard by food insecurity and "food deserts", where residents must walk more than 15 minutes to buy "green" produce.

Drawing on the experiences from communities on the ground, Feeding Liverpool contributes to and influences policy debates locally and nationally, especially through its Good Food Community Advocacy and Policy Group. It also promotes greater public understanding of food systems, policy and related issues through network gatherings. It has supported the creation of Community Food Spaces across the city, led by community members and local community organizations, and is playing a part in tackling local food waste, helping people to save money on food bills and connecting with activities beyond food.

Interfaith engagement beyond *Faith in the City*

The report also highlighted the need for shared working with other faith groups. Interfaith relations in Liverpool began to take shape in the early 1980s, with Christian and Jewish representatives meeting informally, and representatives of Liverpool's Muslim community joining in later. This group has grown, and the Bishop of Liverpool now convenes and hosts regular meetings of the Faith Leaders Group in the city. There is a good working relationship between the faith leaders, who can offer a united voice when the communities face crises. During the riots in the summer of 2024, faith leaders were able to co-ordinate with each other, visit places together, and work with the local authorities to help speak to the communities. Despite all this, the interfaith engagement is not an area we have focused on well, and the diocese is planning to invest in this area further.

Faith4Change
Faith4Change was established as an environmental charity in 2004 with the encouragement of the then Bishop of Liverpool, James Jones. It is based in the diocesan offices. Its core values reflect its deep commitment to sustainability, social justice and environmental justice. Its stated mission is to work in partnership with people of different world faiths and none, to develop trusted relationships and skills that ultimately transform lives, communities and neighbourhood environments, and to advance the education of the public in the conservation, protection and improvement of the physical and natural environment, particularly within disadvantaged communities.

A core area of its work is to foster connections within and across faiths. This work focuses on the values and beliefs we share across faith and cultural traditions, building on key motivations to support action on climate change, often drawing on secular sources of expertise and action to grow and inform change. Community Climate Action projects are co-created in partnership with residents, communities, other groups and organizations and interested people. Together they create spaces to learn, share and develop skills, enhancing their knowledge and awareness and informing their behaviour and actions to reduce the impacts of climate change, including biodiversity loss.

Through its schools and community service, Faith4Change can create a tailored delivery package that meets the specific needs of each organization. From planting and maintaining kitchen gardens to designing faith trails, it works closely with each school or community to create the right space for them, and works with each group through every aspect of development and delivery, whether that's embedding maths into gardening sessions, using creative arts to engage with the environment, offering gentle therapeutic exercise through being outside, or training volunteers in horticulture. In partnership with Myerscough College, it can offer fully funded Level 1 and 2 City and Guilds Practical Horticulture qualifications to adults.

Its Net Zero Carbon 2030 (NZC2030) initiative, in collaboration with the Diocese of Liverpool, is another great example of assisting churches in working towards carbon neutrality. Through the NZC2030 programme, Faith4Change has been engaging congregations in climate actions using the Eco Church framework. Collaborating with leaders from several faiths and denominations has helped extend these efforts beyond their immediate networks.

Conclusion: Beyond the 40th anniversary

Forty years on, this anniversary presents an opportunity for the Church to pause, reflect and consider our role and purpose for the decades ahead. Churches Together in Merseyside Region and Together Liverpool have come together to deliver a project that focuses on telling the story of local groups, developing a "Manifesto of Hope" and culminating in an event in November 2025. A co-ordinator for the project was employed in late 2024. One focus throughout 2025 would be on fostering deeper and broader partnerships between faith communities and social justice activists. A Social Action Network Conference is planned in July. Another focus will be the empowerment of churches and faith communities to engage in social action and civic duties, supported by initiatives like Together Liverpool. Guidance for parishes and organizations on engaging with political representatives and civic leaders is being produced.

The challenges in Liverpool are as grave as they were 40 years ago. The diocese itself has become poorer in relative terms, and we are unable to make more monetary investment in ministry. Yet we have given expression to our commitment to serve our communities in response to the recommendations of the *Faith in the City* report. Diocesan and ecumenical initiatives as detailed in this article continue to play a vital role in addressing the needs of the community, not least the poor and the vulnerable. All our projects are growing and developing in their capacity and outreach, thanks to the generous support from the churches who are otherwise struggling financially, and the growing number of volunteers drawn from our congregations and wider community.

6

Urban mission and ministry: The challenge for the Church of England

Terry Drummond

Introduction

In the period between the early 1970s and the late 1990s, there was a wide-ranging discussion within all the Christian denominations of what constituted urban theology, as well as its importance in underpinning urban ministry across the UK.

The publication of *Faith in the City* by the Archbishop of Canterbury's Commission on Urban Priority Areas in 1985 was an important event in the period under consideration, because of the impact it had on both the Church and wider society. While in hindsight it may now seem to be a "product of its time", it was, nevertheless, a catalyst for an important debate on issues relating to faith in the city, which has continued to this day.

In what follows, I will consider the Church's response to *Faith in the City*; the theology of *Faith in the City*; the Church Urban Fund; diocesan responses to *Faith in the City*; critical responses to *Faith in the City*; the Urban Bishops' Panel; *Faithful Cities*; and Urban Mission and Ministry: Local Contextual Development, before reaching conclusions.

Faith in the City: The Church of England's response to urban realities, 1985-2006

Issues concerning urban mission and ministry had been highlighted for the Archbishop of Canterbury, Robert Runcie, by the publication of the government-commissioned "Scarman Report" into the social disorder that resulted in the riots in Brixton in 1981.[1] His response was the commissioning of a report into the reasons for the urban unrest. The commission was launched on 6 July 1983, its core terms of reference being:

> To examine the strengths, insights, problems and needs of the Church's life and mission in Urban Priority Areas and, as a result, to reflect on the challenge which God may be making to Church and nation: and to make recommendations to appropriate bodies.[2]

The report, published on 4 December 1985, opened with a chapter on theological priorities, in which it noted that in the Church there was a preference for "ambulance work" in meeting the needs of the poor because "to be the protagonist of social change may involve challenging those in power and risk the loss of one's own power".[3]

However, the report reflected a commitment to bringing about social change, intended to improve the lives of those that had been adversely affected by economic adversity during the period it had examined. It did this by speaking truth to power, challenging the government to change course on some of its policies. It made 38 recommendations to the Church of England, and 23 to the government. However, the government was unwilling to change course in ways that were contrary to the neoliberal, *laissez-faire* economic and political philosophy that it had embraced.

---

[1] L. Scarman, *Scarman Report* (1981); <https://www.gloucestershire.gov.uk/your-community/black-history-month/black-history-month-2020/race-relations-acts-1965–2000/scarman-report/>, accessed 3 February 2025.

[2] *Faith in the City*, p. iii.

[3] *Faith in the City*, p. 49.

The commissioners had spent time meeting with representatives of residents in urban parishes, alongside taking evidence in person and in written submissions from organizations working in urban communities. The introduction to the report included a description of this process:

> We decided at the outset that we must spend some time in the UPAs to see for ourselves the human reality behind the official statistics. In the course of a series of visits we saw something of the physical condition under which people in the UPAs are living, and we listened to their own accounts and experiences at open public meetings and in smaller invited groups.[4]

Through the visits, the commissioners were able to hear at first-hand about the problems people were experiencing, by meeting with individuals, families and groups. In this way, the research represented a collection of statistical evidence that was rooted in first-hand experience which, while limited, gave substance to its analysis and recommendations.

In addressing the question, "What Kind of Church?" (Chapter 4), the emphasis was placed on the fact that God is at work in society, which means that Christians are called to work with God in a partnership of clergy and laity working together for the good of local communities:

> A Church which only "parallels" society—which exists alongside but is separate—needs to become a Church that is involved in society. The outward-looking Church should identify what its members are doing in and for the local UPAs, whether in their full-time work or as volunteers, and should recognise this work as part of its mission, and give its members the fullest support in their work.[5]

This understanding highlights the importance of local churches being active in addressing the social problems of the parish. In this way, urban mission can be seen as social action and pastoral care.

---

[4] *Faith in the City*, p. xiv.
[5] *Faith in the City*, p. 76.

The recommendations that were addressed to the Church covered three critical areas, with chapters on:

- Organizing the Church (Chapter 5)
- Developing the People of God (Chapter 6), and
- Supporting a Participating Church (Chapter 7)

The chapter on organizing the Church reviews the different ministries that are available alongside stipendiary clergy, including deaconesses and church army officers. There is an acknowledgement of the importance of the deployment of stipendiary clergy to UPAs, who, it was envisaged, would work alongside an increased number of stipendiary lay ministry; that is, "community workers or administrators—not necessarily tied to one parish". It went on to state: "We hope that the Church Urban Fund we propose might make such ministries possible."[6]

Faith in the City was also radical in its critique of government policy. Indeed, Eliza Filby has since written, with much justification, that *"Faith in the City*... would prove to be one of the most incisive and important critiques of Thatcher's Britain."[7] The recommendations made to the government on urban policy issues were indeed radical, and included areas such as housing policy, unemployment, law and order and support to local government, all of which had considerable economic implications, and turned out to be largely unacceptable to the government.

The theology of *Faith in the City*

The underlying theological thinking in *Faith in the City* was typically Anglican. Chapter 3, on "Theological Priorities", opens with a review of the tradition of urban parish ministry. It emphasizes the importance of community ministry; in particular, the importance of understanding and reflecting on political and social concerns, and on focusing on the contribution that local churches can make to remedying them, by offering

---

[6] *Faith in the City*, p. 91.
[7] E. Filby, *God and Mrs Thatcher* (Hull: Biteback Publishing, 2015), p. 172.

both spiritual and practical help to the community. It places a primacy on meeting the needs of the poorer members of the community, even when they are not members of the Christian community. In this way, it draws on the tradition of urban ministry which had developed in Britain from the beginning of the 1850s. In addition, it refers to the development of Anglican social theology by a distinguished line of Anglican theologians who had wrestled with the ambiguities and challenges around social action, and from which much could be learned.[8]

The chapter also draws attention to the influence that Latin American liberation theology had on the writers of the report. The New Testament theologian Anthony Harvey, a commission member responsible for that chapter, later wrote:

> The significant influence here was liberation theology. This had demonstrated that a theology appropriate to particular social and economic conditions could be formulated by local people in a way that was authentic to their situation.[9]

The suggestion is that its incorporation in the report reflected a shift in theological models used by the commission, no longer relying solely on Anglican theological lineage but instead using liberation theology in ways that could be applied to specific local circumstances, including on the need for poverty alleviation and improvements in social housing provision. Thus, *Faith in the City* represented a specific attempt to take these issues seriously, and to challenge government in a manner that did not leave any room for ambiguity of purpose or action. Indeed, its theological reflection identified liberation theology as a catalyst for social renewal, with its emphasis on the importance of local community reflection and action. In this regard, a key element of its thinking on liberation theology was what it describes as "the preferential option for

---

[8] For more on this see S. Spencer (ed.), *Theology Reforming Society: Revisiting Anglican Social Theology* (London: SCM Press, 2017).

[9] A. Harvey, *By What Authority?: The Churches and Social Concern* (London: SCM Press, 2001), p. 23.

the poor"; that is, the need to place a primacy on listening to the poor and on meeting their needs.

The chapter on theology concluded in a way that was positive about the importance of finding God at work in urban communities, stating: "We believe that God, though infinitely transcendent, is also to be found, despite all appearances, in the apparent waste lands of our inner cities and housing estates."[10] This has since been further recognized by the development, in 2019, of the Estates Evangelism Task Group in the Church of England, which focuses on working with those living on estates to help them meet and overcome the social and economic challenges that they face.

The Church Urban Fund

A key recommendation in *Faith in the City* was a need for a Church Urban Fund (CUF) to be created, to ensure that financial support was made available for the funding of innovative projects in areas with high levels of social deprivation. The report stated it this way, that "A Church Urban Fund should be established to strengthen the Church's presence and promote Christian witness in the urban priority areas."[11] It was a recommendation that was to have long-term implications for ministry in urban parishes and the wider community.[12]

The fund was launched in April 1988, with an initial payment from the Church Commissioners of £1 million. (The dioceses launched fundraising appeals with the aim of raising £18 million in two years.) The Church Commissioners' positive attitude to the CUF became crucial for ensuring continuing funding, and it stood by its commitment to providing financial support for its administration (CUF was based in the commissioners' offices). However, in 1991, the Church Commissioners'

---

[10] *Faith in the City*, p. 70.
[11] *Faith in the City*, p. 363.
[12] A progress report by the Archbishop of Canterbury's Advisory Group on Urban Priority Areas, *Living Faith in the City* (London: General Synod of the Church of England, 1990), p. 63.

annual general meeting voted for a proposal that would reduce its annual grant of £1 million to £500,000. Despite this setback, the fund continued its work through fundraising and becoming an independent charity. In this regard, it continued to make grants and commission research on the outcomes of its work, alongside publishing reports on the value of church-based social action as a way of tackling social problems relating to poverty, social deprivation and exclusion.[13]

An important development that originated in the office of the then Archbishop of Canterbury, the Rt Revd Rowan Williams, became the Near Neighbours programme, launched in 2011, which was later developed into a CUF programme with government funding. Devised by Guy Wilkinson, the then Archbishop of Canterbury's interfaith officer, the intention was to create an interactive project which local faith communities could develop as an interfaith partnership. Hence, Near Neighbours brought together representatives and members of local faith communities, with the following purpose in mind:

> [To] bring people together to build relationships and associations that help them to bond together at deeper levels and to nurture trust, mutual support and a sense of peace and security. The proposals will help to create relationships across differences and provide support for people with a deeper sense of their connection to others. They will provide places for these relationships to develop and thrive to become the foundation for trust.[14]

Near Neighbours, while limited to parishes with a cross-section of faith communities, was able to show the Church of England in a strong light, by being active and effective in bringing faith groups together to improve

---

[13] A. Chandler, *The Church of England in the Twentieth Century: The Church Commissioners and the Politics of Reform, 1948-1998* (Woodbridge: Boydell Press, 2006), p. 386.

[14] Church of England, *Faithfully Interactive Near Neighbours Proposal*, 15 October 2010, p. 2.

the quality of their lives, and CUF continues to be an important part of the Church of England's commitment to urban mission and ministry.

Diocesan responses to *Faith in the City*

The dioceses responded to the publication of *Faith in the City* in several ways; in particular, by launching appeals for the CUF which were to bring in many millions of pounds, thereby providing vital support for new projects in urban parishes. Dioceses also appointed link officers to promote and develop urban mission and ministry. The officers would meet up at annual conferences, and the archdeacon and *Faith in the City* officer for the Diocese of Southwark, Douglas Bartles-Smith, has described an address at one of them by the Archbishop of Canterbury at the time, George Carey, as follows:

> He seemed much more interested in the Decade of Evangelism,[15] which failed to increase church attendance, than standing up for the inner cities. He came to the Faith in the City National Conference where he was poorly received. He tried to suggest to the conference that the Church did not speak with special expertise on political and economic matters; everyone was infuriated that he said this to a conference which had included the Anglican economist Will Hutton amongst others.[16]

---

[15] The decade of the 1990s was declared the Decade of Evangelism by resolution of the Lambeth Conference of 1988. It called the provinces and dioceses of the Anglican Communion, in co-operation with other Christians, to make this a time of "renewed emphasis on making Christ known to the people of his world". Cf. <https://www.anglicancommunion.org/resources/document-library/lambeth-conference/1988/resolution-43-decade-of-evangelism?subject=Evangelism&tag=lambeth+conference>, accessed 4 February 2025.

[16] Douglas Bartles-Smith, *Fighting Fundamentalism* (Shrewsbury: Saxty Press, 2007), pp. 65ff.

This response by Bartles-Smith to the address might also reflect a changing perspective (seen at that time and since) in the Church of England's leadership, whereby urban mission and ministry has no longer been at the forefront of the Church's agenda. An example of this change of approach has been how more and more emphasis has been placed on tackling the decline in the number of worshippers than on tackling social issues relating to inner-city deprivations (a trend that was particularly apparent under the primacy of Archbishop Justin Welby).

In some dioceses, reports were produced that explored the issues relating to social deprivation that had been identified in local contexts. These included *Faith in the City of Birmingham* (1988),[17] a book-length report that describes in some detail the life of the Church in Birmingham which was produced by a committee chaired by Sir Richard O'Brien. In Chapter 4, "Christian Responses: A review of action by Birmingham Churches", there is a convincing explanation of how urban evangelism and community service can be combined, with a specific emphasis on serving those in UPAs who lack contact with the Gospel and the local church.

The Diocese of Winchester formed a group, chaired by Professor Raymond Plant, which produced a pamphlet, *Faith in the City: Theological and Moral Challenge*.[18] This addressed some of the philosophical and practical impacts that conservative political thinking associated with the "New Right", and which was linked to the political philosophy of the governments led by Margaret Thatcher, was having on local communities, particularly those that were being adversely affected by its application.

In Chapter 1, "Conservative Capitalism", the difficulties are described in some detail, and, in some respects, can be seen as being related to the debates and discussions on social justice in the Church of England

---

[17] *Faith in the City of Birmingham: A Report of a Commission set up by the Bishop's Council of the Diocese of Birmingham* (Exeter: The Paternoster Press, 1988).

[18] *Faith in the City: Theological and Moral Challenge* (The Diocese of Winchester, 1988); <https://hampshire.spydus.co.uk/cgi-bin/spydus.exe/ENQ/WPAC/BIBENQ?SETLVL=&BRN=661011>, accessed 4 February 2025.

that can be traced back to the times of Charles Gore and, later, William Temple:

> In "*Faith in the City*", there are many references to inequality, social justice and community, and it is precisely in these areas that some of the New Right thinkers and politicians have posed central questions which any plausible social theology has to confront.[19]

One implication of this insight is that community development work is vital and has to be championed as an alternative to the neoliberal, individualist philosophy of the "New Right". Community development work seeks to enable people to work together to shape their local environment. In so doing, they escape isolation and the feeling of powerlessness that poverty and unemployment often induce. This is an important means of advancing the interests of people and thus serving the common good.

Critical responses to *Faith in the City*

The *Faith in the City* report was followed by several other reports on social and welfare issues. These included one by Frank Field MP, a committed Anglican with years of experience of research on wealth and poverty, who wrote: "The report on the inner cities illustrates the folly of thinking political influence can be exerted as though the Church still commanded the dominance which it enjoyed in the mid-nineteenth century."[20] A theological response came from Nigel Biggar (Latimer House, Oxford). Biggar writes:

> the report concentrates inordinately upon recommending programmes of reform to government and church bureaucracies,

---

[19] *Faith in the City: Theological and Moral Challenge*, p. 5.
[20] F. Field, *The Politics of Paradise: A Christian Approach to the Kingdom* (London: Fount, 1987), p. 113.

and has virtually no moral vision or practical advice to give individual citizens and Christians and local bodies. This omission has provoked quite widespread criticism, and must be reckoned one of the report's most serious defects.[21]

John Atherton, of the William Temple Foundation, and an adviser to the commission, was critical of the chapters that dealt with economics. He suggested that:

> The need to be alert to compromises which avoid real change is particularly important for Christian social vision in Britain. For, if we rightly reject laissez-faire and state systems, the danger is that we end up in the soft centre of consensus politics, of Butskellism, or neo-Keynesianism. Much of Faith in the City never really rises above this level.[22]

Malcolm Brown (who was to become the Director of Social Responsibility and subsequently Director of Mission and Public Affairs of the Church of England) describes the problems for the Church in addressing the issues encapsulated in *Faith in the City* as follows: "In terms of recent history, the encounter between the churches and the Thatcher government in the 1980s was explicitly about economic issues and the social consequences."[23] He goes on to suggest that the publication of *Faith in the City* failed to recognize that the models of social witness associated with Temple were no longer appropriate.

Whatever the perceived inadequacies, however, *Faith in the City* was highly significant for the Church of England. It put UPA parishes on the map, encouraged vocations to urban ministry, and stimulated urban

---

[21] Nigel Biggar, *Theological Politics: A critique of "Faith in the City", the report of the Archbishop of Canterbury's Commission on Urban Priority Areas* (Oxford: Latimer House, 1988), p. 21.

[22] J. Atherton, *Faith in the Nation: A Christian Vision for Britain* (London: SPCK, 1988), p. 67.

[23] M. Brown, *After the Market: Economics, Moral Agreement and the Churches' Mission* (Bern: Peter Lang, 2004), p. 20.

projects in communities. For a season, urban mission and ministry was recognized as a key aspect of the work of the Church. However, after 20 years it had somewhat run out of steam, and began to be less significant.

The Urban Bishops' Panel

In addition to the establishing of CUF, the Archbishop of Canterbury appointed a priest, Patrick Dearnley, to promote and support follow-up work across the dioceses. Runcie also appointed the Archbishop of Canterbury's Advisory Group on Urban Priority Areas, which, by 1985, had become the Bishops' Group on Urban Priority Areas. Both groups were chaired by Tom Butler, Bishop of Willesden and later Bishop of Leicester (subsequently Bishop of Southwark). In 1990, the group published *Living Faith in the City* (GS 902), which reviewed the follow-up actions stemming from the publication of *Faith in the City*, with a focus on the responses made by the Church of England and by government to the recommendations.

In 1995, the group published *Staying in the City: Faith in the City Ten Years On* (GS 1811), which, following on from the previous report, outlined the continuing importance of urban mission and ministry in the life of the Church of England in the context of local communities. In an essay published as an appendix to the report, Gill Moody writes:

- Is God at work only within committed Sunday congregations?
- What are our human, material and spiritual resources: those of committed church goers or those given by God to the whole of His creation? What model of stewardship best uses all of these gifts?
- What sort of Church do we want to be? What financial systems are appropriate to resource the Church? What sort of model of stewardship best serves the Church?[24]

---

24 A Report of the Bishops' Advisory Group on Urban Priority Areas, *Staying in the City: Faith in the City, Ten Years On, GS 1811* (London: Church House Publishing, 1995), p. 123.

These questions reflected issues that would be discussed in the years that followed, as the commitment to urban mission and ministry would become seen as less important in the Church, with a renewed emphasis being placed on mission as evangelistic outreach, and as a way of reducing the decline in the number of worshippers. The two reports represent a critical analysis of the response to *Faith in the City*, by undertaking a detailed review of the key findings and their outworking within the dioceses.

Between 1988 and 1999, the Urban Bishops' Panel was chaired by the Bishop of Hume, Stephen Lowe, who, in 2006, was released from episcopal duties to be the Bishop for Urban Life and Faith, and was succeeded as chair by the Bishop of Ripon, John Packer. During this time, the contrast between the Church of England's approach to advancing social justice in deprived areas and that of the national government may be seen in the government initiatives that promoted urban policy, including the introduction of initiatives such as Action for Cites, Inner City Action Teams, City Action Teams and, from 1994 to 2002, the Single Regeneration Budget (SRB) initiative, all of which, in different ways, were focused on improving economic and social conditions for those living in deprived urban communities. However, these government programmes were time-limited (hence transient), whereas the Church of England, by retaining its parish presence in urban areas, was able to give a long-term commitment to working with people experiencing social deprivation, and in ways that were often effective and permanent.

An additional contribution, made by the Church of England at a local level, was the co-opting of clergy to local Regeneration Boards, where they were able to contribute to urban policy-making and to support the delivery of local projects, which, in some cases, would have a positive impact on their parishes. The experience of being a board member of an SRB partnership is described by Neil McKinnon, Rector of St Matthew's at the Elephant and Castle in the London borough of Southwark.

The next application for SRB funding was successful. There would be an Elephant Links Partnership Board responsible for the spending of the SRB monies. The council would be the "Accountable Body", but the meaning of "Accountable Body" varied. A number of council officers considered that the money could only be spent on what they approved.[25]

In 2000, the government published an Urban White Paper outlining proposals for new developments. In response, in December 2001, the Urban Bishops' Panel published a draft paper called *Towards an Urban Strategy for the Church of England*[26] (it was produced for the House of Bishops to consider). The paper noted that the Church of England continued to use language which could be seen as alien to urban culture:

> Many hoped that the enthusiasm and activity of *Faith in the City*, would change the Church's concerns, its structures, its mind-set (we still speak of rural deans and pastoral counselling), its training programmes and leadership, but these all still deny that for the vast majority in England today, their lifestyle and experience are urban.

It concluded with a proposal:

> An Urban Resource Unit would maintain capacity and knowledge on urban issues as it monitors and develops an overview of government policy, and the resources of the Church through its national and local presence.

It also proposed to review priorities during the following five years:

> We have argued for an urban renaissance in which the Church reclaims its healing, redeeming and transforming tasks, and with this vision before us, the Urban Bishops' Panel will seek, during the next five years and beyond, to set the objectives and recommendations for a Church seeking to build on its established

---

[25] N. McKinnon, "Thinking Long Term: Keeping God at the Elephant and Castle", in M. Torry (ed.), *Regeneration and Renewal: The Church in New and Changing Communities* (Norwich: Canterbury Press, 2007), p. 41.

[26] House of Bishops, *Towards an Urban Strategy for the Church of England*, 2001.

priorities and reputation in urban communities and responding to these unprecedented challenges and opportunities.[27]

The Urban Bishops' Panel ceased its work in 2013. It was succeeded by a short-lived working group of clergy and laity which lacked formal acknowledgement by the bishops or the General Synod, in contrast to Rural Ministry, which had a standing committee. This was symptomatic of how the importance of urban issues and ministry ceased to have the priority that the paper submitted to the House of Bishops (as above) had suggested it should have, and it slipped off the agenda until the creation of the Estates Evangelism Task Group in 2019.

Faithful Cities

The publication of *Faithful Cities* (2006)[28] was a very different report to *Faith in the City* and reflected a changed perspective on urban life and faith. *Faith in the City* was published at a time of economic decline in manufacturing industries. *Faithful Cities*, however, was the product of a period of increasing globalization; that is, unrestricted free trade across the globe, including increases in freedom of movement of goods, services, capital and labour. This is important as it had implications for employment levels, pay levels and investment levels in indigenous economic initiatives (this is not an all-encompassing list) that were not always favourable to local, urban communities, some of which were "left behind" and have not fully recovered in the period since.

The content of *Faithful Cities* offered a different set of challenges to that of *Faith in the City*, in that it was addressed to all the Christian denominations. It also identified the needs of a new, urban generation who were outside the institutional church structures (though, oddly, it did so without making reference to *Mission-Shaped Church*,[29] which had

---

[27] *Towards an Urban Strategy for the Church of England*, p. 50.
[28] Commission on Urban Life and Faith, *Faithful Cities* (London: Church House Publishing and Peterborough: Methodist Publishing House, 2006).
[29] *Mission-Shaped Church* (London: Church House Publishing, 2004).

been published by the Church of England two years earlier, and was the subject of a wide-ranging and important debate within the dioceses at that time). While it addressed issues associated with cities and, by definition, the urban environment, *Faithful Cities* also addressed questions for local churches to consider in both suburbia and rural communities. The emphasis of the report was on urban and public policy seen in the context of government policies on economic and social regeneration. It also marked a shift in theological definition, by replacing the use of the term "urban theology" with the term "public theology". In addition, the term "Faithful Capital" is identified as being a key element of the church's ministry, though the theological foundations are not discussed.

The fact that all regeneration projects should be based on explicit, social values is often underestimated as being an imperative for their success. The developer will be looking for a profitable return, while the local authority may be caught between serving the good of the local community and raising standards across an entire borough or city, and with limited resources at its disposal. The local residents are often the poor relation in this context, and can become the subject of change without being able to make a critical contribution to what is being proposed. *Faithful Cites* points out that: "Our major cities are no longer abandoned husks of post-industrial decay, but hubs of vital economic and cultural activity often focused on city centre and river and dockland development."[30] There remains a need for the property developers in urban communities, whose primary motive is often a need to make large profits (sometimes taking a priority over other considerations), to be challenged by the churches, with a view to persuading them to ensure that the developments represent an holistic understanding of society and people's needs, and not just a way of amassing wealth for their shareholders. The building up of a "good city", the report suggests, should therefore be based on an understanding that the creation of better and safer communities must include recognition of the needs of everyone who will live and work within them. To this end, it is important that the churches, in partnership with other faith groups, promote an understanding of what community means.

---

[30] *Faithful Cities*, p. 10.

It may be, at the simplest level, a regular "drop in" for elders where they can make friends over a cup of tea or a light lunch. In some places, for example, it has been churches that offer "winter shelters" for the homeless, including a rolling programme of churches opening their halls on a different night each week from November to March. In these initiatives, we see impressive examples of churches reaching out and responding to the gospel imperative of caring for the dispossessed. One element of this voluntary work is that there is a financial cost involved in community service, which is given freely by people who are committed to serving others, thus reflecting their commitment to their cause. In addition, the financial commitment of the churches (whose clergy are often on paid stipends working alongside church members who are giving their time free of charge to voluntary activity) *is* a financial contribution, made by urban parishes to community development, and which will often be seen as such by those who benefit from these initiatives. The result is that churches are often seen by members of these communities as "having a stake" in their success, by the very fact that they have been willing to financially invest in them. *Faithful Cities* also suggests that the contribution made by Christian churches in this context must entail being able to actively stimulate and engage in dialogue across faiths and with the wider community. It is all too easy to be caught up in what is referred to as the "clash of civilizations", when what is called for is mutual understanding and dialogue.

In the national context, the impact of *Faithful Cities* was short-lived. This was, in part, due to the fact that the Church of England was entering a period in which discussions were becoming more focused on addressing and reversing the decline in the number of worshippers. While social capital was still recognized as being an important contribution to community development, for some in the Church of England it did not appear to attract new worshippers and hence came to take a "back seat" in their priorities.

A critique of the findings of *Faithful Cities* from an evangelical perspective has been made by Jon Kuhrt, in *Crossover City* (2010), in which he suggests that the report failed to address the importance of the evangelical approach to issues of justice and social outreach:

It failed to effectively engage with the evangelical perspective and experience in urban mission. It was dominated by the liberal agenda which, while it succeeded in challenging structural inequality and giving interesting sociological analysis, was unable to understand the commitments driving the growing evangelical agenda for an integrated approach to social action, evangelism, and church growth and unity.[31]

The period following the publication of *Faithful Cities* in 2006 was, for the Church of England, a time of introspection, in which it increasingly became concerned with the problems of decline and internal theological debate. In looking outwards, its commitment was now to explore new approaches to mission-based activities that were rooted in evangelistic outreach. This was in contrast with the approach taken in *Faith in the City*, which offered insights into local, practical action, drawing on the importance of local parishes. *Faithful Cities* reflected a new public theology that insufficiently appreciated the significance and value of urban mission and ministry. In addition, the publication of *Mission-Shaped Church* (2004) overshadowed *Faithful Cities*, for a Church that was increasingly becoming influenced by issues of evangelism, outreach and church growth.

In his report, *The Urban Church Three Years on from Faithful Cities* (GS 1745), Stephen Lowe makes this point in the introduction:

> The context has been very different. Faithful Cities has not had the impact on the conscience of the Church and Nation of its predecessor, although three years on many of its predictions have already been fulfilled. But the Church of England still holds on to the parochial system maintaining a ministry to every inhabitant of this country, when the overwhelming majority live in urban communities. It has taken this responsibility seriously and has used its historic resources to maintain that ubiquitous presence,

---

[31] J. Kuhrt, "Going Deeper: Resisting Tribal Theology", in A. Davey (ed.), *Crossover City: Resources for Urban Mission and Transformation* (London: Mowbray, 2010), p. 16.

not only because of the obligations of 'Establishment' but because theologically it believes it is vital to sustain a ministry to the needier, marginalised parts of our nation.[32]

Lowe goes on to describe political and social issues that had been of particular importance during his period in office, including asylum and migration, which had been widely discussed by government and policy-makers, making the point:

> Changing patterns of migration continues to reshape local populations amidst cultures of suspicion and fear perpetuated by harsher control rhetoric from politicians, and the extreme right. The situation of those at the end of the asylum process has become increasingly dire ... [33]

Lowe felt that this situation required careful consideration by both the national and local Church.

Urban mission and ministry: Local contextual development

The local context remains the key to urban mission and ministry, which is rooted in the tradition of parish ministry; of clergy being inducted to the "cure of souls", which continues to be the most important contribution it makes to the worshipping community, offering a space for everyone living within the geographical boundaries of the parish. While most residents would have no contact with the clergy and worshippers, the local church remains available to all. In many communities there remains a residual memory; a sense of that being "my church, the one I don't go to".

---

[32] S. Lowe, *The Urban Church Three Years on from Faithful Cities* (GS 745) (London: The Archbishops' Council, 2009), p. 1, para. 2.

[33] Lowe, *The Urban Church Three Years on from Faithful Cities*, para. 16.

It is this approach to ministry that is described by Malcolm Brown, Director of Mission and Public Affairs for the Church of England, in a briefing following a consultation on Estates Ministry, which brought together representatives of estate ministry from across the Church of England:

> "A Christian Presence in every Community"—that's what it says on the Church of England's website. But it is far more than a strap line—it is at the heart of our identity as a church committed to all of the people of the nation, living out the vocation primarily through our parish structure.[34]

While Brown recognizes the problem of linking size with success, the emphasis in the majority of the policies of the Archbishops' Council has been (and remains) on the need for church growth, by increasing the number of new disciples and worshippers. This is encapsulated in the commitment of the Archbishops' Council and Church Commissioners to prioritizing financial support for ministry in dioceses which are focused on church growth across all geographical areas.

The 2016 annual review of the Church Commissioners, *Investing in the Church's Growth*, describes examples of projects given support—an example of urban mission and ministry is a grant of £1.45 million allocated to a City Centre Resource Church in 2014-16, based in Salford in the Diocese of Manchester. The description offers an insight into the background to this and similar developments:

> ... the Resource Church has already run three Alpha Courses and started a youth group, a parent and toddler group and English classes as well as hosting several events for the New Wine Church network. The church was started with a focus on young adults

---

[34] M. Brown, "The 'E' Words, Estates and Evangelism", p. 1. Published online but no longer available.

and the poor, and as with other City Centre Resourcing Churches aims to itself start new churches in due course.[35]

The development of Resource Churches has become an important element of the Strategic Development Fund, though the word "Resource" can be seen to have had different interpretations. It has sometimes seemed to mean being dedicated to the extension of an evangelical style of worship and ministry, rather than to supporting parishes within the diocese that may have a different style of ministry and worship, but which would benefit from extra financial provision. The development of "New Wine"[36] is a pointer to the importance that this evangelical grouping now has in the Church of England, by being an important network for groups of churches within that tradition.

In the context of urban mission and ministry, another example of grant aid that became available was funding specifically addressed to *"Developing Church Growth in Deprived Areas"*, which was the subject of an evaluation report in 2016. A description of examples of ministry that were being developed through this funding was engagement of the wider community through Church outreach or mission-growth in the mission field. The report stated:

> Many of the projects were engaged in activities contributing to the common good, which might in the longer term develop a wider mission field: such as running a Food Bank, providing debt counselling, running cafes or drop-ins for young people or holiday clubs, as well as organising more social activities like BBQs, and fetes . . . [37]

---

[35] The Church Commissioners' Annual Review 2016, *Investing in the Church's Growth* (London: The Church of England), p. 7.

[36] New Wine Movement is an evangelical development of growing churches.

[37] Achill Management, *Developing Church Growth in Deprived Areas: Evaluation Report (Revised)*, August 2016, p. 15; <https://www.churchofengland.org/sites/default/files/2018-04/developing-church-growth-in-deprived-areas_evaluation-report_august-2016.pdf>, accessed 4 February 2025.

However, this report fails to recognize that many of the examples of the initiatives being described are examples of traditional ministry being delivered in most parishes, which are organized with or without specific financial support through time-limited grants.

An example of creative urban mission and ministry in response to a local crisis was the Grenfell Tower fire in June 2017; a tragedy which included 72 deaths and led the local parish, St Clement's Notting Dale (Diocese of London), to respond with immediate action that supported those caught up in the aftermath. Alan Everett, the vicar of St Clement's, described the parish response in an article in the *Church Times*:

> One suggestion has been made that other churches came to the rescue. Although other Anglican churches made a welcome contribution to the deluge of volunteers, this is a profound misreading, which urgently needs to be corrected. The parish, and the parish alone led—and continues to lead—the St Clement relief effort.
>
> How is this possible? Almost entirely through the partnership between the church and its sister organisation the Clement James Centre.
>
> This partnership is not new, but represents decades of outreach and care. The church and centre work so effectively together because we have been doing so for years. And, more important still, the social gospel that has borne such fruit has its roots in the very foundation of the church.[38]

This example of the response to the Grenfell fire reflects the tradition of parish ministry—that is, of urban mission and ministry being *immediate* to specific problems within a local community—and also represents both an ecumenical and interfaith response which Everett describes as follows:

> More significantly still, the centre's work has taken the parish deep into the Muslim community—a community that has

---

[38] A. Everett, "Grenfell Tower Fire: Why the parish church was able to help so quickly", *Church Times*, 26 June 2017.

suffered grievous losses. Muslims trust us. They have turned to us for help; they have worked with us as volunteers.[39]

Conclusion

Urban mission and ministry in the Church of England has been an important element of the Church's ministry, beginning from the time of the Industrial Revolution and the growth of cities. The publication of *Faith in the City* outlined an analysis of the contribution made by the Church of England to delivering social justice, and the importance of its mission practice, that challenged the problems associated with UPAs. It led to 20 years of commitment to social action and theological reflection that, by the beginning of the twenty-first century, had shifted to a renewed interest in mission based on a personal evangelistic approach in which individual faith and personal growth became more important than challenging the social problems in urban parishes. The shift was reflected in the commitment to church planting and its methodology as outlined in the report published in 1994, *Breaking New Ground* (GS 1099), and in the publication of *Mission-Shaped Church*, both of which contributed to that change of emphasis; that is, to the commitment to evangelistic mission and church growth as compared with the social and practical commitment to remedying problems being caused by economic and social injustices of the kind that were addressed in *Faith in the City*.

In addition, *What Makes a Good City*, published to develop the themes of *Faithful Cities*, suggests that:

> The urban church must be prepared to argue for the gospel and missionary significance of our cities; it must be adequately resourced and trained; and it must have a clear vision of how (and why) it collaborates with other participants in the urban drama.[40]

---

[39] Everett, "Grenfell Tower Fire".

[40] E. Graham and S. Lowe, *What Makes a Good City?: Public Theology and the Urban Church* (London: Darton, Longman & Todd, 2009), p. 132.

This is the essence of what is now required in the recovery of the understanding of urban mission and ministry by the Church of England; an approach that draws on historical precedence. The publication of *Mission-Shaped Church* in 2004 focused on a specific, evangelistic approach to worship and ministry, addressing the importance of identifying methods for attracting new Christians which is reinforced by the Renewal and Reform programme (2015),[41] an approach that can be dated back to *Towards the Conversion of England* (1945)[42] and the Decade of Evangelism in the 1990s. In shifting the emphasis, issues of urban mission and ministry that had been so central to the Church of England's approach following the publication of *Faith in the City* have been replaced by a new church-growth theology and strategy, which undermines the tradition of parish ministry and privileges evangelism and personal outreach over and against the tradition of pastoral care and action for the good of everyone living in a parish.

In a study of urban ministry published 25 years after *Faith in the City*, Adrian Newman (Bishop of Stepney 2011-18) states:

> For 20 years we have been focused on halting (and reversing) decline. This has been a period in which the church has become increasingly inward-looking (some would say self-obsessed), concerned at its marginalisation within mainstream society and worried about its declining numbers.[43]

---

[41] Under the umbrella of Renewal and Reform, this work sought to enable the Church's vocation, and to give renewed voice and hope to the people of God and the communities they serve: becoming a church growing in numbers, discipleship and depth of community impact—a growing church for all people and places; <https://cofecomms.tumblr.com/post/107894352727/in-each-generation-a-programme-for-reform-and >, accessed 4 February 2025.

[42] *Towards the Conversion of England* (London: The Press and Publications Board of the Church Assembly, Westminster SW1, 1945).

[43] A. Newman, *So Yesterday: Urban Ministry 25 years from Faith in the City, A Sabbatical Review* (2011), p. 3; <https://www.unlock-urban.org.uk/docstore/40.pdf>, accessed 4 February 2025.

The commitment to urban communities that had followed the publication of *Faith in the City* seems to have become less of a priority. It has become, in the words of an unnamed senior member of the clergy, "so yesterday".[44]

The years between the publication of *Faith in the City* and *Mission-Shaped Church* can be seen as the high point of the Church of England's commitment to ministry in urban communities. Analysis of the changes since 2004, both in the practical outworking of parish ministry and in the theological reflection on urban ministerial practice, shows they are important areas for renewed reflection, based, I would argue, on a need for a review of *Mission-Shaped Church* and *Renewal and Reform*. Both documents underpin the changes in diocesan worship and ministerial practice that we have been considering, and which, in my view, have resulted in a diminished level of delivery of, and focus on, urban mission and ministry that has been regrettable and needs to be reversed.

---

[44] *So Yesterday*, p. 3.

7

Paradoxes of the parochial: The urban parish and a new, progressive political theology

Susan Lucas

A week, it is said, is a long time in politics; the 40 years since the publication of *Faith in the City* seems an eternity in the life of the Church of England and of the nation, yet, in another way, like an evening gone and as a watch that passes in the night.[1] The commission that produced *Faith in the City* was set up to report on the Church in Urban Priority Areas, to reflect on its strengths, insights, problems and needs, on the challenges it was having to meet, and how it was responding to social change. The terms of reference of the commission also authorized it to "enquire into the social and economic conditions which characterize the areas in which these churches are set".[2] Commissioned the month following Margaret Thatcher's second election win in 1983, and published two years into that parliament in 1985, it stood at a pivot point in terms of the social and economic conditions of its time. It was the point at which the post-war consensus based on Keynesian interventionist economics gave way to the neoliberal consensus that today appears almost as economic common sense; a rationality that has inserted itself into every aspect of life, configuring "human beings exhaustively as market actors, always,

---

[1] Psalm 90:4.
[2] *Faith in the City: A Call for Action by Church and Nation* (Report of the Archbishop of Canterbury's Commission on Urban Priority Areas) (London: Church House Publishing, 1985), pp. iii-iv.

only and everywhere as *homo oeconomicus*".[3] In the decades since, that neoliberal rationality has totally reconfigured the social and economic conditions in which urban parishes are set, sometimes in surprising and paradoxical ways. *Faith in the City* made 61 recommendations, 38 to the Church of England and 23 to the government,[4] and it caused quite a stir! Several government ministers labelled it "'pure Marxist theology' ... [exemplifying] a broader secularist narrative that sought to restrict religion to the private sphere".[5] According to Greg Smith, it represented the "last hurrah of the William Temple tradition, [that had] assumed the Established Church has considerable soft power and could influence national policy".[6]

In what follows, I argue that, in the reconfigured social, economic and political space of today, the theological basis of *Faith in the City* continues to point to a theological-political space of hope, albeit in a more complex, contested and paradoxical way than its authors could have envisaged. After several decades of the neoliberal hegemony configuring social, economic and political life in the UK and beyond, the significance of place, of the local and the geographical, has begun to reassert itself as a locus for a new theologico-political imaginary. So I argue that it is the parish, albeit a re-imagined parish, that has begun to assume new significance as the focus for the work of both challenging unjust structures, and doing so in a way that does not neglect the personal, the pastoral and the local. As neoliberalism has disrupted and reconfigured spatialities through economic rationalities, the very sense of what it means to be an *urban* parish has shifted; much of what was distinctively urban in *Faith in the City* is now at least as characteristic of (some) suburban and (some) rural contexts. If a somewhat beleaguered

---

[3] W. Brown, *Undoing the Demos: Neo-Liberalism's Stealth Revolution* (Brooklyn, NY: Zone Books, 2015), p. 31.

[4] *Faith in the City*, passim, but particularly pp. 361-6.

[5] G. Smith, "Is there still faith in the city, four decades on?", *Church Times*, 23 June 2023; <https://www.churchtimes.co.uk/articles/2023/23-june/comment/opinion/opinion-is-there-still-faith-in-the-city-four-decades-on>, accessed 4 February 2025.

[6] Smith, "Is there still faith in the city, four decades on?".

and contested Established National Church no longer has the soft power to influence national policy it once had, or at least imagined it had, its parishes remain loci of an alternative narrative to a ubiquitous, if increasingly itself stressed and beleaguered, neoliberal consensus. That narrative is spatial, local and located, relational, incarnational, and based in the generosity of God. As such, it is a place of paradoxical, practical, progressive political theology, and of hope.

The global and local ("glocal") context: Neoliberalism then and now

While the first theorists of the neoliberalism[7] in the 1930s and later 1960s were, in the Euro-Atlantic world, dismissed by many mainstream economists as cranks and mavericks, as Kojo Koram points out,[8] the neoliberal economic play book was established colonial practice, well before "a grocer's daughter, a former film star and Europe's greatest chicken farmer [had unravelled] 40 years of state expansion".[9] According to Koram, when, in the mid-1970s, "the academics passed the ball to the policy wonks, and the policy wonks to Thatcher and Reagan who caught the pass and scored",[10] the movement from maverick to mainstream of

---

[7] Although the term was probably first used by Milton Friedman in *Neoliberalism and its Prospects*, in R. Leeson and C. G. Palm (eds), *Collected Works of Milton Friedman*; <https://miltonfriedman.hoover.org/internal/media/dispatcher/214957/full>, accessed 4 February 2025.

[8] K. Koram, *Uncommon Wealth: Britain and the Aftermath of Empire* (London: John Murray, 2022), *passim*, but particularly the Introduction: "Seeing the Boomerang".

[9] "New brooms: How three Viennese thinkers changed the world", book review of D. Stedman Jones, *Masters of the Universe: Hayek, Friedman, and the Birth of Neo-Liberal Politics* (Princeton, NJ: Princeton University Press, 2012), in *The Economist*; <https://www.economist.com/books-and-arts/2012/10/13/new-brooms>, accessed 4 February 2025.

[10] "New brooms", *passim*.

neoliberalism was actually a "boomeranging"[11] of economic policies first tried out as colonial practice, back into the European and Atlantic world.

At one level, neoliberalism is a radical appropriation of the laissez-faire economics of Adam Smith and the language of traditional seventeenth- to nineteenth-century liberalism. The regulating mechanism of the economy is seen as market competition, and economic freedom becomes both the guarantee of all freedoms and a rationality which shapes, and in some ways distorts, public life and reason. One writer puts it this way:

> All conduct is economic conduct: all spheres of existence are measured by economic terms and metrics, even when those spheres are not directly monetized ... we are always and everywhere homo oeconomicus, which itself has a historically specific form ... [as] an intensely constructed and governed bit of human capital.[12]

A different way of configuring neoliberalism is as a form of political economy characterized by a hyper-financialized form of capitalism. This is the view of the Marxist geographer David Harvey.[13] Harvey sees neoliberalism as focusing particularly on the "circulation" phase of capital, rather than on its production phase, placing faith less in the "supply side" controls on production that were Keynesian orthodoxy, but on stimulation of demand and desire through accelerating the circulation of capital through the rise of ever more complex variants of the highly liquid "money form". Harvey is surely right that Marx was prescient that the financialization of capital would give rise to ever more complex forms of transaction and financial instruments and products.[14] It has given rise to a world that is very recognizable in day-to-day life in the London of

---

[11] Koram, *Uncommon Wealth*.
[12] Brown, *Undoing the Demos*, p. 10.
[13] See D. Harvey, *A Brief History of Neoliberalism* (Oxford: Oxford University Press, 2005) and *The Enigma of Capital* (Oxford: Oxford University Press, 2010).
[14] D. Harvey, *A Companion to Marx's Capital Volume 2* (London: Verso Books, 2013), pp. 205–6.

the 2020s. One simple example is the ubiquity of electronic payment. Since the Covid-19 pandemic of 2020-2, cash transactions have all but disappeared from everyday life, even in many places in the East End of London in which I serve, but certainly in central London, just six short miles away, where many stores are entirely "cashless". Harvey is right to see a certain contradiction in the hyper-financialization of capital:

> Money, which supposedly measures value, itself becomes a kind of commodity ... it can be used to produce more value (profit or surplus value). Its exchange value is the interest payment which in effect puts a value on that which measures value (a highly tautological proposition!). This is what makes money as a measure so special and so odd. Whereas other standard measures, like inches and kilos, cannot be bought and sold in themselves (I can only buy kilos of potatoes, not kilos full stop), money can be bought and sold in itself as money capital (I can buy the use of $100 for a certain period of time).[15]

The effects of this hyper-financialization are felt in urban contexts, particularly sharply but not exclusively, in London, in terms of housing. A house can have many aspects of use value: a home, a place of safety and comfort, a place to cook, eat, make love and raise children; it can be a place of memory and, for some of us, if we're clergy, it's a space for work, provided "for the better performance of our duties".[16] A house might be a Proustian harbourer of memory, or, like some of Frank Lloyd Wright's houses, of architectural significance. It can be a status symbol, or a designer showcase. And it can be a drug den, a house in multiple occupancy, a sweat shop, or a brothel. Its use value, Harvey points

---

[15] D. Harvey, *Seventeen Contradictions and the End of Capitalism* (London: Profile Books, 2014), p. 28.

[16] *Guidance on Housing Flexibility for Clergy Office Holders* (Church of England National Church Institutions: Archbishops' Council Remuneration and Conditions of Service Committee, 2023), <https://www.churchofengland.org/sites/default/files/2023-04/guidance_on_housing_april_2023_final.pdf>, accessed 4 February 2025.

out, is multi-faceted, myriad, possibly infinite and sometimes highly idiosyncratic. But what of its exchange value? Here, things get more complex; Harvey points out that, in the contemporary capitalist world, housing exchange values are determined speculatively.[17] Sure, they are set to some extent by the costs of production, the mark-up for the speculative builder, but increasingly by speculative exchange value, driven by market and social forces, and the tortuous financial instruments that purport to enable people to own property.

The housing market is a particularly sharp contradiction in East London, where I live and minister. Hackney, Shoreditch and Hoxton have long ago become "gentrified", making exchange values for modest housing—the traditional two-up, two-downs that were once the housing of the poor—eye-watering. Former council and social housing has also shot up in price, leading to a shortage of available council and social housing. But the perfect storm has been the effect of all this on rental prices in East London. In the winter of 2022-3, when fuel prices rocketed worldwide (another consequence of the febrility of exchange values), a family of four in Newham on a household income of £45,000 (hence, well within professional salary scales), who were renting a property, were in danger of being in fuel poverty, unable to withstand the shocks of turbulence in global fuel prices.[18]

So, in urban contexts like East Ham, an effect of neoliberalism's emphasis on growing financial capital has been to make even those firmly within professional income brackets effectively at risk of being in poverty, not least because of the effect it has had on raising rents in the property market. What is more, on other metrics, poverty in Britain is persistent and growing. In 2016, the Joseph Rowntree Foundation was forced to add the category of destitution to its research, and found that 2 per cent of the population of Britain, some 1.25 million people, including 300,000 children, were struggling to eat, heat homes, keep

---

[17] Harvey, *Seventeen Contradictions*, p. 4.
[18] Research commissioned by Newham Council from Civitas, shared at a Zoom meeting on community responses to fuel poverty.

clean and find a bed for the night.[19] And unlike the world that confronted William Beveridge in the 1940s, most people who are poor are in work. Nearly half of all working families in Britain are supported by benefits topping up wages that are insufficient, and only 1 per cent of benefits support the unemployed.[20] In parishes like mine, many of those in work have long working weeks, with around 10 per cent of the population of Newham recording in the 2021 Census that they work 49 hours or more per week.[21] A phenomenon of living in East Ham is seeing the tube trains from central London empty hundreds of people returning from work, often late into the evening. Many work long hours, but it is still not enough for them to make ends meet. Hilary Cottam suggests that "the fundamental contract on which our welfare state is based—that work is always a route out of poverty—is broken".[22]

If property prices in London put those on middling professional salaries at risk of poverty, there is a yawning gulf between a small elite at the top and the so-called precariat: those at risk of destitution, with an attendant lack of experience and possibility, resulting in an "hourglass"-shaped distribution of wealth.[23] The elite not only have higher incomes,

---

[19] <https://www.jrf.org.uk/news/flagship-study-finds-a-million-children-experienced-destitution-in-the-uk-last-year>, accessed 4 February 2025. Cf S. Armstrong, *The New Poverty* (London: Verso, 2017).

[20] Quoting Office for National Statistics figures for 2016 in ONS, *Families and Households in the UK 2016*. The same paper shows this figure is lower than is estimated by the general public. See also A. Hood and N. Keiller, *A survey of the GB benefit system* (London: Institute for Fiscal Studies, 2016); <https://ifs.org.uk/publications/survey-gb-benefit-system>, accessed 4 February 2025.

[21] See "How Life Changed in Newham: Census 2021", available at: <https://www.ons.gov.uk/visualisations/censusareachanges/E09000025>; accessed 4 February 2025.

[22] H. Cottam, *Radical Help: How We Can Remake the Relationships Between Us and Revolutionise the Welfare State* (London: Virago, 2019), p. 39.

[23] Cottam, *Radical Help*, p. 39, quoting M. Savage, *Social Class in the 21st Century* (London: Pelican, 2015). For the specific case of the London labour market, see *The Hourglass Economy: An analysis of London's labour market* on the London Assembly website; <https://www.london.gov.uk/who-we-are/

but higher wealth in the form of property and investments; they are also cushioned by those they know, having good social and professional connections and social standing. The work of Kate Pickett and Richard Wilkinson on equality is by now very familiar, and has been recently updated, suggesting that living with such sharp inequality makes us all anxious.[24] Those who are rich develop their own anxieties, trapped in what the economic historian, Avner Offer, calls the "hedonic treadmill",[25] or, in words familiar from Anglican hymnody, perhaps "spirits oppressed with pleasure, wealth and care".[26]

The paradox of property exchange values is visible in other ways in Newham.[27] My own parish, for example, is just outside the 10 per cent most deprived parishes in the nation, at 11 per cent on the overall indices of mass deprivation. This overall figure, however, masks several anomalies. Large swathes of housing in the parish are privately owned and rented (the largest form of tenure of housing in the parish is privately rented at 35 per cent; it is even higher for the deanery at around 37 per cent).[28] However, the parish is slowly gentrifying, as families from areas like Hackney, Hoxton and, to some extent, Walthamstow look to buy larger properties as their families grow (the parish is a short cycle

---

what-london-assembly-does/london-assembly-publications/hourglass-economy-analysis-londons-labour>, accessed 4 February 2025.

[24] K. Pickett and R. Wilkinson, *The Spirit Level: Why Equality is Better for Everyone* (London: Allen Lane, 2009); updated for 2024; <https://equalitytrust.org.uk/the-spirit-level/>, accessed 4 February 2025.

[25] Cottam, *Radical Help*, p. 40, quoting A. Offer, *The Challenge of Affluence: Self-Control and Well-Being in the United States and Britain Since the 1950s* (Oxford: Oxford University Press, 2006).

[26] T. Dudley-Smith from "Lord for the Years": Hymn 409 in *Complete Anglican Hymns Old and New* (Stowmarket: Kevin Mayhew, 2000).

[27] Newham is both the deanery and the local authority within which my parish is based. In the Barking Episcopal Area of the Diocese of Chelmsford, deanery boundaries for the most part are co-extensive with municipal ones.

[28] Source: 2021 Census Data at Parish Level; <https://parishreturns.churchofengland.org/census-dashboards/?diocese=8&search=Newham>, accessed 4 February 2025.

ride along the Greenway Cycle Path to the corporate offices in Canary Wharf, making it attractive for professional, corporate types). In part, all of Newham has been affected by the "Stratford Effect", the massive rebuilding of what has become the Olympic Park (there is even a new E20 postcode), a legacy of London's hosting of the 2012 Olympics.

When I first arrived in the parish, a local independent estate agent said to me, "when the Olympics came to Stratford, we knew it would be good for our business. But we didn't realize how good." It might have been good for estate agents' business, but it has meant that buying a property is now beyond the reach of most ordinary working people. The result is a paradoxical mix of progressive gentrification in owner-occupied property, as the bankers and corporate lawyers move in, and property bought, often speculatively, as buy-to-lets. Despite its inflated cost, there is high demand for privately rented property in my own parish and in Newham more widely, resulting from a shortage of social housing, an increasing population, and lack of sufficient equity on the part of many of Newham's working population, thus impeding their ability to buy a property. The rate of home ownerships actually decreased between 2011 and 2021, and private renting accounted for almost 40 per cent of the population. Between 2011 and 2021, the population of Newham increased by 14 per cent, to just under 351,000.[29] The high demand for private rentals is, in part, because most of Newham is in Transport for London Zone 2 or 3 (my parish being at the outer edge of Zone 3), thus considerably reducing transport costs for those working in central or other parts of London. Despite Newham Council introducing landlord registration in 2023,[30] much of this private renting is unregulated and unofficial (this has meant that among the worshipping communities in the parish, for example, are extended family members sharing a house or a flat).

The progressive gentrification in owner-occupied property and the high demand for private rental property come together paradoxically

---

[29] Cited in <https://www.ons.gov.uk/visualisations/censusareachanges/E09000025>, accessed 4 February 2025.

[30] Cited in <https://www.newham.gov.uk/landlords-newham/rented-property-licensing/6>, accessed 4 February 2025.

in the roads around Central Park, the green space that—in quite literal geographical terms—*is* the centre of my parish. Cheek by jowl in the roads around the park are properties that are clearly being developed and upgraded to accommodate growing families, while next door are houses in multiple occupancy (three-bedroom houses that in some cases house 15 or 20 men sleeping in bunk beds). These are often people of Eastern European origin, working for sub-contractors on the big transport infrastructure projects like Crossrail. Some of these people may not appear in any of the official statistics of the borough, but they are a visible part of the life of East Ham and can often be seen as groups of young men drinking in parks and on street corners. Mostly Eastern Europeans, they hang around in the car park of a nearby builders' merchants, hoping for work for a day. They are a twenty-first-century variation of the casual labour drawn so vividly in the parable of the labourers in the vineyard.[31] To add insult to injury, further north, in Stratford, until property prices steadied a couple of years ago, properties were often bought and left empty, simply to appreciate in value.

Not least of the influences of neoliberalism since the early 1980s has been the effect it has had on the welfare state. By the time of the publication of *Faith in the City*, the welfare state (itself influenced in its origins by the Anglican Social Teaching of William Temple) had come under financial stress in the 1970s. The welfare state was originally a cross-party project, the economic crises of the 1970s, in which high inflation had taken hold, polarized views. On the right, neoliberal ideas were gaining traction, while on the left, socialists dug in and continued to advocate for the transformative power of the state to provide universal care. By 1983, with Thatcher starting her second term in office in the UK and Reagan two years into his first in the US, the neoliberals were in the ascendant and beginning to define the terms of the debate. In terms of welfare provision, they advocated a neoliberal approach which came to be known as "new public management".[32] Under this method, state

---

[31] Matthew 20:1-16.

[32] C. Hood, "A Public Management for All Seasons?", *Public Administration* 69 (Spring 1991), pp. 3-29; <https://onlinelibrary.wiley.com/doi/abs/10.1111/j.1467-9299.1991.tb00779.x>, accessed 4 February 2025.

bureaucracies would be controlled through commercial management practices, competition, audit, innovation and testing, numerical targets and rigorous cost controls. The practices of new public management were widely adopted, and have come to be seen, not as ideological, but as common sense. The Blair Labour government of 1997 embraced this methodology, so much so that Margaret Thatcher, in response to a question about what she considered to be her greatest achievement, said in 2002 that it was: "Tony Blair and New Labour. We forced our opponents to change their minds."[33] Today, most public services, from bin collections to social care, from traffic wardens to aspects of healthcare, from prisons to hospital catering, are commissioned through competitive tendering frameworks. One writer remarks that, at times, it seems as though we have forgotten any other model ever existed.[34] The extent to which neoliberals' "new public management" has delivered better outcomes or cost savings is highly contested: those who tend to support this approach argue that numerical targets have indeed delivered better outcomes; the more sceptical suggest that the model is in fact inherently wasteful, with a high percentage of public resource absorbed by the tendering process itself.[35]

Beveridge's original vision for the welfare state was one of a shared project that benefited everyone. But the services it provided were not ends in themselves: people were educated in order to participate in society; were housed in order to feel safe and comfortable; were healthy in order to enjoy life and contribute to the common good. New public management has reconfigured this so the services provided are ends in themselves—"free, perfect and now".[36] This has normalized the idea

---

[33] Quoted in C. Burns, "Margaret Thatcher's Greatest Achievement: New Labour", available as a blog on Conservative Home website at <https://conservativehome.blogs.com/centreright/2008/04/making-history.html>, accessed 4 February 2025.

[34] Cottam, *Radical Help*, p. 28.

[35] Cottam, *Radical Help*, p. 28.

[36] Cottam, *Radical Help*, p. 45, quoting R. Rodin, *Free, Perfect and Now: Connecting to the Three Insatiable Customer Demands: A CEO's True Story* (New York: Touchstone, 2000).

that for every problem there is a solution, and, ironically, the supposed rationalization of welfare through new public management has actually driven up demand. I am part of a patient and community participation panel at Newham General Hospital, which is just outside my parish. I was drawn to this as a piece of work because of my own (largely positive) experience of caring for my elderly mother at home at the vicarage for the last two years of her life. I combined this with my pastoral practice with parishioners, who are often elderly, and with the complexities that the multiple morbidities of old age bring. One thing that has emerged from conversations with front-line medical and nursing staff is the need to manage people's expectations of what it is possible for medicine to do, which are sometimes unrealistic. I was very struck by the remark of a palliative care nurse, for example, in response to my mum's desire to remain being cared for at home, that "many people have big and unrealistic expectations of what hospitals can do". Alongside these kinds of "quasi-consumer" expectations, the importing of new public management ideas into the welfare state has resulted in marketized organizational cultures that are arm's length and transactional.

It was, of course, William Temple who coined the phrase "welfare state" in the Scott Holland Lecture he delivered in 1928, drawing a contrast with the "Power-State" of pre-First-World-War Prussia, in which the state controlled the lives of its citizens to its own ends. Temple's early vision of a welfare state, which in turn influenced Beveridge, reversed this, and the state was to serve the welfare of its citizens.[37] In 2008, Rowan Williams drew out the rich implications of this in a lecture at St James' Church, Piccadilly:

> I take it to mean something like this: the state deals with human beings in their fullness, their capacity for creativity, self-motivation and self-management. That is, the state deals with human beings in their *freedom*, not just in their *need*.[38]

---

[37] W. Temple, *Christianity and the State: The 1928 Scott Holland Lectures* (London: Macmillan, 1929).

[38] R. Williams, "From Welfare State to Welfare Society: The Contribution of Faith to Happiness and Wellbeing in a Plural Civil Society", *Crucible: The*

Unfortunately, there was a difference between Temple's broad principle of the state existing for its citizens in their freedom, and the actual implementation of the post-war welfare state. The extent to which the actual implementation of the welfare state embodied the implications of creativity, self-management and self-motivation that Williams identified in the above quotation, or whether what emerged in practice was a more distant, monolithic and transactional bureaucracy, is contested. The more bureaucratic and state-centred model is expressed in a remark made by Malcolm Brown, "that [y]ou had an essentially state centralized model of welfare delivery".[39] Joseph Forde offers a different interpretation, arguing that, in the post-war period, there is much historical evidence of the state welfare sector and voluntary welfare sector working in co-operation and, indeed, in partnership, in the delivery of welfare, in the way that Temple and Beveridge had envisaged.[40] So, while the extent to which the actual implementation of the welfare state was a bureaucratic, monolithic enterprise is contested, I am of the view that distance and transactionality were exacerbated and exaggerated by the neoliberal marketization of welfare from the 1980s. Hilary Cottam says this:

> Our welfare services usually start... with an idea in a government office. Public servants or consultants respond to a perceived need, perhaps the findings of a focus group, or a ministerial pledge, and they decide that a new service or a reform must be organised. Reports and budgets will be put together following a logic that looks good on paper, and at some time in the future

---

Journal of Christian Social Ethics (January–March 2009), pp. 51–60, also available online at <http://rowanwilliams.archbishopofcanterbury.org/articles.php/1160/archbishops-lecture-celebrating-60th-anniversary-of-the-william-temple-foundation.html>, accessed 4 February 2025.

[39] In response to a semi-structured set of interview questions put to him by Joseph Forde, forming part of the research for *Before and Beyond the 'Big Society': John Milbank and the Church of England's Approach to Welfare* (Cambridge: James Clarke & Co., 2022). The remark is quoted on p. 205, in response to Question 3 around the theology of the state on p. 269.

[40] Forde, *Before and Beyond the 'Big Society'*, p. 205.

> ... a new programme will be launched ... the result is nearly always an expensive failure. The elegantly conceived idea meets a more complex, messy reality, and much too late, the flaws in the plan are revealed.[41]

Many in urban parishes know too well the effects of faceless and bureaucratic welfare services, which are driven by targets and competition but too often fail to meet their needs. Take Ellen,[42] for example, a lady who lived in the sheltered flats immediately next to one of our churches. A housing association manages the flats; a colleague remarked to me that housing associations have been firmly annexed by the neoliberal paradigm of managed reality, and long since ceased to be agents of social change. Just before my arrival in the parish in 2016, the housing association had reclassified this block of flats as general purpose, rather than sheltered, housing. That gave residents the responsibility to organize their own social care if they needed it, or not if they were deemed not to need it. Many are not, in the strict sense, in need of personal care, but are still vulnerable. For example, Ellen had long-term health conditions, which deteriorated to a point when she began to struggle to eat and to maintain her personal hygiene. As a parish church, we were able to intervene, to help her arrange some care, to get her properly assessed medically, to contact a long-lost relative who was prepared to support her in navigating all this, and ultimately to support her to move to another location where her needs could be better met. Or take Mary, a tiny, bird-like lady in the same block, who came into our parish office one day terrified because she thought she had had a massive electricity bill. Her concern was fairly easily solved by my parish administrator, who took just a minute or two to read the bill and realize that Mary had overpaid, and the massive figure was actually a rebate. There are other stories that make the impersonal and transactional reality of neoliberalism in people's lives obvious. We run a low-cost food pantry in one of our churches, for example, and the effects of the high cost of housing, fuel and transport mean that we receive regular visits from professionals such as nurses,

---

[41] Cottam, *Radical Help*, p. 8.
[42] Some names have been changed in telling people's stories.

teachers and others, firmly within the category of those seeking assistance with meeting their food needs. The global hegemony of neoliberalism has very real and concrete effects on the ground to the people we see, know and care for in the day-to-day workings of the parish, including those in professional jobs.

Looking back to *Faith in the City*: Theology transforming society

I have suggested that the neoliberal hegemony that was just beginning to take hold at the time of *Faith in the City* is by now ubiquitous, and embodies an economic and market rationality in every area of life that, to some, seems like no more than common sense, even if it has had significant, and sometimes devastating, effects on real people's lives. Part of the report's ambition was to find a theological basis for how the Church might mediate change in the way society is structured, through changing relationships between social groups.

If, as is being suggested, the urban context has changed significantly in the period since its publication, that ambition, and that project, remains more urgent than ever for the Church of England to engage with, not just as regards meeting material and pastoral needs, but in formulating a critique of the economic rationality of neoliberalism, and in advocating a credible alternative to it.

Even now, such a critique has not been fully articulated or heard outside of academic circles, in ways that invite consensus and excite the public imagination, still less have effective alternatives been offered. What has not changed is that now, as then, "the teaching of Jesus makes demands on us ... Jesus' call to show compassion on those in need is one of those".[43] The *Faith in the City* report poses the question whether the injunction to "remember the poor ... should be confined to personal charity, service and evangelism towards individuals, or whether it can legitimately take the form of social and political action aimed at altering the circumstances which appear to cause poverty and distress. We shall

---

[43] Cited in *Faith in the City*, p. 47.

argue that these are false alternatives: a Christian is committed to a form of action which embraces both."[44] It is surely right to go on to say that what remains true for Christians is the profound social, political and economic implications of Jesus' teaching of the Kingdom, exemplified perhaps in the Magnificat, "in which the normal priorities of wealth, power, position and respectability would be overturned".[45] These reversals today find expression in the Fourth Mark of Mission: "To seek to transform unjust structures of society, to challenge violence of every kind and to pursue peace and reconciliation."[46] The "both/and" of the personal and structural finds expression in the report:

> Whatever the implications for society as a whole ... the characteristic sphere of Jesus' ministry was that of personal relationships and individual responses.[47]

Set against the theological, missional and vocational imperative to be both prophetic, in seeking to transform unjust structures, and to be deeply relational, *Faith in the City* was prescient, at the dawn of the neoliberal era, in recognizing both its configuration of human beings into "specks of human capital",[48] and the neutral, depersonalized and transactional model already inherent in the welfare state:

> The techniques of modern government depend upon the identification of socio-economic groups of anonymous individuals; the social sciences attempt to predict human behaviour according to patterns that are derived from the observation of collectivities. Even the services from which

---

[44] Cited in *Faith in the City*, p. 48.
[45] Cited in *Faith in the City*, p. 48.
[46] *The Five Marks of Mission*—summary produced by Anne Richards and the Mission Theology Advisory Group; <https://www.churchofengland.org/sites/default/files/2017-11/mtag-the-5-marks-of-mission.pdf>, accessed 4 February 2025.
[47] Cited in *Faith in the City*, p. 48.
[48] The phrase is Wendy Brown's in *Undoing the Demos*, p. 33.

the most personal attention might be expected—health and welfare—often reduce their clients to the status of 'cases' or 'applicants' with little concern for the ways in which individuals may differ from one another.[49]

The gospel imperative both to challenge unjust structures and to be relational, that is, to have concern for how those structures impact differently in different circumstances and with different people, remains at least as significant in 2025 as it was in 1985, and I shall argue that the parish is a progressive, political and paradoxical space in which this relational and structural vocation can effectively be lived.

Parish: Progressive, political—and paradoxical

At the end of my curacy in the Liverpool Diocese, a wise and experienced priest remarked, both with seriousness and with a twinkle, "Always remember, Sue, that these are the people God has given us to love." That wry remark encapsulated why, in the complexities of a public space shaped by a neoliberal rationality, it is a renewed commitment to the parish that offers hope of a different imaginary of the public. This must have built into it the imperative to remember the poor, both in the sense of caring personally and pastorally, and in challenging unjust structures.

So, first, the parish is geographical; it is mission and ministry that is shaped above all by *place*. It is not unimportant that the vast majority of serving clergy in the Church of England, from the curate serving their title to the archbishops, are "someone of somewhere".[50] That title reflects a commitment to the cure of souls in a particular place, that we are given a share in, with and by the bishop, when we are licensed to a post. So, before we lift a finger—before we start any initiative, open a low-cost food offer or community cafe—our very presence represents an alternative to what David Harvey calls "uneven geographical developments and the

---

[49] Cited in *Faith in the City*, p. 49.
[50] I owe this insight to the Revd Lucy Winkett, in conversation.

production of space".⁵¹ Harvey remarks that capital configures space in such a way that it becomes "a loosely connected mosaic of unevenly distributed geographical development within which some regions tend to become richer while others become poorer".⁵² Harvey, writing from a US perspective, uses examples of the displacement of economic activity from areas like Detroit from the 1960s onwards (in Britain, we can point to examples such as the former mining communities in the North-East, post-steel industry Sheffield, or the end of the significance of the docks in Liverpool). London is an "exceptional case", however, because some of the former sites of industrial economic activity in London's Docklands have recently come full circle, to be centres of the new financial economy, Canary Wharf being one example. Capital, then, configures space instrumentally, moving in and out as supply and demand of labour and capital evolve, and sometimes leaving a trail of devastation and devaluation behind. To engage in parish ministry, however, is to be called and committed to inhabit space and place; that is, in a way that is non-instrumental, at one level, just to be there, but to be there actively and with open eyes, ears, heart and mind. This is part of our ordination declarations to be "watchmen"⁵³ or sentinels. Simply being present in this place is a sign of a non-instrumental configuration of place, which stands against neoliberal models that configure it instrumentally—and disposably—as ways of fixing surplus capital and labour.

Second, parishes are relational places. It is in more relational, local and contextual models that alternatives, both to the monolithic, bureaucratic state configuration of welfare and the market models of neoliberalism, are gradually beginning to bubble up, not just in academia and activism, but within organizations and business consultancy. One writer who has sought to configure and experiment practically with such models in welfare is Hilary Cottam. She argues that neither the State nor the

---

[51] D. Harvey, *Seventeen Contradictions and the End of Capitalism*, p. 146 and passim.

[52] Harvey, *Seventeen Contradictions and the End of Capitalism*, p. 149.

[53] Common Worship, Ordination of Priests; <https://www.churchofengland.org/prayer-and-worship/worship-texts-and-resources/common-worship/ministry/common-worship-ordination-0>, accessed 4 February 2025.

market has succeeded in delivering better lives, putting an end to the five "giants" Beveridge wanted to slay, of want, disease, ignorance, squalor and idleness. Cottam argues that, in a sense, what is needed was always already there, but marginalized by the bureaucratic and transactional form the welfare state eventually came to take:[54]

> This new way of working and being starts in a different place. The question is not how we can fix these services, but rather, as I stand beside you, how can I support you to create change.
>
> At the heart of this way of working is human connection ... when people feel supported by strong human relationships, change happens. And when we design systems that make this sort of collaboration and connection simple and easy, people want to join in. This is not surprising, and yet our current welfare state does not try to connect us to one another, despite the abundant potential of our relationships ... This is an approach that upends the current emphasis on managing scarcity.[55]

Cottam's principles for reform of the welfare state are relational, both in the sense of working through relationship and building on capability inherent in existing relationships, as well as deep listening to diagnose real need, and building on inherent capacity rather than operating from a narrative of scarcity. Her approach circles back to the Temple tradition of an intermediate, civic, public institution which is neither the immediate family nor the State. But this kind of relational, deep listening, capacity-building approach is already in the DNA of many parishes, and perhaps particularly UPA parishes. In one church in my parish, for example, a community cafe is a welcoming space where people can gather, socialize, dream, and sometimes argue! It is open to all: from the knitting group which includes a Muslim woman who, as a labour of love, found a source of sackcloth and repaired, by hand, every one of the church's hassocks; to the parents and toddlers of all backgrounds using the day nursery in another part of the building; to the bereavement

---

[54] This is a theme running through *Radical Help*.
[55] Cottam, *Radical Help*, p. 15.

group who laugh long and hard together as well as weep; to some very vulnerable people, often with mental health issues, who simply seek a safe space. We also offer space to a charity that provides genuinely low-cost psychodynamic counselling. The service is fully booked up, although the charity continues to do assessments and "triage" potential counselees onto a waiting list.

This is a parish church with a community centre which offers public space, with just the kind of bias towards the participation of all that Cottam sees, as a way to move beyond transactional welfare. It is also a paradoxical space, precisely because it is one in which a very diverse group of people could, in a memorable phrase of Hannah Arendt's, feel "at home in the world".[56] I am often struck by the question of what being "at home" in the world in East Ham is like: few in the parish were born here, and the white East Enders have overwhelmingly moved on to Essex. Indigenous Asian families are also beginning to move on, recognizing the possibility of "more house for your money" in Essex. Here, it seems, the overwhelming drivers are economic, even beyond the religious and cultural ties that bind particular communities. Yet, the particularity of East Ham's diverse communities makes common ground difficult and contested. In a way, this is precisely what a parish is; it is both a place of being at home in the world, and one in which we are perpetually in exile—the very word *par-oikos* means "outside the walls". At one level, this etymology serves to remind (re-mind) parishes that mission is built into what they are.

Perhaps more deeply, however, the parish represents an interpersonal space, a space of freedom, which is contested and shaped by dissensus as much as by common ground. Cottam again sees this kind of "dissenting relationality" as vital in reimagining a new model for welfare, beyond the monolithic state and the market; the experience of the parish perhaps shows that its building is more widely needed for a new public and political imaginary. She writes of this kind of dissenting relationality:

---

[56] H. Arendt, "Understanding and Politics", in J. Kohn (ed.), *Essays in Understanding 1930–1954* (New York: Harcourt, Brace & Co.), pp. 203–327.

> Sociologists differentiate between what they call "bridging relationships" those that connect us to people and experiences different from ourselves—and "bonding" relationships that are formed between people of similar backgrounds. Bonding relationships can be useful. These are the ties that lead to strong [relationships] ... but bonding relationships can also serve to keep others out ... bridging relationships [help] create distance from ... negative experiences.[57]

If bridging relationships, or dissenting relationality, help distance us from negative experiences, they also help distance us from the preconceptions and filters of our own chosen "tribes". And, as Cottam says, "it is becoming harder to build these critical bridging relationships ... and as they become rarer, so they make us more uncomfortable".[58] If the parish, the *paroikos*, has built into its missional DNA this sort of dissenting relationality that "comforts the afflicted and afflicts the comfortable", its paradoxical parochiality, its non-instrumental configuration of space, makes it a site for a reframing of a new, and more progressive (and pastoral), public and pastoral imaginary. As such, initiatives like the cafe, community counselling and the food pantry are not simply what *Faith in the City* calls a "preference for ambulance work";[59] in other words, for meeting needs without addressing deeper injustices. Instead, they are a ministry that is both personal and political; one that meets the needs of people where they are located, in ways that acknowledge their freedom as well as their need, and in so doing opens up spaces of contested relationality that can become the site of a new political imaginary.

It is, no less in 2025 than in 1985, a challenge to earth in practice; a very different paradigm from the dominant one. So, in parishes, we start with where we are, and the resources that God has given us, always hopeful that even small initiatives can be significant, and with the recognition

---

57 Cottam, *Radical Help*, p. 87.
58 Cottam, *Radical Help*, p. 87.
59 Cited in *Faith in the City*, p. 49.

that, in a parish, this place, and this people, are what we have been given.[60] So, it is an encouragement that, even in the time that *Faith in the City* was published, this parish was, even then, at the forefront of initiatives that built spaces for just this sort of contested relationality. A predecessor as rector was part of a group of local Christians who, with support from the Tavistock Institute, pioneered a vernacular, grassroots conciliation service based in the parish. Although there was some professional support, the model began with local volunteers. The reflective paper written by one of the original consultants to the project describes how, over the initial two years of the project, the volunteers increasingly owned their role with lighter and lighter professional support.[61] Its original values insisted that it was genuinely based in conciliation rather than the more familiar pattern of mediation; that is, on finding ways for people to "be at home in the world" and with one another, and to live creatively with conflict, in a contested space, rather than seeking closed solutions. It recognized that to focus on mediation "would increase the likelihood of success ... it would mean taking on only such cases in which both parties were prepared at least to meet".[62] The project was firmly rooted in the ideas of diversity and contestation, and therefore in the ever-present possibility of conflict not being immediately or easily resolvable. It was this very patient willingness to tolerate dissent that held out the possibility of constructive change and a re-imagined future. The project initially ran for two years and was sustainable for some years beyond that. However, as Miller's paper recognizes, it was always fragile, and in the end was not sustainable:

---

[60] The Parable of the Mustard Seed springs to mind of course. See Matthew 13:31-2. See also S. Wells, *God's Companion: Reimagining Christian Ethics* (Malden, MA: Blackwell, 2006), p. 1: "God always gives ... enough to sit and eat with him and be his friends", and for direct comment in relation to engagement in diverse community contexts, see S. Wells, *On Being With* (Diocesan Interfaith Advisors' Conference, Lambeth Palace, 2016).

[61] E. J. Miller, "Conflict and Resolution: The Newham Experiment" (London, Tavistock Institute, Tavistock Occasional Papers 9, n.d.).

[62] Miller, "Conflict and Resolution", p. 9.

> The volunteers, having underestimated... what they were taking on may ... [have undervalued] what they have achieved ... funding is insecure; the morale and commitment of volunteers are at times fragile and need consolidation ... However, the evidence of this experiment indicates ... the potential to go further.[63]

The Newham of 2025 is more diverse, more crowded, more conflicted than the Newham of 1986, when the Conflict and Change project first ran, just a short year after *Faith in the City* was published. Yet the imperative to "remember the poor", as a dual calling both to minister pastorally and personally to need, and to challenge unjust structures, is more urgent than ever, in a public, political and economic space that has been shifted in puzzling and paradoxical ways by a neoliberal hegemony.

As a national church, we are a place of contestation: over the Prayers of Love and Faith, over our historic failures to respond well to safeguarding, and over our legacy of racial injustice. Perhaps contestation is the point, and that part of our vocation as a national church in our time is to learn how to travel well together in our own version of dissenting relationality.[64] Perhaps, too, surfacing dissensus is not unhealthy, and, if there is a role for a humbler national church, it might be to provide a place from which we can encourage good dissensus in public life. However, it is in the grassroots work of the parish, that paradoxical place of being, both at home and in exile, of belonging yet being outside the walls, of choosing to love those God has given us even if we don't much like them or they're not much like us, of being sentinels, that offers the fragile hope of a new, emerging political imaginary that is both personal and prophetic. It is a place in which we can be at home and in exile, and so notice and emulate where God is at work in it, and where an image of public life that is diverse and relational can emerge; a public life that embodies a little more the image of a triune God who is, of course, diverse and relational.

---

[63] Miller, "Conflict and Resolution", p. 26.
[64] A model for how to do this is in the values adopted by my own diocese, Chelmsford. See <https://www.chelmsford.anglican.org/about-us/travelling-well-together/>, accessed 4 February 2025.

8

More than bread—More than words: Good news on our estates

Sophie Valentine Cowan

Introduction

"The exclusion of the poor is pervasive and not accidental. It is organized and imposed by powerful institutions which represent the rest of us."[1]

These words, captured by the *Faith in the City* report, may not be intentionally directed at the Church of England, though it is difficult to read them without being aware of the implications for the national Church. As the Church of England continues to struggle with its identity and purpose,[2] estate churches persistently go without the basic provisions that are needed to support their communities and to share in the work of Christ.[3] The exclusion of the poor from the abundant resources[4] of the Church of England exemplifies the national problem of greed and entitlement: too often the wealthy obfuscate the financial situation in order to protect their own interests. Perhaps I speak too plainly, though

---

[1] *Faith in the City*, p. 360.

[2] Demonstrated most vividly in Archbishop Justin Welby's resignation in 2024 and the subsequent uncertainty over future leadership.

[3] For more on this see "Church on the Margins", *Church Action on Poverty*; <https://www.church-poverty.org.uk/what-we-do/cotm/>, accessed 4 February 2025.

[4] A. Barrett (ed.), *Finding the Treasure: Good News from the Estates* (London: SPCK, 2023), p. 2.

this might be expected from a working-class Christian called to be a priest.

This chapter presses for an institutional fast so that churches in the most financially deprived areas can finally be equipped to freely offer the life-giving Gospel in word and deed. I begin by considering what it means to wait expectantly for change on estates; then there is an exploration of the scriptural imperative of a ministry that provides both bread and word; I then move on to offer a short reflection and response; and finally conclude with a prayer for a strategic fast by the decision-making bodies of the Church of England. The intention is to promote a fast that reinvigorates the desire to bring Good News in the truest sense; to re-inspire the Church of England to be a structure that supports estate churches to impart more than bread and more than words.

The main themes of this chapter were first formed as a talk for a webinar for the Vision and Strategy of the Church of England.[5] I write this with the deep-held belief that the Church of England has much to offer and much to gain by unashamedly prioritizing the ministry and mission of estate churches.

Expectant waiting

Council estates have been and remain a huge part of my life and subsequent calling to ordained ministry; hence, I speak from this positionality. The *Faith in the City* report was written before I was born, and is still understood to be a foundational text in the life of the Church.[6] This extensive piece of work, published in 1985, summarizes the way in which the Church

---

[5] For more on the Vision and Strategy of the Church of England webinars, see <https://www.churchofengland.org/about/vision-strategy/vision-strategy-webinars>, accessed 4 February 2025.

[6] See P. Sedgwick (ed.), *God in the City: Essays and Reflections from the Archbishop of Canterbury's Urban Theology Group* (London: Mowbray, 1995). See also "Commission on Urban Life and Faith", *Faithful Cities: A Call for Celebration, Vision and Justice* (London: Church House Publishing and Peterborough: Methodist Publishing House, 2006).

of England has sought to engage with urban priority areas (UPAs), and, in a three-part overview of UPAs, it presents recommendations to both Church and State. The underlying assumption woven throughout this seminal text is that the Church ought to have a voice in the national response to the development of urban areas. However, 40 years later, the situation is quite different. There are now freshly asserted questions being asked about the validity of the Church of England's position in the nation's governance.[7] The institution seems less respected than it once was, and, as the veil of "respectability" is torn, there is, perhaps, an opportunity to meaningfully address the hierarchical issues within the Church, which, arguably,[8] compound the problem of class division, and participate in supporting structures that maintain inequality for those most in need. It may be that some of the waiting is over.

To be expectant is part of the Christian vocation; our wait for Christ's return compels our ecclesial action and determines our interactions with those who are yet to know Christ for themselves. However, the waiting weighs differently on an estate where there are so many people surviving without their basic needs being met.[9] The context of the estate is something that might be difficult to fully understand for many Christians in Church of England churches, who will not have encountered estates in their day-to-day lives. Yet, estate churches are part of the body of Christ, just as much as the wealthy parish churches that make up much of the Church of England. The difference is that estate churches are waiting for Christ while also waiting for provision, and this is often combined

---

[7] For more on this see "Lords Spiritual in the House of Lords Explained"; <https://lordslibrary.parliament.uk/lords-spiritual-in-the-house-of-lords-explained/>, accessed 4 February 2025.

[8] E. Schüssler Fiorenza, *Wo/Men, Scripture, and Politics: Exploring the Cultural Imprint of the Bible* (Eugene, OR: Cascade Books, 2021).

[9] See "Child Poverty", Joseph Rowntree Foundation; <https://www.jrf.org.uk/child-poverty>, accessed 4 February 2025.

with waiting to be heard,[10] waiting to be understood,[11] and waiting to be included.[12] The waiting is multi-dimensional, and frustrations arise through a lack of understanding and a lack of interest on the part of some of those in the Church and wider society.[13]

While the *Faith in the City* report speaks of UPAs, I prefer to speak of "estates", as this is the term used by people living in the areas where I grew up and lived for most of my life. As I understand them, council estates are areas of housing that have been built by the local authority for the purpose of providing housing for those people who encounter financial hardship, or who are legally entitled to accommodation in line with the Housing Act 2004.[14] Estates are places that bring together those most in need, and are intended to offer stability and dignity. Many of these estates are now something of a mixed economy, given that council tenants have had the right to buy council houses since the passing of the Housing Act

---

[10] For more on listening to the voices of women on estates, see E. Clark-King, *Theology By Heart: Women, the Church and God* (Peterborough: Epworth, 2004).

[11] To begin to understand estate ministry, see L. Green, *Blessed Are the Poor? Urban Poverty and the Church* (London: SCM Press, 2015).

[12] A helpful insight into what real inclusion might look like is offered by the contributors to the following text: L. Larner (ed.), *Confounding the Mighty: Stories of Church, Social Class, and Solidarity* (London: SCM Press, 2023).

[13] Such tensions are explored in M. Charlesworth and N. Williams, *A Church for the Poor: Transforming the Church to Reach the Poor in Britain Today* (Colorado Springs, CO: David C. Cook, 2017).

[14] For more on this see <https://www.legislation.gov.uk/ukpga/2004/34/contents>, accessed 4 February 2025.

1980.[15] Since then, over 2 million council properties have been sold.[16] In 1979, local authorities and housing associations let 5.5 million homes.[17] This number declined by around a quarter over the following 40 years, reaching 4.1 million in 2022.[18] The wait for a council house can be years, and can lead to increased vulnerability and suffering for those who have no other option. This is something I know from personal experience and from working in the field of social housing before becoming ordained.

What can now be seen on our estates is a complex social picture where there is, of course, no one "type" of resident, though there are discernibly three key groups:

- People renting through the council (local authority) on relatively secure tenancies.
- Those renting from private landlords—the landlords having procured these properties over time, often charging 30–50 per cent more than a council rental agreement.
- And those who have bought their properties, either through Right to Buy or from a sale further down the line because of an initial sale through Right to Buy.

---

[15] For more on this see "Right to buy: Past, present and future", House of Lords Library; <https://lordslibrary.parliament.uk/right-to-buy-past-present-and-future/>, accessed 4 February 2025.

[16] For more on this see "Gov.UK, Social Housing Sales and Demolitions, 2022–2023, Right to Buy Sales"; <https://www.gov.uk/government/statistics/social-housing-sales-and-demolitions-2022-23-england/social-housing-sales-and-demolitions-2022-23-right-to-buy-sales#:~:text=PRP%20Right%20to%20Buy%20sales,the%20end%20of%20March%202023>, accessed 4 February 2025.

[17] For more on this see "Social rented housing in England: Past trends and prospects", House of Commons Library; <https://commonslibrary.parliament.uk/research-briefings/cbp-8963/#:~:text=How%20has%20the%20supply%20of,reaching%204.1%20million%20in%202022>, accessed 4 February 2025.

[18] "Social rented housing in England: Past trends and prospects".

It is within the tensions created by the above disparities that estates exist, as simultaneously tight-knit communities *and* areas where the fractures in wider society can be highly visible;[19] where there is much waiting for better days to come *and* a sense that such change may never emerge.[20]

My own vocation has been informed and shaped by having been brought up on estates in Corby, and having lived and served on estates as part of my ministry. Estate ministry is part of who I am, and part of what God has called me to do and to be. It is to be expected, then, that I approach this topic from the grassroots, and with the pavements of the estates in mind. I do not glorify estate communities; nor do I condemn them as crime-ridden, benefits-dependent areas.[21] However, I am very aware that in places where there is little investment in infrastructure, education, healthcare, etc, and where life expectancy can be 20 years less than in wealthier areas,[22] the results often include much discontent, and this can easily be evidenced in higher than average crime rates. My own expectant waiting for Christ, and for the earth to be as it is in heaven, contends with the frustration of these difficulties, which are further compounded by Church structures that are set up to exclude people

---

[19] For more on this see "Housing Models and Types", Crisis; <https://www.crisis.org.uk/ending-homelessness/key-homelessness-policy-areas/housing/housing-models-and-types/>, accessed 4 February 2025. M. Stephens and J. Perry, "How the Purpose of Social Housing Has Changed and Is Changing", in M. Stephens (ed.), *Housing Policy in a Changing World* (Coventry: Chartered Institute of Housing, 2023), pp. 65-75. R. Powell, "Housing, Ethnicity and Advanced Marginality in England", in J. Flint and R. Powell (eds), *Class, Ethnicity and State in the Polarized Metropolis* (London: Palgrave, 2019), pp. 187-212.

[20] The following book offers an insight into the complexity of estate life: L. McKenzie, *Getting By: Estates, Class and Culture in Austerity Britain* (Bristol: Policy Press, 2015).

[21] This is the constant (and, in my opinion, lazy) narrative of the press. For more information see L. Hanley, *Estates: An Intimate History* (London: Granta Publications, 2023).

[22] For more on urban areas and the challenges that exist, see "CUF Look up Tool"; <https://cuf.org.uk/lookup-tool>, accessed 4 February 2025.

like me; and that seem to ask the question, "Can anything good come from the estates?" Nevertheless, I try to be expectant as I wait faithfully on God and the Church through the rough and tumble of ministry. I am often able to rejoice, for just as those who "found faith in the city" I, like many others, am privileged to meet Christ on the estates, precisely because I seek Christ there daily.

In the parish where I serve, we hold a community pantry, which provides food and supplies for around 60 households a week and over 600 individuals each month. We do not do this alone but as part of a network across our town,[23] with many volunteers making this possible, and with numerous grant applications. There is often a lot of waiting in hope and a determination not to despair. We rely on charity because we have no other choice. I have found that a significant part of this ministry is keeping people unified and prayerful, as we face one struggle after another. It is far too easy to let the endless waiting turn people against one another. In this kind of context, discord is much too easily sown, and bitterness too swiftly takes root. We each must be especially disciplined and patient in our ministry and mission as those who know the promises of God (Isaiah 61).

As the pantry opens, I register and welcome people; we get to know each other, and to care for one another. Our community gathers for supplies: bread, fruit and vegetables, tins, hygiene essentials, and more. At the end of our serving tables is a "help yourself" table, full of flowers that the supermarkets have thrown away. I notice the smiles of the people as they walk out with bunches of flowers held closely to their chests, and I, too, leave at the very end with my own bunch: a small portion of joy. There is a hopeful expectancy in the waiting that is momentarily captured in the gift of roses or carnations bundled into buckets (even if a little bruised). It reminds me of the political notion of "bread and roses",[24] though there

---

[23] For more on community pantries see "Food bag scheme praised in university research", *BBC News*, 2 December 2024; <https://www.bbc.co.uk/news/articles/clyxn13gzvxo>, accessed 4 February 2025.

[24] For more on this see J. Oppenheim, "Bread and Roses"; <https://chawedrosin.wordpress.com/2008/05/09/bread-and-roses-by-james-oppenheim/>, accessed 4 February 2025.

is something more to this expectancy than radical determination. For, before we begin calling the numbers and inviting people to fill up their shopping bags in turn while we wait for the commotion to begin, we pray. And even though not all are Christians, everyone joins in (or waits respectfully), as we give thanks for what has been provided, and speak words of scripture and bless our community. *Together* we lift our hopes in prayer, and stand in solidarity with one another, knowing that poverty lingers, despite the wealth of country and Church.

Some time ago, I wrote the prayer below for the National Estate Churches Network website.[25] It speaks of our expectant waiting, and the eternal hope we have in the One we trust, despite the persistence of poverty, and Whose love we know to be stronger than death:

> Holy One you are outside of time
> and we are so often out of time
> out of luck and out on the edge
> of all that looks like blessing and satisfaction.
> Eternal God, stand with us while we wait.
>
> Lord Jesus you taught us well
> and gave us words that fill us up, more than food,
> so, as we queue for tins and nappies,
> for a space to give what we too can bring,
> Eternal God, stand with us while we wait.
>
> Spirit of life, flame of heaven,
> You are warm and energising,
> but this world, Your world, can be cold and empty,
> these people Your people, can be brittle and flaky,
> Eternal God, stand with us while we wait.

Council estates and the Church of England share a history, not least because of the parish system, which has ensured the inclusion of

---

[25] This can be located at <https://estatechurches.org/2020/09/prayer-from-the-estates/>, accessed 4 February 2025.

social-housing estates in the ministry of the Church of England and, if protected and invested in, they will continue to be places of importance as regards ministry. As the Church of England seeks to include estate churches in the national conversation and engages more actively with urban and working-class theologies,[26] it is important to acknowledge that much good work has already taken place,[27] and to realize that it is still the case that Anglicans living on estates are often forgotten and marginalized by members of their own denomination. God stands with us while we wait.

Exploration: Scriptural imperative

The Bible has so much to say about poverty and wealth,[28] and the Church often seems bound by a tension between prioritizing serving scripture and serving sustenance; those who fall on one side or the other often do so with strongly held convictions. Here I share something of what it means to me to balance the focus of ministry on both the words of the gospel and the action of the gospel.

My congregations often hear me say, "the best thing we have to offer is Jesus". I say this because I mean it. Nothing we do as the Church should minimize the meaning of the death and resurrection of Christ Jesus, or the importance of scripture's true depiction of the Incarnation, through to the Empty Tomb and the pouring out of the Spirit for our Christian

---

[26] For more on this see "Let Justice Roll down like Waters: Exploring the wellbeing of Working-Class Clergy in the Church of England: A Rally Cry for Change"; <https://www.churchofengland.org/sites/default/files/2023-10/focussed-study-4-working-class-clergy-wellbeing.pdf>, accessed 4 February 2025.

[27] One example of such engagement can be found in the following autobiography: J. Williamson, *Father Joe: The Autobiography of Joseph Williamson of Poplar and Stepney* (London: Mowbray, 1963).

[28] For more on this see G. Gutiérrez and L. Müller, *On the Side of the Poor: The Theology of Liberation* (Maryknoll, NY: Orbis, 2015).

faith. Even so, the Good News is to be more than told; it is to be shared around tables, and it is to care for the body as well as the soul.

I have come to this understanding through reading many verses in scripture; however, the one that stands out is Jesus' reference to Deuteronomy, when the tempter aims to provoke him by saying,

> "If you are the Son of God, command these stones to become loaves of bread." Jesus answered, "It is written: 'One does not live by bread alone, but by every word that comes from the mouth of God.'" (Matthew 4:3-4; cf. Deuteronomy 8:3).

There is clearly a need for both the words of God spoken through the prophets and recorded in the Bible, and bread as a minimum human requirement. Even so, the words of scripture are evidently not the same as the Word of God (John 1:1-5); Who *is* Jesus Christ? There is a spiritual understanding to both terms (B)read and (W)ord. Jesus says, "I am the bread of life. Whoever comes to me will never be hungry, and whoever believes in me will never be thirsty" (John 6:35). This may become a text of judgement, if it is assumed that those who have bodily hunger and thirst lack belief.

We are helped to avoid such confusion by being taught to pray, "Give us this day our daily bread" (Matthew 6:11), no doubt with the anticipation of both accepting Christ in communion (1 Corinthians 11) and having our hunger met (perhaps even by miraculous provision) with daily bodily sustenance (Matthew 14:13-21; Mark 6:30-44; Luke 9:10-17; and John 6:1-14). Some may argue that it is not the work of the Church to meet basic human needs: we may pray, we may point people toward Jesus, and we may help where possible, but that is as far as it should go. In the context of the estate, this could easily be the most straightforward conclusion; after all, which estate church could afford to try to solve poverty anyway?

On estates, we are accustomed to weighing up the cost, so when we read of Jesus telling his disciples to feed the crowds, we can readily understand their response:

> '... Are we to go and buy two hundred denarii worth of bread, and give it to them to eat?' (Mark 6:37).

The dilemma becomes a political and/or theological debate, and our decision to become focused on bread more than words, or words more than bread, is evidenced in the agendas of our PCCs, Deanery Synod debates, Diocesan Strategies, Church Commissioners' budgets, etc. In conversation, referencing foodbanks, pantries, top up shops, etc., I have heard various people asking, "do they really need it?" "Why should we be paying for this?" And congregants saying: "We cannot pay our parish share let alone provide food for our parish." I was once told of "Jesus Loves You" stickers that were tacked onto loaves of bread in a large church's foodbank with no explanation; the recipients were left bemused and insulted because they did not understand how Jesus could love them, and also make it possible for them to have to seek out charity for food. There was, perhaps unwittingly, an underlying suggestion that a lack of faithfulness has led to a lack of food.

The Church often appears to try to understand financial deprivation from the outside: observing the queues of shoppers; seeming to wonder if they could try harder to change their lot; hoping for an "aspiration transformation" that will lead people out of a poverty mindset and into the "middle-class kingdom of God". This can sometimes seem to be the position of the Church of England, even after *Faith in the City*.

Conversely, in Acts, a different vision and a different strategy are portrayed:

> Day by day, as they spent much time together in the temple, they broke bread at home and ate their food with glad and generous hearts, praising God and having the goodwill of all the people. And day by day the Lord added to their number those who were being saved. (Acts 2:46-7)

> On the first day of the week, when we met to break bread, Paul was holding a discussion with them; since he intended to leave the next day, he continued speaking until midnight. (Acts 20:7)

More than bread and more than words are offered as the standard. Furthermore, those journeying on the road to Emmaus provided bread for a stranger, listened to his words, and found:

> ... Then their eyes were opened, and they recognized him; and he vanished from their sight. They said to each other, 'Were not our hearts burning within us[k] while he was talking to us on the road, while he was opening the scriptures to us?' ... They were saying, 'The Lord has risen indeed, and he has appeared to Simon!' Then they told what had happened on the road, and how he had been made known to them in the breaking of the bread. (Luke 24:31-2, 35)

These early Christians show us that, to be Church, we are compelled to offer more than bread and more than words. This is real Christian community: to know and love God and one another, living intentionally as the Body of Christ. How many of us would let our brother or sister go without food if we had something to spare? And which one of us does not long for those who do not know God to come to know the love that God has shown to us through Jesus Christ; to experience real salvation?

Our strategy can neither be to feed everyone nor to force our faith on anyone. However, the Church of England can find authenticity in sharing the Good News through both bread and word. We must not buy into the idea that the Church is supposed to be a mixed economy; the poor living contentedly alongside the rich: this is a vision that is as mis-sold in our politics as it is in our churches. We know that people living on council estates may face financial hardship, and some may not. We know that there will be poverty (Matthew 26:11), and that God's people may be financially poor (Philippians 4:12). Of course, financial poverty does not equal spiritual poverty; it is simply symbolic of a need to share what God has already given for all of us. Our churches must offer both material and spiritual sustenance if we are to imitate Christ, and if we are to value the contribution of the early Church.

Reflection: More than bread—more than words

When I reflect on how to deliver the Good News on our estates, I am reminded of those I know who have little or no interest in what the Church is about. I wonder, what would Good News look like to them? In her recent book *Underclass*, Jessica Taylor writes:

> Religion barely played a role on our council estate. The churches were used for mums and toddlers groups, weight watchers and children's clubs . . . I do wonder why God didn't feature in our lives on the estate. . . . Where was God whilst we struggled to make ends meet? God wasn't going to answer your prayers by paying the gas bill. . . . God wasn't there when my brother died. God wasn't there when Ben drove his car off a cliff edge and his body didn't wash up for months. . . . Good things don't happen to good people. Bad things don't happen to bad people. . . . No one cares if you live or die. No one is coming to rescue you. . . . No Christmas miracle is going to put the latest toys under the tree for your kids at the eleventh hour. You had to learn to survive, and you had to realise you were on your own.[29]

This is the sentiment of many I know on estates. However, when I speak of the work being done to feed the hungry, to strive for dignity for those in need, and of the ministry we offer to the dying and bereaved, and the hours spent trying to make ends meet by whatever means possible, one of the first things I am asked is: "Why do you have to do all of this when the Church of England is so rich?" For those who can cope with the dissonance resulting from poor churches being located within a wealthy institution, they often come to faith in Christ with an immediate (and warranted) mistrust of the institution. They already know that "[t]he exclusion of the poor is pervasive and not accidental".[30]

Reimagining a well-known biblical scene, Richard Carter writes about wealth in the Church:

---

[29] J. Taylor, *Underclass: A Memoir* (London: Constable, 2024), pp. 80-1.
[30] *Faith in the City*, p. 360.

I remember many years ago a rich member of my father's congregation coming to ask him if he thought it immoral when there was so much poverty in the world if he spent £50,000 on a new car he wanted. My father was not one to judge. He looked at the man with love and said that he thought it was immoral. The man went away with sadness and bought the car.[31]

It should go without saying that the Church cannot claim to be faithful to God when it prefers to "future-proof" itself by amassing funds, rather than actively contributing to, and caring for, those who are most vulnerable and in need within its congregations. If there can be a genuine acceptance of estate churches as being just as much a part of the Church of England as any other within this national organization, there ought to be a strong desire to give fairly (and not through a sense of superiority or pity) because, where there is excessive wealth, there is poverty. This connection is not there by chance; hence, not only is redistribution needed, but repentance.

Response—Resource the faithful

A strategic fast does not easily provide SMART goals, much as these may be popular in business models within the Church at the current time.[32] A fast begins with seeking God and being prepared to repent. Such a task is not as easily measured as a list of bullet points. Regardless, I am keen to learn what might happen if boards of finance were asked to read the text below before their meetings commence; and asked to reflect on how they had met this calling at the end. For the Church of England to have integrity in our poorest regions, a transformation of our priorities is required. Only then will its ministers be able to live out our faith in word and deed; with more than words and more than bread. The

---

[31] R. Carter, *The City Is My Monastery: A Contemporary Rule of Life* (Norwich: Canterbury Press, 2019), pp. 64-5.

[32] "SMART" means: Specific, Measurable, Achievable, Relevant and Time-Bound.

Church's structures must be regularly challenged and shaped to support the authentic mission and ministry of the Church. If this were to happen, the identity of the Church of England might be less enraptured by themes of style, ancient grievance, and questionable morality, and thus might offer the real substance that is so vital. "Poor" churches need not exist in England; the fact that they do reflects a point of failure in the institutions that claim to support the structure of the Church.

"The exclusion of the poor is pervasive and not accidental. It is organized and imposed by powerful institutions which represent the rest of us."[33]

Conclusion and prayer

Many of our churches demonstrate that the Good News of Christ is more than bread and more than words; it is time for the Church of England's structures to bear witness to this, and share wealth and resources in humble repentance before God, for what has been hoarded and mismanaged both personally and institutionally. The Church of England must end the unnecessary waiting, and bring encouragement to those most in need, by supporting and funding those churches already offering ministry on estates. This may take any number of practical forms. One suggestion might be to bolster those churches that already provide food for their communities with a fund that can be accessed annually (and without lengthy forms to fill in). It might be that wealthier dioceses begin to relinquish their assets in favour of those serving poorer counties. Smaller gestures and larger gestures are needed.[34]

I am suggesting that the starting point for a genuine and sincere response is a strategic fast; not for those who do not have enough, but for the parts of the Church of England where financial wealth can be found.

---

[33] *Faith in the City*, p. 360.

[34] For more on this see S. Cowan, "Estate ministry could use a gift or two", *Church Times*, 7 June 2024; <https://www.churchtimes.co.uk/articles/2024/7-june/features/features/estates-ministry-could-use-a-gift-or-two>, accessed 4 February 2025.

This fast ought to directly resource those faithfully serving on estates; that is, those already living among God's people, grappling with what to prioritize, knowing that there is more that should be offered, but finding that there is not enough of anything that is needed. For scripture states:

> I do not mean that there should be relief for others and pressure on you, but it is a question of a fair balance between your present abundance and their need, so that their abundance may be for your need, in order that there may be a fair balance. As it is written, "The one who had much did not have too much, and the one who had little did not have too little." (2 Corinthians 8:14–15; cf. Exodus 16:18)

As Christians within the Church of England, we must ask ourselves: what is God's vision, and what is God's strategy for sharing Good News on our estates? God's strategy, I suggest, may be found in the following adaptation of Isaiah 58:6-12 by the Northumbria Community,[35] with my own small addition in square brackets. If we can accept these words as relevant to the Church of England today, may they lead us to implement the changes that are needed, to bring us back to our God with sorrow for our failure, and to share freely what we have when we have been given so much. I suggest we should read these words aloud wherever we assemble to make decisions about wealth and finance, and be compelled to offer more than bread and more than words, so becoming the Church that Christ seeks here in England, and especially on our estates:

> The Fast [of the Church of England as a Strategic Response]
> Is this not the fast that I have chosen:
> to loose the bonds of wickedness?
> to undo the heavy burden?
> and to let the oppressed go free?
> that you break every yoke?
> Is it not to share your bread with the hungry?

---

[35] For more on this see "Welcome to the Northumbria Community"; <https://www.northumbriacommunity.org/>, accessed 4 February 2025.

that you bring to your house those who are cast down?
when you see the naked person that you cover them?
and not hide yourself from your own flesh and blood?
Then shall your light break forth as the morning;
healing shall spring forth speedily;
and your righteousness shall go before you;
the glory of the Lord shall be your rearguard.
Then you will call; and the Lord will answer.
You shall cry, and He will say,
"Here I am"...
Your people will rebuild the ancient ruins
and will raise up the age-old foundations;
you will be called
Repairer of Broken Walls,
Restorer of Streets with Dwellings...
[*Finally, you will offer
more than bread,
and more than words.*]

The unwillingness to provide financial support for estate churches is pervasive and not accidental. It is organized and imposed within our own institutions which represent each of us.

9

"Building a People of Power": Community organizing and parish mission in East London

Angus Ritchie and Averil Pooten Watan

Introduction

> The Churches in the twenty-first century will be in a crucial position to influence opinion, and to awaken hope ... The nurturing of hopeful commitment requires effort, prayer, struggle and persistence. In their response to poverty and despair, the Churches need to reject the widespread assumption of a general goodwill, the idea that most people—including the government—are on the same side, and that, if only the evidence were presented, all will be well. *Faith in the City* seemed to assume this, and it may therefore be the last document of its kind. I have never believed it. I have never believed it, and see it as one of the most fatal naiveties of the liberal tradition. The sooner we realise that people and groups have conflicting values and interests, the better.
>
> Fr Kenneth Leech[1]

Kenneth Leech's critique of *Faith in the City* concerned its underlying assumptions about how and why power was exercised.

---

[1] K. Leech, *The Sky is Red: Discerning the Signs of the Times* (London: Darton, Longman & Todd, 1997), p. 107.

In the conclusion of *Faith in the City*, the commissioners write that:

> The critical issue to be faced is whether there is any political will to set in motion a process which will enable those who are at present in poverty and powerlessness to rejoin the life of the nation.[2]

As Leech observes, the assumption seems to be that the injustices identified in the report will be remedied primarily by appealing to the goodwill of those who are already powerful. Yet the biblical witness repeatedly shows God acting through, and not just for, those who are oppressed and marginalized.

In the Gospels, it is repeatedly those who experience poverty and marginalization—the Syrophoenician woman, the woman with the haemorrhage, the blind beggar Bartimaeus, lepers and children—who grasp the true meaning of the Kingdom. Often the wider crowd, and even Jesus' disciples, seek to silence their cries, but they are invariably rebuked by the Lord. Those he commends in encounters such as these for having "faith" are almost invariably people who are poor, and are crying out for healing and grace.

Faith in the City did urge the Church to recognize the spiritual and theological gifts of inner-city congregations, and called on the wider Body to create new pathways for leadership and theological reflection. But it did not conceive of those who experience injustice as the primary agents in addressing it. With Leech, we would argue that this is not only a possibility but an imperative—both because it is the primary pattern for God's action in the Scriptures, and because it transforms power relationships in a way that is essential to creating a more just society.

Given his critique of *Faith in the City*, and the wider culture of the Church of England, it is not surprising that Leech was drawn to the work of Saul Alinsky (1909-72). Alinsky understood that the surest way for poorer communities to secure a more just future was for them to "get organized" so that they had a seat at the decision-making table—and that the transformation of power relationships would necessarily involve a

---

[2] *Faith in the City*, p. 360.

considerable amount of tension and conflict. In the back streets of 1930s Chicago, Alinksy pioneered the practice of broad-based community organizing. As Leech explains, he was "one of the first people in the modern period of urban life to recognize the organizational potential of the churches, especially of the Roman Catholic church, with its solid working-class and immigrant base".[3] Churches and trade unions were the key building-blocks of Alinsky's "People's Organizations". Funded by the dues of member institutions (so that their agenda was determined by the people, not by external funders), these broad-based alliances identified common interests and common concerns. Through bold, non-violent action, they secured tangible improvements in local people's lives.

Twenty-five years after *Faith in the City*, Adrian Newman wrote a sabbatical reflection on its reception. Entitled "So Yesterday", it pondered the failure of the report to live up to what had been perceived as its early promise.[4] As he observes, "the vapours of liberation theology that periodically erupted from below the surface of the report" were "quietly forgotten" in its implementation.[5]

> The church's overwhelming response to *Faith in the City* was to invest in the Church Urban Fund and enter into partnerships, but in so doing we managed to leave the power relationships in the church unchanged.[6]

Newman's analysis reveals a double dilution. In the first place, *Faith in the City* had only "vapours" of liberation theology. It lacked the systematic theological analysis of agency, interests and power that Leech rightly saw as essential for effective action. Secondly, these "vapours" were further

---

[3] K. Leech, *The Eye of the Storm: Living Spiritually in the Real World* (London: HarperCollins, 1992), p. 184.

[4] The title of the reflection was drawn from a comment by one of the senior clergy Newman interviewed, on the decline of urban mission as a priority of the wider Church of England.

[5] A. Newman, *So Yesterday: Urban Ministry 25 Years on from Faith in the City, A Sabbatical Review* (2011), p. 7.

[6] Newman, *So Yesterday*, p. 8.

diluted in its implementation, because of a reluctance to embrace the tensions inherent in transforming relationships of power.

If such relationships are to be transformed, there needs to be prophecy as well as partnership. Newman identifies community organizing as a key practice in this space:

> Organising is more a prophet than a partner. It works on the basis of numerous alliances, certainly, but it is an essentially prophetic movement designed to challenge, confront and change the established power structures that perpetuate injustice. Perhaps this explains why the Church of England has a somewhat ambivalent attitude to Organising, because we remain—notionally at least—part of the very establishment that needs to be confronted in the name of justice.[7]

Community organizing in East London

Community organizing came to East London in 1996, with the founding of The East London Communities Organisation (TELCO). This is the oldest chapter of what is now Citizens UK, a national community organizing movement. As in the US, churches stood at the heart of the alliance. Like its American counterpart, the Industrial Areas Foundation, Citizens UK is best known for its campaigns—most prominent and successful of which is the Living Wage.[8] It began in the UK at a time when many East Londoners could see HSBC's international headquarters being built in Canary Wharf, taking advantage of huge governmental investment in infrastructure.

Local people wanted to ensure those who would work in the tower as cleaners, caterers and security guards would receive some of the benefits

---

[7] Newman, *So Yesterday*, p. 20.
[8] Unlike the statutory minimum wage, the Living Wage was calculated according to the cost of living of a family living in London. There are now two "real Living Wage" rates, one for London and one for the rest of the UK; <https://www.livingwage.org.uk/>, accessed 4 February 2025.

of this investment. A range of religious and civic leaders in TELCO therefore wrote to the bank's chairman, Sir John Bond, requesting a meeting. When the letter was ignored, the nuns from one member institution (St Antony's Catholic Parish in Forest Gate) came up with an imaginative solution. The 2,000-strong congregation banked with HSBC, and usually deposited St Antony's copious quantities of candle money when the local branch was at its quietest. The nuns instead saved up the money over several months, and paid it in just before Christmas—coin by coin—as part of a delegation from TELCO that succeeded in "tying up" the Oxford Street branch of HSBC just weeks before Christmas. The high-profile action, involving members of a number of churches and mosques, was conducted in full view of the media. It was one of a series of imaginative actions which secured a meeting with the HSBC chairman, and in time a commitment to pay the Living Wage. For Angus (who was at the time serving his title in Plaistow and Canning Town, at one of TELCO's founding parishes), the campaign showed how churches could embody a more faithful approach to conflict and reconciliation. The writings of Kenneth Leech offered a powerful critique of false narratives of "reconciliation" which preached "peace when there is no peace" (cf. Jeremiah 6:14). As he argued, the faithful practice of the gospel will inevitably generate adversaries—and in the face of systemic injustice, the journey of reconciliation first involves prophetic confrontations.

The story of the Living Wage began with prophetic confrontation. But in time companies like HSBC, Barclays and KPMG moved beyond a grudging acceptance of the need for fair pay to a point where they began to recognize a "business case" for the Living Wage, because of its positive impact on retention and productivity. Prophetic confrontation was not an end in itself but the first stage in a journey in which the voice and agency of low-paid workers was recognized, and the behaviour of employers changed in concrete ways. There was a reconciliation, but one built on justice and not on its avoidance. For those of us who engaged in the Living Wage campaign through local churches, one of the striking features of the experience was that it was a practice that *both* called us to engage deeply with people of other faiths and beliefs ("walls down") *and* drew us into a more faithful embodiment of the gospel ("roots down").

In this chapter, we will explore three other ways in which the "roots down", "walls down" approach of community organizing can help the local parish to live out its God-given mission. In particular, they help the parish to develop a form of social witness that centres on God's action through those the wider culture (and indeed the Church) too often marginalizes or underestimates.

- First, community organizing takes the local congregation seriously—as a place that can "influence opinion and awaken hope";
- secondly, community organizing sees action as something which develops new leaders, particularly those the dominant culture overlooks and belittles;
- thirdly, community organizing can help parishes forge a deeper connection between prayer and action, so that the gospel is experienced as "good news" and not just "good advice".

In writing this, each of us is drawing on our own direct experience of this work (for Averil in her ministry as a lay leader and churchwarden at St Barnabas and St James' parish in Walthamstow) as well as the experience and reflections of many others in the movement.

Averil is a trustee, and Angus the director, of the Centre for Theology and Community. CTC was founded by church leaders in East London to ground churches' organizing more deeply in their faith and lived spirituality, and to harness the potential of community organizing to contribute to the whole life and mission of the local parish. CTC is an ecumenical charity, with a particular depth of work in Roman Catholic parishes and Pentecostal congregations. In 1985, *Faith in the City* noted the relative strength of Roman Catholic and Black-led Pentecostal churches in urban priority areas, and this is at least as true today.[9] Community organizing is one way in which East London's Anglican parishes are deepening their partnership in mission with Catholic and Pentecostal neighbours.

---

[9] *Faith in the City*, p. 44.

From 2020 to 2023, CTC piloted a project with TELCO and the Barking and Stepney Episcopal Areas entitled "Harnessing the Potential of Community Organising for Growth" (abbreviated in this essay to "Organising for Growth"), which helped six smaller, sacramental parishes to grow in number, depth and impact. As Bishop of Stepney, Adrian Newman was a key figure in the development of the project, along with Bishop Peter Hill across the River Lea in Barking. Since 2024, CTC and Citizens UK have been working with the Church of England to share this approach more widely[10]—and it is encouraging to be working with the Church Urban Fund on the sharing of the learning from this project.

Our chapter will draw on testimonies and data from the East London project, and from another piece of research conducted by CTC with Catholic and Pentecostal as well as Anglican members of TELCO.[11] They tell the story of how faith-filled community organizing is helping to build a people of power in East London today.

Valuing the local congregation

In 1930s Chicago, Alinsky recognized that the parish and the union branch were places that nurtured face-to-face relationships, conversations about common interests and the building and tending of a common life. They were therefore the building-blocks of what community organizing calls the "relational power" which is an essential counterbalance to the power of the state and the market. In the century that has followed, these local institutions are under huge pressure. Against the grain of

---

[10] The pilot project was funded by the Church of England's Strategic Development Fund, and the national project (which has a particular focus on children and young people) is funded by the Strategic Ministry and Mission Investment Board.

[11] See M. Brittenden and A. Ritchie, *Organising for Growth: Growing inner-city churches in number, depth and impact* (London: CTC, 2024) and M. Brittenden et al., *Not only with words: Synodality, Community Organising and Catholic Social Action* (London: CTC, 2024); <https://www.ctcuk.org/resources/research-reports/>, accessed 4 February 2025.

much progressive activism, community organizing takes local religious congregations seriously as agents of transformation. It must be recognized that some of the decline in participation in faith communities has been caused by the abuses of power which have occurred within them. Indeed, one of the urgent tasks in institutional renewal is a greater transparency and honesty about where power is concentrated, and how it is exercised. As we shall see, community organizing offers some practices which can help to make this happen. But it believes that healthy local congregations are an essential part of a healthy society.

In her essay on "Collectives with soul: building sustainable communities through organizing", Alison Webster explains why this is so. Community organizing "starts from an awareness that while the market and the state are organized for power and success (not least, to make money), the so-called Third Sector is not organized to anything like the same extent. Collectives of all kinds have waned in importance under neoliberalism, and this has weakened participatory democracy and undermined ways of building 'people power.'"[12] Webster draws on the work of pastoral theologian Bruce Rogers-Vaughn to analyse the impact of the rise in the power of the market relative to these relational institutions. "Competitive individualism, and a notion of 'freedom' that prioritizes the 'freedom to consume', is eroding our identities as citizens, creating and perpetuating massive inequalities between and within nations."[13] In this context, Rogers-Vaughn argues, the strengthening of institutional life has an important role to play in human flourishing:

> Prior to neoliberalism, domination was exercised by means of the disciplinary powers of institutions. Today domination occurs through the suppression of these institutions. Prior to neoliberalism, domination required replacing a particular type

---

[12] A. Webster, "Collectives with soul: building sustainable communities through organising", *Anvil* 38:2 (November 2022).

[13] Webster, "Collectives with soul".

of subject with a new form of subject. Today it occurs through the fragmentation and dispersal of the subject altogether.[14]

One way of defining an institution is that it is the set of structured relationships which emerge when human beings agree to be faithful to one another across time. That is what the "institutions" of a Scout group, trade union, marriage and mosque have in common. It is one of the characteristic myths of competitive individualism, and its particular vision of "freedom", that such commitments make us less free. In fact, our institutions are vital to our freedom, wellbeing and flourishing. They enable us to build relationships of solidarity and trust across boundaries of age, race and religion. Without them, we are isolated individuals, and our lives and communities are dominated even more by the power of the market and the state.

As face-to-face relationships across difference decline, and citizens feel less agency over daily life, a succession of recent crises have led on to a sharp rise in divisive and destructive forms of far-right populism on both sides of the Atlantic.[15] But there is a more constructive populism, in which ordinary people come together in institutions anchored in their communities, to build alliances and win social justice. Laura Grattan's 2016 study explores this form of "radical grassroots democracy" in the United States,[16] while Pope Francis has likewise made a contrast between the constructive populism he had experienced in Latin America and the populisms of 1930s Europe, which have disturbing echoes in our own times:

> In Latin America, it means that the people—for instance, people's movements—are the protagonists. They are self-organized.

---

[14] B. Rogers-Vaughn, *Caring for Souls in a Neoliberal Age* (New York: Palgrave Macmillan, 2016), p. 122, cited in Webster, "Collectives with soul".

[15] These crises include the financial crash of 2008, the Covid-19 pandemic and the surge in energy prices after Russia's invasion of Ukraine.

[16] See L. Grattan, *Populism's Power: Radical Grassroots Democracy in America* (New York: Oxford University Press, 2016).

> When I started to hear about populism in Europe I didn't know what to make of it, until I realized that it had different meanings.

In Francis' words, 1930s Germany represented a disordered form of populism in which people did not "talk among themselves" but rather sought refuge from their fears in a "charismatic leader".[17] Pope Francis' remarks go to the heart of the issue: one kind of populism involves the people handing over their power, whereas in the other they are the "protagonists". We might call the former "fake populism", for in our own times the "charismatic leader" who is given the power is usually drawn from the economic elite. By contrast, community organizing exemplifies an "inclusive populism" in which ordinary citizens are the "protagonists".[18]

Two decades ago, veteran US community organizer Ernesto Cortés Jr argued for the vital role of local congregations and other grassroots institutions in the health of a society. Reading his essay in 2025, it is sobering to reflect on how much the wider context has worsened:

> It is not a constitution that makes a democracy, but the habits and practices of empathy, relationality, deliberation, negotiation, confrontation, argument, and ultimately compromise. This is the stuff of democracies. To a surprising degree, a plutocracy has emerged in our culture: one in which certain groups of people can manipulate the system to serve their interests and exempt themselves from normal requirements and restraints... The only way to curb such a shift is to rebuild the democratic institutions that develop in people their capacity to engage one another in

---

[17] Pope Francis, "The Danger is that in Times of Crisis We Look for a Savior", *El Pais in English*, 22 January 2017.

[18] See A. Ritchie, *Inclusive Populism: Creating Citizens in the Global Age* (South Bend, IN: University of Notre Dame Press, 2019), pp. 4-5, and Pope Francis, "Video Message of the Holy Father to participants in the International Conference 'A Politics Rooted in the People'", 15 February 2021.

the kind of reflection, relationships, and deliberations that are requisite for the functioning of a decent society.[19]

In a later conversation, Cortés explained why institutions like the local parish are vital to the task at hand:

> Citizens are formed through the process of organizing. It requires institutions which can incubate this process by passing on the habits, practices, and norms necessary for humans with different opinions and temperaments to flourish together: to compromise, to talk to and not just about one another, to act in the light of one another's views and needs and not just unilaterally or selfishly.[20]

In the sections which follow, we will explore in more detail how community organizing can assist in renewing parishes for this work, and for their wider mission.

Community organizing in the local parish

When a parish joins its local Citizens UK chapter, lay and ordained leaders begin "one-to-one" meetings within and beyond its walls. Out of these many conversations come the actions which deliver change within and beyond its walls. The "one-to-one" is a conversation which does not seek to enlist the other party into a predetermined activity, but rather explores their gifts and passions. It explores questions such as:

- What relationships are central to this person's life?
- How do they spend their time and money, and why?
- What are the motivations for key decisions they have made?

---

[19] E. Cortes Jr, "Towards A Democratic Culture", *Kettering Review* 48 (Spring 2006), p. 48, in A. Ritchie (ed.), *Inclusive Populism: Creating Citizens in the Global Age* (South Bend, IN: University of Notre Dame Press, 2019), pp. 66-7.

[20] Conversation with Angus Ritchie, cited in *Inclusive Populism*, p. 19.

- What institutions are they involved in, and why?

Alongside the one-to-one, churches engaged in community organizing are taught to conduct a "power analysis". The tool is used as a way to understand the dynamics of an institution. The power analysis reflects the following questions:

- Who is officially at the centre of your organization? (Often this is the priest, or the person with the most decision-making power.)
- What is the real decision-making process? Does the person at the centre make the final decision? Or is there another process? Are there people close to the official decision-makers who are able to influence their decision?
- Who are the people that can make decisions about money?
- What are the different groups in the organization? (e.g. prayer groups, toddler groups, youth groups, senior groups, the Parochial Church Council.)
- Who are the most relational people? (These are the people who are close to different groups of people, are known by everyone, and are often invited to participate in different groups.)
- Where are you in this power analysis? What are your most significant relationships?

Power analysis helps us think strategically about our congregations and how to ensure one-to-one meetings are occurring at both the existing core of the church and among those currently on the peripheries of decision-making. It also encourages us to reflect on who we spend our time with and why we choose certain people. Typically, we select those closest to us, people with whom we feel comfortable; while this is not inherently problematic, we must consider whether we are fostering a culture of indifference or a culture of encounter.[21]

Community organizing invites us to foster a culture of encounter, urging us to reflect on how we interact with others, especially those who

---

[21] These terms are drawn from Pope Francis, *Fratelli Tutti: Encyclical on Fraternity and Social Friendship* (2020), §30.

are not closest to us. Undertaking such a power analysis ensures that one-to-ones are not only conducted with those who currently dominate the congregation's life. The organizing process ensures that attention is given to the gifts, passions and development of the people whom the dominant culture (and sadly, all too often, the institutional Church) overlooks and marginalizes. As Alec Spencer and Lynne Cullens observe, an intentional focus on diversifying leadership flows from the witness of Scripture:

- What might we learn from God's own choice of leaders that might benefit our discernment today? Who does God raise up to build his kingdom?
- Often the most unlikely people in the society of the time; the young, the gentiles, the women and the sinners. Selected by God because their lived experiences inspire others, adding insight and rich depth to their witness and journeys of faith.
- In God's kingdom, those leaders who are powerful and of noble birth are few. As Church we must seek to correct the long-standing disparity between those whom we have consistently appointed as leaders, and the principles to which scripture points.[22]

As the experience of the Organising for Growth project demonstrates, when the Church is intentional about broadening its leadership, it generates a "powerful missional and motivational effect". We explore this in more detail in the next section.

Developing leaders through action

The Organising for Growth project provided a clearer framework, and more intensive resourcing, so that inner-city parishes could harness more of the potential of community organizing to support their journey of renewal. A key leader (usually the incumbent) from each participating church had to commit to undertaking three one-to-one meetings a week,

---

[22] A. Spencer and L. Cullens, "(Un) likely leaders", September 2021; <https://cuf.org.uk/news/unlikely-leaders>, accessed 4 February 2025.

and a fortnightly learning community offered a spiritual and theological framework for the organizing process—and guided participants in undertaking a power analysis of their church, identifying and developing new leaders, and developing them through action. A trained community organizer provided on-the-ground support for the participants and the leaders being identified and developed.

A key theme of Organising for Growth is that the whole process needs to reflect St Paul's instruction to "pray without ceasing" (1 Thessalonians 5:16). The Cycle of Prayer and Organising (see Figure 1) is a key teaching tool.

One vivid image used in CTC's training expresses this call to a deeper process of discernment: "Is our prayer like the icing on a cake or the yeast in the dough? Do we make our plans and bring them to God in prayer only when they're fully baked and ready, asking for a blessing, or is prayer integral to how our plans are formed?"

The one-to-one relational meeting is the first step in this process: identifying the individual gifts, interests and vocations of church members so that each can grow as a missionary disciple. This requires creating an environment built on trust where members feel valued and heard. By employing one-to-one listening and/or group discussions ("house meetings"), the church leadership and its members can discern the passions and skills within the congregation. In this process, listening is not primarily a matter of identifying new tasks to undertake, but new leaders to develop. Proceeding in this way involves trusting that God has given his people the gifts they need (whether within the existing congregation or the wider community) to undertake the mission which he has entrusted to them. Recognizing first and foremost that each member has a God-given gift cultivates a sense of purpose and belonging. Not only does this personal connection strengthen the individual's spiritual life but their growth as disciples enriches the entire community's faith journey.

Figure 1: A Cycle of Prayer and Organising

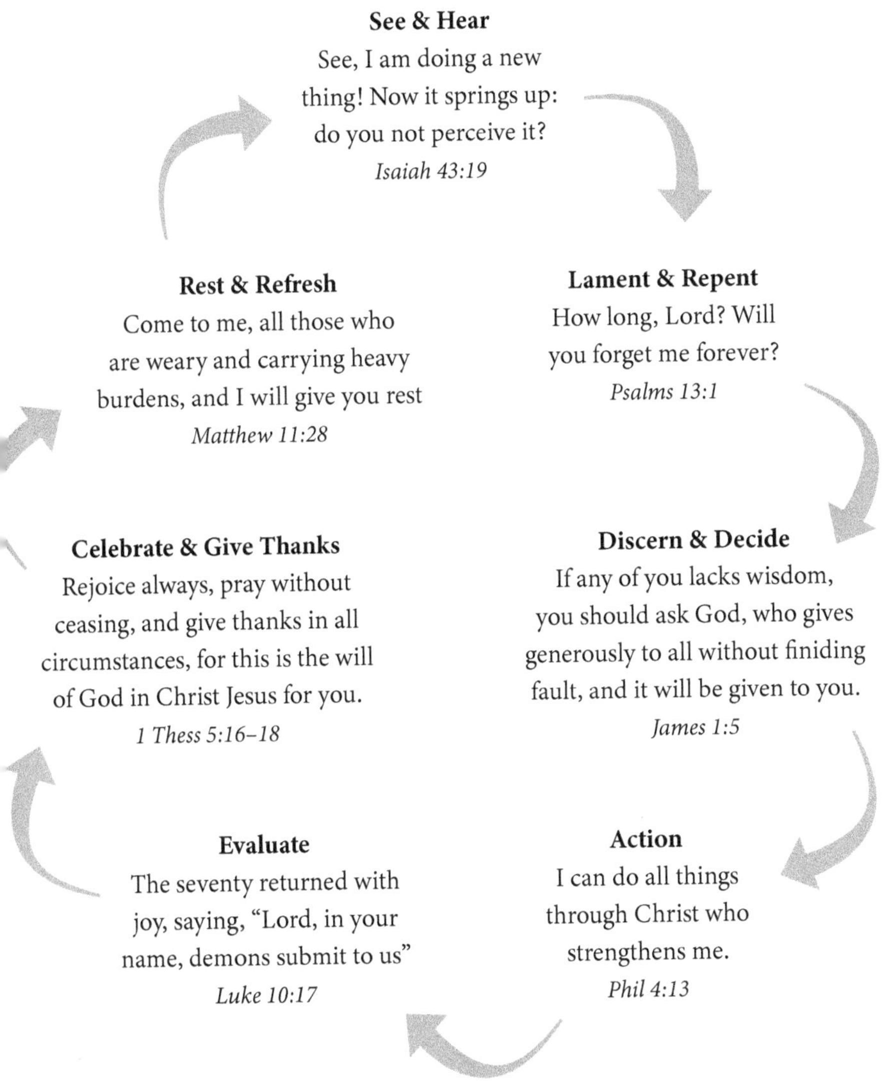

See & Hear
See, I am doing a new thing! Now it springs up: do you not perceive it?
Isaiah 43:19

Rest & Refresh
Come to me, all those who are weary and carrying heavy burdens, and I will give you rest
Matthew 11:28

Lament & Repent
How long, Lord? Will you forget me forever?
Psalms 13:1

Celebrate & Give Thanks
Rejoice always, pray without ceasing, and give thanks in all circumstances, for this is the will of God in Christ Jesus for you.
1 Thess 5:16–18

Discern & Decide
If any of you lacks wisdom, you should ask God, who gives generously to all without finding fault, and it will be given to you.
James 1:5

Evaluate
The seventy returned with joy, saying, "Lord, in your name, demons submit to us"
Luke 10:17

Action
I can do all things through Christ who strengthens me.
Phil 4:13

Leadership training grounded in individual vocation

Once these vocations and gifts are identified, community organizing provides opportunities for leadership training. In a way that seeks to reflect Jesus' pedagogy in the Gospels, the training provided seeks to accompany people on a journey of action, learning through their experience and reflection upon it. This approach ensures that leadership development is not a top-down process but one that grows organically from the interests and talents of church members. It empowers individuals to see their discipleship as integral to the Church's broader mission, fostering a leadership style that is authentic and grounded in real-life experiences.

This also leads on to a valuing of the small and seemingly insignificant, especially in the church's social action. In a neighbourhood where low pay and a lack of affordable housing affects the wellbeing of great numbers of residents, it is tempting to be dismissive of a campaign to win lighting in a park, and to rush to address larger structural issues. But these small-scale campaigns have a vital role in developing the agency and confidence of new leaders—so that they (and not those already used to taking a lead) can play a part in more strategic actions. This slow and patient approach, which puts 'people before programme', is key to sharing power and broadening leadership.

CTC's approach draws heavily on Pope Francis' maxims in *Evangelii Gaudium* on the Common Good and Peace in Society—in particular that "realities are greater than ideas" and "time is greater than space". He writes that

> one of the faults which we occasionally observe in sociopolitical activity is that spaces and power are preferred to time and processes. Giving priority to space means madly attempting to keep everything together in the present, trying to possess all the spaces of power and of self-assertion ... Giving priority to time means being concerned about initiating processes rather than possessing spaces ...
>
> What we need, then, is to give priority to actions which generate new processes in society and engage other persons and groups who can develop them to the point where they bear fruit

in significant historical events. Without anxiety, but with clear convictions and tenacity.

Sometimes I wonder if there are people in today's world who are really concerned about generating processes of people-building, as opposed to obtaining immediate results which yield easy, quick short-term political gains, but do not enhance human fullness.[23]

The Church amplifies its capacity for internal spiritual growth and external social action by interlinking formation as disciples and vocational discernment with leadership development. Internally, when members lead from a place of their spiritual gifts and passion, it inspires a more vibrant, engaged community life. Worship becomes more participatory, small groups more impactful, and overall, the spiritual vitality of the congregation flourishes. Equipping church members with community organizing skills prepares them to address social injustices effectively. Leaders learn to mobilize their congregation in service and advocacy, rooted in a deep understanding of the gospel's call to love and justice. This dual focus ensures that the church does not become insular but remains a relevant, powerful force for social change in the broader community.

Case study: St Barnabas, Walthamstow

St Barnabas and St James the Greater ("St Barnabas") is an Anglican church in the Anglo-Catholic tradition that has served the community of Walthamstow, in the East London borough of Waltham Forest, for over 100 years. The church sits close to a large housing estate, also served by a local mosque. The congregation of St Barnabas itself is ethnically mixed—including several African-Caribbean members who moved to Walthamstow in the 1950s and 60s as part of the Windrush generation, as well as a sizeable Filipino community who have arrived over the last 50 years. The church's diversity is part of its legacy, owing

---

[23] Pope Francis, *Evangelii Gaudium: Apostolic Exhortation on the Proclamation of the Gospel in Today's World*, 24 November 2013, §§222-3.

to successive priests who have supported diversity, inclusivity and community organizing within the church. The church has been a dues-paying member of TELCO for several years and, in 2022, participated in Organising for Growth.

In 2016, following the induction of new leadership, the church contributed significantly to the creation of the Waltham Forest Citizens UK alliance. Averil (the churchwarden, and a key proponent of the Citizens UK community organizing method) played a proactive role within church activities, internally and externally, but faced challenges in establishing a "core team" or broader group of church leaders beyond her spouse, Mark Watan, to lead on church ministries or community advocacies.

From the beginning, their commitment to fostering intentional discipleship started with cultivating personal relationships within the congregation. The churchwarden focused on addressing external needs, while her spouse concentrated on internal needs. Internally, this approach led to several active ministries, including a guitar ministry that evolved into two separate community choirs, for young people and adults, and an extended worship service encompassing *praise, worship* and *reflection* aptly named Hour of *PoWeR*. Externally, this enabled the deployment of some of the first pop-up vaccination clinics in London that did not require ID, proof of address or NHS numbers, supporting friends with irregular immigration status during the height of the Covid-19 pandemic.

Their combined efforts laid a solid foundation so that the church was well prepared to realize its potential for spiritual and community development when it engaged in the Organising for Growth project. In particular, during an Hour of *PoWeR* extended worship session, they introduced CTC's Flow of Discipleship tool (see Figure 2). This tool enabled church members to assess their spiritual journey and envision their goals within the church context, fostering a reflective and growth-oriented outlook on their spiritual journey and relationship to St Barnabas. This reflection and CTC's lay leadership training enabled church leaders to develop spiritually and empowered them to take action as missionary disciples.[24]

---

[24] For a fuller account of the role of the Flow of Discipleship in the Organising for Growth programme, see Brittenden and Ritchie, *Organising for Growth*,

Figure 2: Discipleship flow

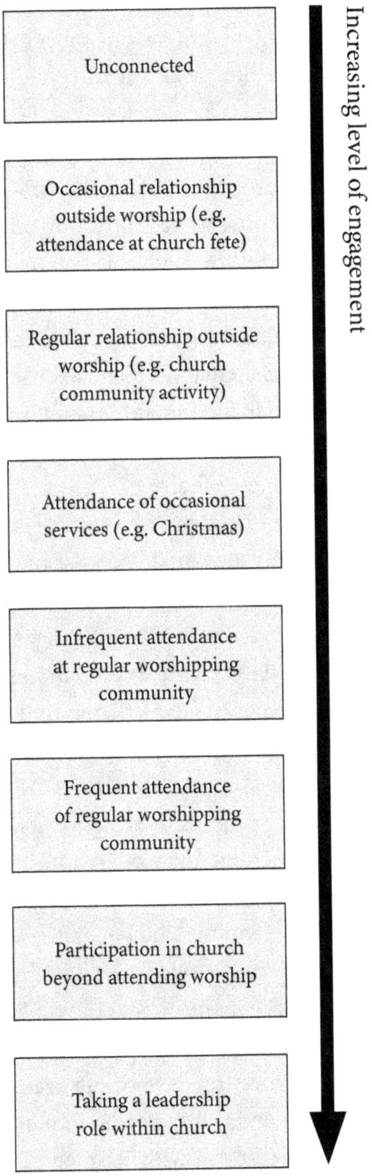

- Unconnected
- Occasional relationship outside worship (e.g. attendance at church fete)
- Regular relationship outside worship (e.g. church community activity)
- Attendance of occasional services (e.g. Christmas)
- Infrequent attendance at regular worshipping community
- Frequent attendance of regular worshipping community
- Participation in church beyond attending worship
- Taking a leadership role within church

Increasing level of engagement →

As a result, the church has seen key leaders emerge within the congregation, one of whom has become employed as a community organizer apprentice and joined the Parochial Church Council (PCC). Another went on to expand her role as a member of the PCC and become the parish safeguarding officer and lead recruiter, and spearhead a community outreach project to redevelop an underutilized space within the church and transform it into a "Warm Welcome" community living room for use by the church and broader community. Mark Watan is now an ordinand in training to be a priest. Averil was selected as the Voluntary Community Sector lead and co-chair of the Borough of Sanctuary Steering Committee. This role involved working with the local authority in Waltham Forest to secure Borough of Sanctuary status, accredited by the City of Sanctuary, which has enabled a weekly drop-in, fully staffed community hub for migrants to support them with questions relating to benefits, housing, education and English for Speakers of Other Languages (ESOL), amongst others.

Lastly, with an increased and broader congregational involvement in TELCO and Citizens UK, the parish stood at the heart of a successful community organizing campaign. As part of the then UK government's efforts to relocate asylum seekers from contingency hotels (including one near the church) the Home Office's accommodation hotel operator, Clear Springs Ready Homes, issued eviction notices to all 400 asylum seekers and refugees, with only a five-day notice to leave the hotel and, for some recipients, to leave London. Because of the outreach St Barnabas had already engaged in, many of these residents were well known to the congregation. Newly trained key church leaders collaborated with Citizens UK to organize a solidarity action outside the hotel. They aimed to convey a strong message to the hotel operator and the Home Office, highlighting the injustice of the eviction. This effort successfully led to the rehousing of all 400 occupants within the capital.

Intentionally developing church leaders using the community organizing method, rooted in developing leaders and the church without a prescribed agenda, transforms individuals and the entire church community. By starting with its members' unique interests,

pp. 8-17.

gifts and vocations, the church becomes a dynamic force capable of profound spiritual growth and impactful social action. This approach ensures that church leadership is not just a title or position but a living, breathing embodiment of the church's mission. Through this intentional development, churches can look forward to a future where their leadership and congregations are fully engaged in deepening their faith and striving for social justice in their communities and beyond.

The process has also seen St Barnabas grow in number and in sustainability with the average weekly congregation rising from 34 (of whom seven were under 18) to 70 (of whom 20 are under 18) in just two years. A greater sense of shared power and responsibility, and a renewed sense of mission, have led to increased giving—and a recent parish vision day has seen those who have developed as leaders beginning to develop others in an ongoing "ripple effect".

St Barnabas' is not an isolated story. As CTC's *Organising for Growth* report explains:

> The project had a target of helping the six churches to have 190 new worshippers by December 2023. In fact, a total of 211 new worshippers were attending by September 2023, 86 of these new worshippers (40%) were under 18. Average Weekly Attendance (for which no specific target was set) had risen by 106 across the six churches. No targets were set for parish share payments, but the project has already led three parishes [including St Barnabas'] to achieve an increase of more than £15,000 per annum with further increases anticipated.[25]

The stories of these churches, and others in the wider Citizens UK movement, show the rich potential of the organizing method—when it is grounded in patience, prayer and the lives and interests of local people.

---

[25] Brittenden and Ritchie, *Organising for Growth*, p. 12.

Rooting the work spiritually

As the Welsh evangelical Martin Lloyd-Jones observed, the Christian gospel is "good news not good advice".[26] Christians act in the confidence that the ultimate victory has already been won, and that God's Spirit is active in the world so that the Kingdom of God, which will only come to completion in eternity, is nonetheless a reality in which we can participate here and now. This is reflected in some of the key gospel texts which inspire us to act for justice: the Magnificat, Jesus' sermon in the synagogue in Nazareth and the Beatitudes are all descriptions of a reality that is dawning rather than ethical or political imperatives. They are spoken by and to people living on the social and economic margins.

Jesus does not offer us a political ethic; he both proclaims and embodies a new reality. All authentically Christian social action must do the same. As Australian pastor Sarah Bachelard warns, many churches' action for social justice has become "functionally atheistic", even in cases in which such action reflects the distinctive theological convictions of the church. Theological orthodoxy is not enough; the process by which a community discerns how to act must involve a living encounter with God. Bachelard writes that:

> in the context of the church's commitment to justice, the recovery of authentic practices of discernment is not just a matter of preference; it is not just that some of us prefer this way of decision-making rather than another... It is a direct reflection of whether the church really does see itself as responsive to another Other—receiving itself and its vocation from God; or whether it is, for all its professions of faith, functionally atheistic.[27]

---

[26] Quoted by Tim Keller in an address to The Gospel Coalition in 2007.

[27] S. Bachelard, "The Ego-Driven Church: On the Perils of Christian Activism", *ABC Religion and Ethics* blog, 19 December 2017; <https://www.abc.net.au/religion/the-ego-driven-church-on-the-perils-of-christian-activism/10095104>, accessed 4 February 2025.

The Cycle of Prayer and Organising

The Cycle of Prayer and Organising grew out of observation and reflection on Christian engagement in community organizing. It articulates a journey which (as we saw above) begins with discernment of the gifts and passions God has put on the heart of his people. As people gather, they listen, identify issues on which there is an appetite and need for action, and discern how God is calling them to act. Fr Richard Springer explained what this meant in another local parish (St George-in-the-East in Shadwell) where nine years of community organizing have grown the average weekly congregation from around 15 to 70. It has seen the parish work with neighbouring mosques and schools in TELCO to win around 70 affordable homes on two plots of land adjacent to the church. In the process of discerning, deciding and acting:

> We heard that the provision of sustainably affordable housing in our neighbourhood is an urgent need, including for people in our congregation and we wanted to respond... and there are people here passionate about doing something practical—motivated by their faith and direct experiences of being homeless or vulnerably housed—and with the right encouragement and support we knew these people could become leaders on doing something.

Alongside this, Fr Richard explained:

> we listened to God reminding us what we already have rather than worrying about what we do not have—a constant temptation in ministry. In our case, God has given us a strip of land we own that could potentially be developed—and some really motivated people.

A key part of this listening to God was reflection on Scripture—a process in which the Holy Spirit was experienced as an active companion and guide:

> I have been greatly encouraged that people across our church have repeatedly come back to Isaiah 58.6-12 which has become a word for this part of our work.
>
> So we connect the needs of our neighbourhood, the passions of our people, the gifts God has given us, and look for signs and words from the Lord including through our reading together of Scripture. It's not complicated, but it's hard work.[28]

Particularly during the pandemic, St George's discovered the importance of the second stage in the cycle—lamentation. It was the cornerstone of "Shadwell Responds"—a neighbourhood organizing alliance within TELCO set up to respond to the Covid-19 pandemic.

At the height of the Covid-19 pandemic, its listening campaign (conducted largely by phone and Zoom calls) identified a deep level of grief and trauma, and need for a communal space for commemoration and prayer. So, in February 2021, 60 local people from ten institutions gathered online for an event co-chaired by Fr Ray Warren OMI of English Martyrs Catholic Parish in Tower Hill and Shaykh Kazi Ashiqur Rahman of Darul Ummah Mosque which featured scriptural reflection from the Bible and Qur'an. In their homes, participants were invited to light a candle or hold up their hands in prayer, and to type in the Zoom chat the names of loved ones they wanted to hold before God. The lamentation was one stage in a process that also led to action (with a successful campaign to change national policy on the operation of free school meal vouchers during the pandemic). If action is to be rooted in the experience of those who experience the sharp end of social injustices, and to genuinely be a response to God's prior presence and activity, it will often need to be preceded by lamentation.

Our former colleague Selina Stone captures this relationship between lamentation and discernment beautifully in her recent book *Tarry Awhile*:

---

[28] Lecture at Ridley Hall, Cambridge with the Revd Alanna Harris, October 2020; <https://www.ctcuk.org/spirituality-and-action-in-shadwell/>, accessed 4 February 2025.

> Tarrying is a time to wait with God and to wait on God ... It is to pause and sit with the one who has made us and who sustains us. It is to sit shoulder to shoulder with Jesus, to be looked upon by God and to be filled ever more with the Holy Spirit.
>
> To wait on God is to continually notice our need for God to hear, to speak and to act. It is a response to lament; we wait on God because we wait for God to answer. In this posture, we expect that this time will not be in vain, but we will leave having received something from the one who has all things to give ... Tarrying is a gathered practice that enlivens the individual. We cannot tarry alone.[29]

In the Cycle of Prayer and Organising, lament and discernment lead on to action. This leads on to evaluation which again is a more distinctive feature of the community organizing process.

The same process of evaluation is of course required within the community organizing movement as well as in the congregations with whom it works. While Kenneth Leech was admiring of Alinsky's approach, he was not uncritical of its practice in East London. For the practice to thrive, it must attend to prophetic voices from within and without.

In his study of community organizing in the United States, Jeffrey Stout writes that:

> In broad-based organizing that aspires ultimately to have a significant impact at the national and international levels, the standing temptation is, as [Ernesto Cortés] puts it, "to skip steps, to take short cuts." If the right sort of micro-organizational work is not being done, the macro-organizational work of connecting citizens' groups with one another in progressively wider networks will create only an illusion of democratic power.

---

[29] S. Stone, *Tarry Awhile: Wisdom from Black Spirituality for People of Faith* (London: SPCK, 2024), p. 33.

This is why effective evaluation (as indeed for an honest power analysis of a church or community organizing alliance) is so crucial to the work of community organizing. As Stout continues:

> If Cortés is right, it seems that high degrees of participation, vigilance, self-constraint, and patience on the part of organizers, leaders, and citizens will be required to scale up the organizational effort without sacrificing either effectiveness or internal accountability.[30]

Undefended leadership can be a catalyst for both effective evaluation and honest power analysis. A key factor in undefended leadership—as opposed to what Bachelard calls the "Ego-driven Church"—is recognizing and resisting "functional atheism" as a constant temptation. To understand and experience the mission and action of the parish church as a participation in the work of God is helpful not only in challenging the temptations of pride and defensiveness but also in reducing anxiety and developing a pattern of ministry that is sustainable.

The final stages in the Cycle of Prayer and Organising—"celebrate and give thanks" and "rest and refresh"—are essential to the cultivation of such a pattern. CTC's teaching on these stages of the cycle draws on St John Paul II's encyclical *Dies Domini*, which emphasizes the role of Sabbath in both giving thanks to God for his goodness towards us and resisting the idolatry of work. As a day of thanksgiving, Sabbath speaks "vividly of 'renewal' and 'detachment'" and its "interruption of the often oppressive rhythm of work" expresses the dependence of human beings and the whole cosmos on God. Without a "constant awareness" of that reality, St John Paul II warns, human beings "cannot serve in the world as co-workers of the Creator".[31]

---

[30] J. Stout, *Blessed Are the Organized: Grassroots Democracy in America* (Princeton, NJ: Princeton University Press, 2010), pp. 8-9.

[31] Pope John Paul II, *Dies Domini: Apostolic Letter on Keeping the Lord's Day Holy* (1998), §15.

Conclusion

Forty years on from *Faith in the City*, Kenneth Leech's critique has stood the test of time. We need to move beyond the naive assumption of a "general goodwill", as if poverty and inequality were problems susceptible to a technocratic solution, rather than manifestations of both structural and individual sin. Leech looked forward to a day when the Church of England—shorn of some of its status and privilege—might precisely through that loss become a more powerful witness to the Kingdom of God. In our East London parishes, we have found community organizing to be a crucial tool in enabling this to happen. Here on earth, such witness will always be imperfect and incomplete. But it can offer us a glimpse in human history of the fullness of life for which God has prepared us.

PART IV

Contemporary challenges

1 0

Church, State and welfare in England today

Joseph Forde

Introduction

Faith in the City is one of the most substantial documents on welfare provision in England to have been published in the post-war period. Issued by the Church of England in the autumn of 1985, it was highly critical of the negative effects its authors believed the economic and social policies being pursued by Mrs Thatcher's Conservative government were having on the poorest members of British society. Robert Runcie (Archbishop of Canterbury from 1980 to 1991) had instituted the Commission on Urban Priority Areas in 1983 to undertake the review that resulted in its publication. This was partly out of a concern that the government's free market (deregulatory) economic and social policies may have contributed to bringing about the inner-city riots that had broken out in some of Britain's poorest areas in 1981/2. Unemployment, in part the consequence of increased deindustrialization that occurred under the Thatcher government's first term, had reached a level not seen since the inter-war depression, topping 3 million in January 1982.[1] This was putting a strain on the welfare state, and causing significant financial hardship for those who had lost their jobs. Runcie was keen

---

[1] See BBC, "On this day", 26 January 1982; <http://news.bbc.co.uk/onthisday/hi/dates/stories/january/26/newsid_2506000/2506335.stm>, accessed 4 February 2025.

to know how the Church of England could best contribute to meeting some of the social challenges that the country now faced, as well as how to advise appropriate bodies on the most appropriate ways of tackling them. Accordingly, the commission's core terms of reference were: "To examine the strengths, insights, problems and needs of the Church's life and mission in Urban Priority Areas and, as a result, to reflect on the challenge which God may be making to Church and Nation: and to make recommendations to appropriate bodies."[2]

When reflecting on *Faith in the City* and its impact, it is important for us to acknowledge from the outset that the Church of England is a very different church from the one that it was back then. It has experienced a steady decline in religious affiliation and observance since the early 1960s, falling from 9.9 million members in 1960 to 5.5 million in 2010, and membership has declined further in the years since.[3] This has been at a time when the UK's population has increased by around 30 per cent.[4] However, the Church of England remains one of the largest providers of welfare in the UK. This is why its approach to welfare matters: to its affiliates; to affiliates of other Christian denominations; to members of faith-based organizations that are not Christian but which see the provision of welfare as a vital component of a civil society; to those of no faith who take the same view; and to all those who find themselves in need of welfare support.[5] In the year that we are celebrating the 40th anniversary of *Faith in the City*, a report that, among other things, was highly critical of government policy on welfare, and which made a number of recommendations for how government and the Church of England could enhance their contributions to its provision, it is surely

---

[2] Cited in *Faith in the City*, p. iii.

[3] See J. Haywood, *The Decline of the Church of England* (2013); <https://churchmodel.org.uk/2013/10/09/the-decline-of-the-church-of-england/>, accessed 4 February 2025.

[4] Cited in <https://www.macrotrends.net/global-metrics/countries/gbr/united-kingdom/population>, accessed 4 February 2025.

[5] For more on this see J. Forde, *Before and Beyond the 'Big Society': John Milbank and the Church of England's Approach to Welfare* (Cambridge: James Clarke & Co., 2022), p. 2.

right that we should examine its role as a provider of welfare today, as well as the level of influence it now has on the shaping of government policy on welfare.

After setting the scene, I will consider its approach to welfare in relation to some of the capacity constraints that it now has to operate within; give thought to its increasing focus on delivering what has been described as "wellbeing" interventions, and the reasons for this shift in its approach; explore the extent to which, in the years since the publication of *Faith in the City*, there has been a decline in the level of influence it once had on the shaping of government policy on welfare provision; and reach conclusions on the direction it might take in its approach to welfare in the years to come.

Setting the scene

Today, 40 years after *Faith in the City* was published, we live in very different times. The social democratic consensus that had characterised politics in England from the mid-1940s to the mid-1970s has long since gone. That was a time when Labour and Conservative governments had bought into the concept of a welfare state, as a means of delivering welfare on a scale not seen before. Their intention was to avoid what had happened after the First World War, when those returning from battle had frequently to endure prolonged periods of unemployment and inadequate healthcare, housing and educational provision for their children. The expanded range of state-provided social security, social housing, secondary education and healthcare provision that the post-war Attlee administration had enacted conformed broadly to the vision of a welfare state that Archbishop William Temple and William Beveridge had championed.[6] It was a vision that captured the imagination of politicians from the left and the right—as well as many of their constituents—and was to remain a dominant feature in British politics until the mid-1970s.

The moment Mrs Thatcher became Prime Minister on 4 May 1979 marked the beginning of a paradigm shift in Conservative party politics;

---

[6] See W. Temple, *Christianity and Social Order* (London: Penguin, 1942).

one that rejected social democracy as an ideology of government, and much of the philosophical underpinning of the post-war welfare state consensus. Her view was that the British people "had given up on socialism—the thirty-year experiment had plainly failed—and were ready to try something else. That sea change was our mandate."[7] Over the following eleven and a half years, the Attlee administration's welfare statist legacy was systematically weakened. The Social Security and Housing Benefit Act 1982 included reductions to social security benefits, and, from 1982 onwards, pensions were increased in line with prices rather than earnings. The Housing Act 1980 reduced local government control over housing by allowing council tenants to buy council houses, without allowing councils to use the money generated to build more houses. The Education Reform Act 1988 weakened local government control over education by allowing schools to opt out of state control and become grant-maintained. Unemployment rose from 5.3 per cent in 1979 to 12 per cent in 1982/3,[8] despite Beveridge's insistence that it should never again be permitted to rise to pre-war levels.[9] Changes such as these to the government's overall economic and social policy direction, and, specifically, its approach to welfare provision, helped shape the backdrop from which the Church of England produced the *Faith in the City* report, published in the autumn of 1985. It made 38 recommendations pertaining to the Church of England and 23 to the government and wider society. These latter recommendations included the need:

> 2. To increase the Rate Support Grant to local government so that it could increase its provision of welfare services....
> 11. To extend state support for the long-term unemployed.
> 12. To increase Child Benefit....
> 16. To expand the public housing programme.

---

[7] M. Thatcher, *The Downing Street Years* (London: HarperCollins, 1993), p. 10.

[8] D. Fraser, *The Evolution of the British Welfare State* (London: Palgrave Macmillan, 2009), p. 307.

[9] Fraser, *The Evolution of the British Welfare State*.

As these were all measures that would increase the resources required of the welfare state and the demands being placed on it, it can be reliably argued that they amounted to a continuation of Temple and Beveridge's vision for a welfare state, at a time when government spending on welfare was being squeezed. However, it was a report that, by and large, failed to convince Thatcher's government of the need to change its direction on welfare.

In the 40 years since *Faith in the City* was published, there have been other examples of Conservative and Labour administrations taking policy decisions which can be interpreted as challenging to the post-war, social democratic vision for a welfare state. In 1990, for example, the National Health Service and Community Care Act brought about competition in the NHS, by establishing an internal market by way of the so-called purchaser/provider split, which, for many, was seen to run counter to the ethos of *co-operation* on which the NHS had been founded. In 2007, Tony Blair's "New Labour" administration enacted legislation that saw a gradual increase in the retirement age from 65 to 68, which, for some, was seen as running counter to Beveridge's vision of the state providing financial security for everyone who had reached an age beyond which they could not reasonably be expected to work.[10] There was a series of cuts to the real-terms funding of parts of the welfare state during the period of austerity launched by David Cameron's coalition government in 2010. These were in response to the fiscal challenges stemming from the financial crash of 2007/8, and which have since been described by the Institute of Fiscal Studies as "the longest, deepest, period of cuts to public services since at least the Second World War".[11] In the years since, many of the cuts—in real terms—have not been reversed.[12] Today, the funding of the welfare state remains challenging, in no small part owing to the cost of living crisis stemming from the Covid-19 pandemic, and

---

[10] W. H. Beveridge, *Social Insurance and Allied Services* (London: HMSO, 1942).

[11] P. Thane, *Poverty and the Rise and Fall of the Welfare State in Britain, 1900 to the Present* (London: Bloomsbury, 2024).

[12] This applies particularly to the cuts in local government that have adversely impacted on adult social care provision, as one example.

the pressures it has put on the public purse. In addition, increases in population size and the longevity of citizens mean the demands that are now being placed on it can sometimes exceed its capacity to meet them. However, I am of the view that there remains much to celebrate about the British welfare state, and its ongoing contribution to meeting the welfare needs of British society.

In the UK, for example, we still have a publicly funded National Health Service free at the point of use, although it is currently under-resourced for meeting some of the demands being placed on it; a publicly funded education system, where over 89.8 per cent of 16- and 17-year-olds are in full-time education or an apprenticeship;[13] a publicly funded system of higher education, where 35.8 per cent of 18-year-olds enrol each year;[14] a publicly subsided level of provision of social housing, in which, for those who do not have the wherewithal to fund a mortgage, 17 per cent of the population live (though this level of provision remains insufficient to meet current demand pressures).[15] Further, we have a publicly funded, inflation-linked, pension scheme for our senior citizens; an economy with relatively low levels of unemployment; and, for those who are unemployed, publicly funded, state-provided, financial assistance. Family allowances are still being paid to mothers with children; state grants are still being paid for funeral expenses for those who can't afford them; statutory maternity, disability and sickness payments are still being made;

---

[13] Cited in Government UK Document (2023), "Participation in Education, Training and Employment age 16 to 18" (Headline Facts and Figures Section); <https://explore-education-statistics.service.gov.uk/find-statistics/participation-in-education-and-training-and-employment>, accessed 5 February 2025.

[14] Cited in Government UK Document (2023) and produced by the House of Commons Library, "Higher Education Student Numbers", p. 5; <https://researchbriefings.files.parliament.uk/documents/CBP-7857/CBP-7857.pdf>, accessed 5 February 2025.

[15] Cited in Government UK Document (2024), "Social Housing Lettings in England, Tenants, April 2021 to March 2022", see Introduction, Section 2.1; <https://www.gov.uk/government/statistics/social-housing-lettings-in-england-april-2021-to-march-2022>, accessed 5 February 2025.

and there is a statutory, minimum holiday entitlement of 28 days for all those in full-time work. Many of these welfare interventions can, in some key respects, be traced back to the thinking of Temple and Beveridge, and their vision of a society where the state becomes, in Temple's words, "the Community of Communities", or what he called "the administrative organ of the community".[16]

However, if the welfare state is to remain a central part of welfare provision in the UK in the years to come, politicians from across the political divide have increasingly come to recognize that it needs reform. Evidence of this is how the Starmer Labour government, since it was elected in July 2024, has embarked on a major programme of reforms to key aspects of education, health, social housing and "welfare to work" provisions (this is not an all-encompassing list), some of which are likely to take several years to deliver. There remains uncertainty about how these reforms are going to be funded in the medium to long term, however, with economic growth levels rising only modestly, and ongoing uncertainty about Britain's access to key markets in Europe and the USA.

There are also concerns that have been voiced by some writers (including by some theologians such as John Milbank)[17] about how they perceive the welfare state as being too remote and overly bureaucratic in its management practices and in its delivery of welfare.[18] Sadly, this perspective, though not without some justification, is too often characterized by the sweeping generalizations that many of its advocates make about professional management practice, without having much in the way of theoretical or applied experience of the discipline, not least with respect to the organizations that they are often writing about. Like any form of professional practice, management will succeed or fail based on the values that underpin it, and how they are applied. Recognizing this, Warren Kinston, in his seminal works on ethical design that emphasize

---

[16] Temple, *Christianity and Social Order*, pp. 70-1.

[17] For a critique of John Milbank's thinking on this (and much else), see J. Forde, *Before and Beyond the 'Big Society'*, pp. 116-66.

[18] See, for example, H. Cottam, *Radical Help: How We Can Remake the Relationship Between Us and Revolutionise the Welfare State* (London: Virago, 2019).

the importance of integrating values into all aspects of decision-making and management practices, remains a pivotal thinker in this field. As well as being an internationally recognized authority on management practice in healthcare settings (he is a medical doctor and was, for many years, a management consultant with whom I had the privilege of working in my own management practice in the NHS), he has consistently shown in his writings and organizational interventions a more nuanced, informed, balanced and sophisticated approach to management theory and practice than many (if not most) of those who write about it from positions that are more critical than his has been.[19] The reality is that there are numerous examples of good and bad professional management practice in the public, private and voluntary sectors (including the churches). However, what distinguishes the public sector from the private and voluntary sectors is the extent to which government plays a role in shaping its strategic direction, including the values that underpin it. If there is a government that, for ideological reasons, does not like the role that the welfare state performs in British society and wants to see it reduced, that will inevitably, and often adversely, impact on its leadership and overall stewardship of organizations such as the NHS, often setting the parameters within which professional management practice has to be conducted. Perhaps that is a price we must pay for the privilege of living in a democracy.

This is the context in which the Church of England now operates as a voice on the shaping of government policy on welfare provision. It is a very different context from the one that produced the *Faith in the City* report in 1985, and, as we have seen, the Church of England is a very different church from the one that it was back then, with a range of capacity constraints that it did not have in 1985. These capacity constraints now impact on its role as a welfare provider, and as an influence on the shaping of government policy on welfare, and thus merit our attention.

---

[19] See W. Kinston, *Working with Values: Software of the Mind: A Systematic and Practical Account of Purpose, Value and Obligation in Organisations and Society* (London: Sigma Centre, 1995).

Capacity constraints

In May 2018, I interviewed Malcolm Brown, at that time the Director of Mission and Public Affairs for the Church of England. He said the following about the *Faith in the City* report: "We no longer do reports like *Faith in the City* . . . because the message has gone out that they are either embarrassing or they fall flat, and we haven't got the money anyway. There is a shift of method and model. . . . We don't do it anymore like that."[20] What Brown was referring to is a shift in the way the Church of England now engages with welfare issues; one that has been described by the Anglo-Catholic theologian John Milbank as "a shift in direction away from the Temple legacy of long reports telling the Government what to do . . . to a more authentic radicalism in which the Church gets involved in all kinds of processes of welfare".[21] This shift partly reflects the steep decline in religious affiliation and observance referred to earlier, and the constraints it has placed on the Church of England's financial and human resources. This pertains not just to its capacity to do things, but also its capacity to understand and comment on areas such as welfare provision, and to do that with authority, despite diminished numbers.

In February 2021, the Church of England produced a report on the housing crisis called *Coming Home: Tackling the Housing Crisis Together*[22] that made recommendations for government and other key actors in the housing market on how things could be improved. The report also identified actions for the Church of England—working with others—that were intended to increase the number of affordable houses. In the period since, much has been done by the Church of England to enable dioceses

---

[20] Cited in Forde, *Before and Beyond the 'Big Society'*, p. 204.

[21] J. Milbank, "Christian Vision of Society puts Economics and Politics in their Place", *ABC Religion & Ethics*, 8 December 2011. Cited in Forde, *Before and Beyond the 'Big Society'*, pp. 119-20.

[22] C. Arbuthnot (Chair), *Coming Home: Tackling the Housing Crisis Together*, the Commission of the Archbishops of Canterbury and York on Housing, Church and Community; <https://www.archbishopofcanterbury.org/sites/abc/files/2021-02/coe-4794-hcc-full-report-v6.pdf>, accessed 5 February 2025.

to provide high-quality, affordable housing on some of its 200,000 acres of land, with a focus on forming partnerships with housing associations and local authorities to help bring this about.[23] However, although worthy in many of its recommendations and follow-ups, the report had only a limited impact on shaping government policy on housing. Similarly, in January 2023, the Church of England produced a report on the crisis in the adult social care sector called *Care and Support Reimagined: A National Care Covenant for England*[24] that was, essentially, a values-based study. Though worthy as a vision of what adult social care might be in an "ideal" world,[25] it was a report that, in my opinion, was less than grounded in the financial and political realities of the moment, and, once again, had only a limited impact in political circles. Neither report was on a scale anywhere close to that of *Faith in the City*, either in scope or impact. This may reflect the point that Brown made about the capacity constraints that the Church of England must now operate within, and, as a consequence, the shift in method and model in its approach to welfare.

Further evidence of this shift has been how, since 2010—partly in response to the social implications stemming from the financial crash of 2007/8—the Church of England has focused more on playing a larger role in providing welfare interventions centred in and around the churches, than on seeking to shape government policy on welfare. In 2014, for example, a biennial national church and social action survey reported that 114.8 million volunteer hours were spent on church social action, an increase of 54.4 per cent from 2010.[26] The same year, a Church Urban Fund survey reported a 45 per cent increase, since 2011, in the number

---

[23] See "Bishop Launches Housing Strategy", *Church Times*, 29 November 2024, p. 5.

[24] A. Dixon and J. Newcome (Co-Chairs), *Care and Support Reimagined: A National Care Covenant for England*; <https://www.churchofengland.org/sites/default/files/2023–01/care-and-support-reimagined-a-national-care-covenant-for-england-full.pdf>, accessed 5 February 2025.

[25] See J. Forde, "Care and Support Reimagined", *Signs of the Times* (autumn 2023), published by Modern Church, pp. 14-16.

[26] See "National Church and Social Action Survey", 2014. This statistic is cited in G. Knott, *Jubilee + Social Action and Church Growth Report*, 2015; <https://

of clergy in the Church of England who considered "engaging with the poor and marginalized in the local area to be a vital activity for a healthy church".[27] It also reported that one third of Church of England churches were involved in foodbanks in 2011, with the number increasing to two thirds by 2014.[28] Consistent with this approach has been the Church of England's announcement in 2022 that it would pump an additional £3.6 billion into its parishes over the following nine years, by supporting social action projects such as foodbanks, and by helping the Church to achieve its target to be carbon net zero by 2030.[29] It envisaged this as being part of a wider effort to stem its decline in membership, by increasing "mission activity" among young people and disadvantaged communities.

Along similar lines, Sam Wells, vicar of St Martin-in-the-Fields, in his writings and ministry, has focused increasingly on the need for more church-based welfare interventions to be provided at a local level.[30] He has done much to develop and promote the Asset-Based Community Development (ABCD) model, which seeks to take more of a "bottom-up" approach to welfare provision, prioritizing community assets and emphasizing the strengths of community-based welfare interventions, while recognizing that the state must retain a vital role in the provision of welfare. The ABCD model is underpinned by a view that the Church has an important role to play in creating "cross-generational community", by adopting an approach to welfare provision that cherishes "people for what they are, not what they are not".[31] Consistent with the growth in popularity of this approach in the parishes has been how, in the years since *Faith in the City* was published, the Church of England has

---

cuf.org.uk/resources/church-in-action-a-national-survey-of-church-based-social-action>, accessed 5 February 2025.

[27] S. Wells, R. Rook and D. Barclay, *For Good: The Church and the Future of Welfare* (Norwich: Canterbury Press, 2017), p. 28.

[28] Wells, Rook and Barclay, *For Good*, pp. 28-9.

[29] See H. Sherwood and K. Makortoff, "The Church of England to pump 3.6 bn into parishes and fund more social action", *The Guardian*, 11 May 2022.

[30] See, for example, Wells, Rook and Barclay, *For Good*.

[31] See Wells, Rook and Barclay, *For Good*, p. 12.

developed a number of locally based, specialist welfare centres that offer expertise, advice and support to those living on the margins, such as the Building Futures campaign for rough sleepers at St Martin-in-the-Fields and the Archer Project for rough sleepers at the Anglican cathedral in Sheffield, both of which incorporate ABCD thinking in their ethos and practices.

Church-based welfare interventions such as these have increasingly come to play an important part in the delivery of welfare to some of the most vulnerable people in our communities. For example, the growth in church-based foodbanks since circa 2010 has undoubtedly helped to alleviate the plight of many of those who have been experiencing food poverty. However, while acknowledging that foodbanks currently provide a vital source of welfare provision—one that is likely to be needed for some time to come to help get Britain through the poverty crisis—many of their providers do not see them as being a long-term solution to the removal of want (one of Beveridge's "Five Giant Evils") in a society as well off as ours (it is a view that I happen to share).[32] Similarly, the support for rough sleepers that church-based projects provide to those who find themselves living on the street is a vital source of assistance to them at a time of immediate need; however, it was noticeable that during the Covid-19 pandemic, when rough sleepers had to be provided with accommodation paid for by the state to minimize the risk of cross-infection, their numbers were reduced substantially,[33] only to rise again in the period since the pandemic ended. There are limits, then, to what

---

[32] This is the view of the Trussell Trust: see its document, "Ending the Need for Foodbanks"; <https://www.trussell.org.uk/our-work/ending-the-need-for-food-banks>, accessed 5 February 2025.

[33] The number of people estimated to be sleeping rough on a single night in autumn 2022 was down 28 per cent from 2019, which was before the Covid-19-related measures which may have reduced people's risk of rough sleeping, particularly in 2020. See Government UK Document (2023), "Rough sleeping snapshot in England: Autumn 2022", Main Findings Section; <https://www.gov.uk/government/statistics/rough-sleeping-snapshot-in-england-autumn-2022/rough-sleeping-snapshot-in-england-autumn-2022>, accessed 5 February 2025.

churches (and the wider voluntary sector) can achieve in the provision of welfare, as there are limits to what the state can achieve. Both have important but different roles to play, reflecting the pluralist nature of British society.

However, we now turn our attention to a further aspect of the shift in focus on welfare that we have seen in the Church of England since around 2010; that is, a shift "from welfare to wellbeing".

From welfare to wellbeing

During the period of austerity, launched by the Cameron-led coalition government in the summer of 2010 and maintained by successive Conservative governments in the 14 years that followed, there was a growth in the number of "wellbeing" interventions being provided by churches from within the Church of England. In a recently published article, Nick Spencer makes out a convincing case for why this has happened: "Humans need attention, sympathy, time, patience, friendship, and love almost as much as they need food, clothing, and a roof over their head [because] . . . a human starved of company, kindness, and compassion will soon see their humanity—their dignity, their personhood—wither and die."[34] Therefore, for Spencer: "Herein lies the 'welfare church' of the future."[35] Similar thinking to this can be found in a book that appeared in 2011, written by John Atherton, Christopher Baker and John Reader, in which they state: "Increasing incomes do not, on their own, produce increasing happiness. Rather, other factors become more significant, and these relate particularly to the more immaterial relational concerns of family, friendships, health, participation and philosophy of life."[36] They point to how—in the post-war period—there has been a trend towards people seeking more opportunities for self-realization, including "an

---

[34] N. Spencer, "New Giants: Church, Welfare and Future", *Crucible: The Journal of Christian Social Ethics* (October 2024), p. 35.

[35] Spencer, "New Giants: Church, Welfare and Future".

[36] J. Atherton, C. Baker and J. Reader, *Christianity and the New Social Order* (London: SPCK, 2011), p. 26.

enhancing of the spiritual dimensions of wellbeing".[37] Further, they point to how increased life expectancy as a result of improved healthcare delivery has resulted in increased availability of time for leisure, and has created a need for more lifelong educational opportunities, particularly for the elderly.

Along similar lines, in an official Church of England document published in 2016, called *Thinking Afresh about Welfare: The Enemy Isolation*,[38] Malcolm Brown argues that Beveridge's report of 1942 had laid the foundations of Britain's welfare state by "identifying 'Five Giant Evils'—Want, Disease, Squalor, Ignorance and Idleness" that needed to be slain. However, Brown identifies another enemy which he argues has threatened "the well-being of our people and which frustrates efforts to address Beveridge's agenda ... It is the Enemy Isolation."[39] By the "Enemy Isolation", Brown means Loneliness, Estrangement and Friendlessness. Its effects can be seen in the isolation that many face: in old age; in those who have been made redundant from work; in a working mother in need of childcare; in a person who has been made homeless; in those who have experienced a breakdown in their marriage; in a person who has experienced estrangement from their families (this is not an all-encompassing list). Crucially, Brown then asserts: "Churches are perhaps the most important schools for neighbourliness that exist in Western societies today."[40] Consequently, for Brown, churches, by being located in the localities, are well equipped to help meet these sorts of wellbeing needs, with members of church congregations (and their clergy) often possessing the interpersonal (and sometimes professional) knowledge and skills necessary for undertaking these sorts of wellbeing interventions. For Brown, moreover, there is also an added dividend for churches engaging in this kind of work. As he puts it: "Trying to remedy

---

[37] Atherton, Baker and Reader, *Christianity and the New Social Order*, p. 25.

[38] M. Brown, *Thinking Afresh about Welfare: The Enemy Isolation*, Internal Policy Document, Church of England, 2016; <https://www.churchofengland.org/sites/default/files/2017-11/the-enemy-isolation.pdf>, accessed 5 February 2025.

[39] Brown, *Thinking Afresh about Welfare*, p. 1.

[40] Brown, *Thinking Afresh about Welfare*, p. 5.

their isolation, people may turn in inappropriate ways to statutory services, GP surgeries or the police. Human isolation adds numerous burdens to social institutions which were never intended to address this basic need, reducing the capacity of those institutions to do the work for which they were designed and funded."[41]

In other words, with the churches increasingly contributing to meeting some of the wellbeing needs of a number of their local residents, this can take demand pressures off state-provided mental health services, thus avoiding them becoming overstretched. This is very welcome at a time when a survey undertaken in 2022 found that 49.63 per cent of adults (25.99 million people) in the UK reported feeling lonely occasionally, sometimes, often or always,[42] and when taking into account that loneliness is a well-known trigger for depression and anxiety. Examples of these wellbeing interventions have included: the Warm Welcome campaign—launched in the autumn of 2022 and supported by the Church of England—that aims to provide "free, safe and welcoming spaces open to all",[43] but particularly those experiencing loneliness or struggling with meeting the cost of heating their homes as a result of the cost of living crisis; lunch clubs for the elderly; knit and natter groups; mums and toddlers' groups; arts and crafts groups; drama groups; music-making groups; "meet-ups in the local pub"; church rambling societies; book reading groups; and English language classes for those for whom it is a second language, to name just a few. Church-based wellbeing interventions such as these can contribute in a positive way to people's sense of their own wellbeing. For many, they offer a welcome break from the "cyber" world of internet surfing and social media, and a welcome vehicle for building friendships and social networks in ways that state-provided wellbeing interventions can't always achieve. As such, they can help to ease demand pressures on state-provided services such

---

[41] Brown, *Thinking Afresh about Welfare*, p. 2.

[42] Cited in "Campaign to End Loneliness" Document: "Facts and Statistics about Loneliness"; <https://www.campaigntoendloneliness.org/about-the-campaign/>, accessed 5 February 2025.

[43] See "Brown to be founding patron of Warm Welcome", *Church Times*, 19 November 2024, p. 6.

as mental health clinics, GP practices and adult social care services. They also have an added advantage for the Church of England as, by being seen to be contributing in ways that make a positive difference to local communities, there is some evidence that this can contribute to congregation-building.[44]

However, we now turn our attention to a further change in the way the Church of England has operated in the field of welfare provision since the publication of *Faith in the City* in 1985; that is, to a noticeable decline in its level of influence on the shaping of government policy on welfare provision and related matters.

A decline in its levels of influence

In 1976, in a foreword written for an edition of Archbishop William Temple's book of 1942, *Christianity and Social Order*, the Rt Hon. Edward Heath, Conservative Prime Minister between June 1970 and October 1974, wrote the following:

> The impact of William Temple on my generation was immense. ... His personal influence was not limited to those of his own way of thinking. It extended to those who held no religious belief and to those whose political views did not match with his own. It embraced the whole spectrum of those who were seriously concerned with the social, economic and political problems of his day.[45]

Temple's book was foundational to the effort that brought about the welfare state in the 1940s, and which *Faith in the City* sought to defend. It would be difficult to think of anyone in the Church of England today who displays that level of influence on the shaping of governmental social and

---

[44] This is a view put forward in H. Rich, *Growing Good: The Future of the Church?* (London: Theos, 2020).

[45] E. Heath, Foreword to W. Temple's *Christianity and Social Order* (London: Shepheard-Walwyn, 1976), pp. 1-3.

economic policy, particularly on welfare provision. The same might be said of High Church Anglican socialist R. H. Tawney, who published two books on political theory in the inter-war years, *The Acquisitive Society* (1921) and *Equality* (1931),[46] that, for many in the Labour Party—then and since—have been seen as foundational for a defence of the welfare state.[47]

Certainly, in the period since the publication of *Faith in the City*, there have been other figures in the Church of England who have campaigned successfully on welfare issues, and who have made significant contributions to improving the lives of the poor and marginalized in their localities. Two that immediately come to mind are Bishop David Sheppard, in the city of Liverpool in the 1980s and 1990s,[48] and Bishop David Jenkins, in the city of Durham during the same period.[49] Both were high-profile, influential welfare advocates, arguing for a compassionate and empathetic approach from government and the churches to meeting the welfare needs of the poor and marginalized. Both had a particular concern for the welfare of those living in urban contexts who had fallen victim to the deindustrialization wave that was sweeping the country at that time, and the high levels of unemployment it had caused. Again, it would be difficult to think of anyone in the Church of England today with that level of influence in political circles on welfare and related aspects. No doubt there will be a number of reasons for this, some of which will fall outside of the remit of this analysis. However, I would like to raise one possible contributing factor, which may have had a bearing on bringing about this decline in the Church of England's level of influence on shaping the direction of government policy on welfare and related matters.

---

[46] R. H. Tawney, *The Acquisitive Society* (1921) (London: Fontana, 1961) and *Equality* (1931) (London: Unwin Books, 1964).

[47] See, for example, R. Hattersley, *Choose Freedom: The Future for Democratic Socialism* (London: Michael Joseph, 1987), which is, in many respects, a defence of Tawney's work.

[48] See D. Sheppard, *Bias to the Poor* (London: Hodder & Stoughton, 1983).

[49] See D. Jenkins, *The Calling of the Cuckoo* (London: Continuum, 2002). It is a useful introduction to his life and work.

Over the last 20 years or so, there has been a discernible shift in the Church of England's centre of attention; one that can be described as a growing preoccupation with addressing internal issues: the ordination of women priests and bishops; debates on gay marriage and gay blessings; the introduction of "managerialism" into its organizational structures and practices; the excessive preoccupation with decline and "mission" attempts to reverse the trend, being just four examples. While these issues have been of considerable importance to those in the Church who have been affected by them, they are less likely to have been seen as having the same level of importance to those who have not been members of the Church of England, including politicians in that category. Saying this, of course, is not to suggest that efforts have not been made by the Church of England to influence the direction of government policy over the last 20 years or so. While the Church of England was under the leadership of Archbishop Justin Welby, for example, we saw how his opposition in the House of Lords to the Rwanda scheme for deporting migrants resonated in some political circles and wider society, as did his opposition to assisted suicide, being just two of a number of efforts. However, it *is* to suggest that these efforts have been fewer in number and have had less impact than before, when contrasted with the levels of influence that Archbishop William Temple had had on shaping the direction of government policy, for example. At a time when the welfare state is under considerable strain following 14 years of austerity policies and the after-effects of the Covid-19 pandemic, there is a case to be made that the Church of England should now refocus its efforts more on addressing external factors, such as influencing the new Starmer Labour government on its approach to tackling the challenges that it now faces on welfare and related matters. A change of approach such as this might also have the added benefit of increasing its perceived relevance in wider society.

With that aim in mind, there is a further factor that the Church of England might want to take into account when considering a possible change of approach. This relates to its adoption of "middle axiom" methodology in its interface with government on politically sensitive matters. Middle axiom methodology can be traced back to the thinking of J. H. Oldham, who, in the preparatory material for the Oxford Conference on Church, Community and State held in 1937, described middle axioms as "attempts to define the directions in which, in a particular state of society, Christian faith must express itself".[50] It is a view that William Temple embraced, believing that "the Church is concerned with principles and not with policy",[51] and "the Christian citizen applies them; and to do this he utilizes the machinery of the state".[52] Temple took this view because he believed: "A policy always depends on technical decisions concerning the actual relations of cause and effect in the political and economic world; about these a Christian as such has no more reliable judgement than an atheist, except so far as he should be more immune to the temptations of self-interest."[53] Using middle axioms has been a methodology that the Church of England has adopted in its approach to Church-State relations since the early 1940s, as a way of avoiding being seen as formulating political policy or allying itself with one particular political party or stance. It has done this by steering a path that focuses more on Christian principles than on policy-making in its advice to governments, for example. However, *Faith in the City* went *beyond* middle axioms in some of the recommendations that it made to government which were clear policy statements, such as the need to increase the Rate Support Grant to local government or to extend state support for the long-term unemployed. That may be one reason why it has since been considered one of the most impactful and politically significant documents to have been published by the Church of England on welfare in the post-war period. Looking to the future, I am of the opinion that there is now a debate to be had in the Church of England on whether, by adopting a similar approach in its advice to government on welfare and related matters to that used in *Faith in the City*, it might produce a more impactful outcome on the shaping of

---

[50] Cited in D. P. McCann, "A Second Look at Middle Axioms", *The Annual of the Society of Christian Ethics* 1 (1981), p. 76. See also J. H. Oldham, *The Church and its Function in Society* (London: G. Allen & Unwin, 1937).

[51] Temple, *Christianity and Social Order*, p. 43.

[52] W. Temple, *Citizen and Churchman* (London: Eyre & Spottiswoode, 1941), p. 83.

[53] Temple, *Christianity and Social Order*, p. 40.

government policy on welfare, than by continuing with its use of the middle axiom methodology.

Conclusion

Since the publication of *Faith in the City* in 1985, the contribution that the Church of England has made to delivering on welfare and, more recently, on "wellbeing" interventions has been considerable, and remains so. It has much to offer in this regard, and, as we have seen, this has often been in ways that have been complementary to those being provided by the welfare state. This approach has been wholly consistent with the thinking of William Beveridge on these matters, as evidenced by his statement of 1948:

> Voluntary action is needed to do the things which the State should not do, in the giving of advice, or in organising the use of leisure. It is needed to do the things which the state is most unlikely to do. It is needed to pioneer ahead of the state and make experiments. It is needed to get services rendered which cannot be got by paying for them.[54]

---

[54] W. Beveridge, *Voluntary Action: A Report on Methods of Social Advance* (London: George Allen & Unwin, 1948), pp. 301-2. Despite the fact that Beveridge had disagreed with the Attlee administration's decision not to permit the friendly societies to distribute state benefits, thus causing them to go into decline, he acknowledged in *Voluntary Action* that: "Throughout the period covered by this review, encouragement of Voluntary Action for improvement of social conditions has been a principle of public policy, reflected in legislation, in administration, and in judicial decisions" (p. 305). He went on to say: "In the present day, State encouragement of Voluntary Action has taken an even more direct form. Grants of public money have been made to voluntary agencies on conditions, leaving them a large measure of independence" (p. 305). Beveridge then called for a continuance and extension of public grants to voluntary agencies (p. 315). This, and other statements that he makes in *Voluntary Action*, flies in the face of those who

However, I am of the view that taking this approach does not mean that we cannot bring an end to foodbanks, which, in the UK, have only been around for 20 years or so. While acknowledging that they currently provide a vital source of welfare provision, one that is likely to be needed for some time to come to help get Britain through the poverty crisis, they need not be a long-term solution to the removal of want in a society as well-off as ours. Indeed, the fact that they were not needed for most of the post-war period demonstrates that the welfare state *can* be the solution to the problem of want for those in need of welfare support, in a society as well-off as ours.

By contrast, since the end of the Second World War, the welfare state has been, and remains, only one source of support to people in need of "wellbeing" interventions, of the kind that we have been discussing. Arguably, when these require specialist, professional expertise, such as in the treatment of a range of mental illnesses, or in the handling of complex medical conditions such as eating disorders, these interventions might more accurately be described as "welfare" interventions. Most people would agree that these are better handled by welfare providers such as the NHS, which have trained staff with the expertise, skills and experience necessary to carry out this work. However, when people are in need of what Nick Spencer has categorized as "wellbeing" interventions, such as the human need for attention, sympathy, time, patience, friendship, love, company, kindness and compassion, this is not always the case. Saying this, of course, is *not* to suggest that these things cannot be provided by state welfare providers, and, in many cases, *are* being provided by them. Having spent a career working in the NHS in the field of employee relations, training and development before taking retirement, hardly a day went by when I did not see evidence of these things. But it is to suggest that the state does not, and should not, have a monopoly of wisdom or a monopoly on praxis when it comes to meeting these "wellbeing" needs. Indeed, for several years now, we have seen much evidence of how the Church of England has been making valuable contributions to meeting

---

have since sought to pit Beveridge against the Attlee administration and its implementation of his report of 1942. For more on this see Forde, *Before and Beyond the 'Big Society'*, pp. 205-9.

them, and how it is well equipped for that purpose.[55] In this respect, then, I agree with Nick Spencer's vision when he says: "Herein lies the 'welfare church' of the future."[56]

Welfare provision remains of vital importance at a time when Britain is slowly recovering from the shocks it has faced in the wake of Brexit, Covid-19, and the climate imperative. The welfare challenges that Britain currently faces are immense: reducing the waiting lists for elective procedures in the NHS; meeting the repair costs to school buildings in need of refurbishment; reducing child poverty; increasing the number of affordable houses; taking measures that will reduce the number of rough sleepers; supporting people to transition from welfare to work, being just a few that the Starmer Labour government is having to address. The contribution that the Church of England can and should make to influence this welfare agenda is important, not least for the reasons that were set out at the beginning of this analysis. It may well be that reports in the style of *Faith in the City* are no longer optimal or affordable, as has been stated by Malcolm Brown. Hence, other opportunities need to be identified for the Church of England to influence the analytical, academic and political debates concerning welfare provision, working in consort with other churches, charities, think tanks and university departments currently engaged in research on welfare and the best ways of delivering it.[57]

In summary, then, when reflecting on *Faith in the City*, and the considerable impact that it had on the political scene at the time of its publication (despite having only a limited impact on persuading the government of the day to change its course on welfare provision), I am suggesting that the Church of England should reconsider the extent to which it might be willing to move beyond using the middle axiom methodology in its attempts at influencing the shaping of government policy on welfare and related matters; that is, along the lines taken by the authors of *Faith in the City*. I am also suggesting that it might wish to consider reprioritizing its efforts, away from what has, arguably, been an

---

[55] For more on this see Forde, *Before and Beyond the 'Big Society'*, pp. 116-66.

[56] Spencer, *New Giants: Church, Welfare and Future*, p. 35.

[57] For more on this see Forde, *Before and Beyond the 'Big Society'*, pp. 227-42.

over-preoccupation with internal matters during the last 20 years or so to one more focused on shaping external ones, such as the Starmer Labour government's strategic and practical approach to welfare provision and poverty alleviation in the years to come. What is more, by taking that approach, I am suggesting that this might increase its perceived relevance in society, at a time when it continues to battle against the decline it has seen in its membership and levels of religious observance, in the period since *Faith in the City* was published.

11

Whose side is the Church on? Dialogue with the Catholic Social Thought tradition

Jenny Sinclair

Introduction

The language-world of *Faith in the City* was the soundtrack of my teens. I left home in 1980, five years before it was published, but Urban Priority Areas, unemployment, jobs, investment, poverty, social justice, welfare, the poor, deprivation, the unions, the Labour Party, the Thatcher government—this was the currency of our kitchen table.

I preferred Liverpool's music scene. As the daughter of Bishop David Sheppard, forging my own path was not straightforward. Earlier, in London in the early 1970s, our home had been the focal point of conversations between those who would later be the key instigators of the report. As a little girl, I watched Eric James, Robert Runcie and others come and go.

As a young adult, estranged from the faith, I avoided everything church-related. I found employment in local government. In my mid-twenties, a dark-night-of-the-soul conversion in 1988 led me to be received into the Catholic Church. I married and worked as a graphic artist and in various charities. While my father's prominence in the Church of England grew, I chose a quiet life.

Things changed in 2011, after both my parents had died. I experienced a movement of the Spirit. This was just before the Tottenham riots, and I was sensing a social instability, the beginnings of the unravelling that is now evident to all. People were comparing the comparatively weak response from the churches with the partnership[1] between my father and Archbishop Derek Worlock in the 1970s-90s. Their 20-year friendship had played a pivotal role in Liverpool at a time of upheaval in the early 1980s. I was being prompted—against my own inclinations—to ask, "what happened to the Sheppard-Worlock spirit?"

Others soon joined me. Over a couple of years of researching the partnership, we found that it had two defining features. First, a joint servant leadership, encouraging an "outward-facing church" that engages with the life of the neighbourhood, and second, their focus on the dignity of the human person and solidarity with poor communities.

This Spirit-movement and historical reflection led to the creation of Together for the Common Good. But while we are inspired by their example, we recognize that this is a new time, with different challenges requiring new approaches. Independent of any denomination, and dedicated to spiritual and civic renewal, we are a small national charity working across the churches, helping leaders and young people discover and fulfil their vocation for the common good. Our understanding, rooted in the tradition of Catholic Social Thought (CST), sees the common good not as a utopian ideal but as "the shared life of a society" that is built "by working together across our differences, each taking responsibility, according to calling and ability".[2]

Assumptions

For many Anglican clergy, *Faith in the City* has a special place in their hearts. For some, it inspired their calling to ministry. For significant parts of the Christian community, its engagement with the realities of British life remains a high-water mark of social concern. Others, better equipped

---

[1] Together for the Common Good, "Our History"; <https://togetherforthecommongood.co.uk/about/our-history>, accessed 5 February 2025.

[2] Together for the Common Good, "Common Good Thinking"; <https://togetherforthecommongood.co.uk/about/common-good-thinking>, accessed 5 February 2025.

to do this than I, have assessed its legacy. But for me, its 40th anniversary offers an opportunity to re-examine the vocation of the Church[3] in our own time.

My father is regarded as one of the prime instigators of the report. It is therefore relevant to note the influence of *Bias to the Poor*.[4] I have lost count of the number of people who have told me that this book was an inspiration for them.

What Catholics call the "preferential option for the poor"[5] is more relevant than ever. But I believe that my father's preferred way of showing that bias and preference is far too top-down to meet the situation we face today. Fundamentally, he believed that the Church and the State, rather than poor people themselves, should be the prime agents of change.

Bias to the Poor called for a government-led wealth redistribution and for a government-mandated social wage for the low paid and unemployed. Such moves now seem to rely too much on easily abused and often dehumanizing centralized state power and fail to address both the underlying economic causes and the extent of their impact. The book's advocacy on behalf of poor communities also sounds paternalistic, overlooking the aspirations and autonomy of the people involved, and underestimating the problems caused by benefit-dependency.

First published on 1 January 1983, *Bias to the Poor* contained some of the key assumptions underpinning *Faith in the City*, which came out just under two years later—assumptions that were to shape the dynamic between the mainstream Christian denominations and poor communities for two generations.

---

[3] I am using the term "Church" to refer to all the churches unless specified otherwise.

[4] D. Sheppard, *Bias to the Poor* (London: Hodder & Stoughton, 1983).

[5] "The Preferential Option for the Poor" is a key principle in CST. Reflected in canon law, it is regarded as a true Catholic obligation. Following the biblical preference given to powerless individuals who live on the margins of society, the tradition includes spiritual as well as material poverty and encompasses all who are marginalized by poverty. See Pontifical Council for Justice and Peace, *Compendium of the Social Doctrine of the Church* (London: Bloomsbury Publishing, 2006), #182–4.

Much has happened since these publications appeared. We see marked decline in attendance across most of the institutional churches, poverty has worsened, and we find ourselves in a moment of unprecedented geopolitical and cultural upheaval. In such a scenario, it is vital for Christians to read the signs of the times with care and attention.

Reading the signs of the times

To begin this process, we need to understand the root causes of the malaise facing the West. If we do not dig deep, our responses are likely to be inadequate. Understanding context is vital. We may address symptoms but fail to comprehend the times. We may approach evangelization without understanding political economy. If Christian leaders make the wrong call, we may inadvertently promote the injustices we wish to eliminate.

The rethinking needs to be profound, because many of our assumptions—political, social, cultural—are likely to be out of date. This is a new time that warrants an honest examination of conscience, a process that will help with the discernment around how God is calling the Church to play its part.

Catholic Social Thought

There is no such thing as a neutral worldview. So let me be clear about the position I am taking. I listen and learn across the Christian traditions and in particular draw on Catholic Social Thought (CST). My interpretation of this tradition is grounded in political reality by reading a wide range of journalism, and by consulting with political thinkers, philosophers and grassroots communities.

Rooted in the gospel, CST is a body of thinking intended as a gift for all people of goodwill, it is a deep theological tradition that draws on social and political expertise, data and lived experience from across the world to help us read the signs of the times.

Sometimes referred to as "the theology of the Holy Spirit in practice", it began at the end of the nineteenth century as a response to the effects of the Industrial Revolution on working men and families. Now, as then, it seeks to uphold the integrity of human beings and creation, and to interrogate structures of power that dehumanize. For many, it stands out as the most coherent theological framework for understanding the world.

At its heart is a notion of justice that demands we look at what is happening to people, to families, relationships, communities, the natural world, in concrete terms right here, where we are. It identifies three sources of power: the two earthly powers of money and state, and the one relational, transcendent power of human beings in relationship with each other and with God.

It recognizes the tension between capital and labour and argues for a balance between them, emphasizing the priority of decent work and the dignity of labour.[6] Within the Catholic tradition, work is seen as something that gives life meaning and through which we are called by God to help shape the world.

The tradition does recognize the importance of wealth creation and that businesses can and do achieve a great deal of social good. However, there is a realism about the damage that capital can do when it is over-concentrated and under-constrained. Its tendency to exploit and dehumanize workers, to commodify human beings and the natural world, must be kept in check.

It is significant that this tradition is non-partisan. It has even-handedly condemned all dehumanizing modern political-economic systems: communist, socialist and liberal as much as capitalist. All of them are judged to be deeply corrupted by the materialist, spiritually empty premises established by the narrow rationalism of the atheistic Enlightenment.

---

[6] John Paul II, *Laborem Exercens*, encyclical letter, Vatican website, 14 September 1981, #14; <https://www.vatican.va/content/john-paul-ii/en/encyclicals/documents/hf_jp-ii_enc_14091981_laborem-exercens.html>, accessed 5 February 2025.

What we see

When we read the signs of the times, first we say what we see.

We see that too many young people cannot afford a home. We see that social trust is breaking down. We see the symptoms of what Pope Francis calls a "malign"[7] culture—consumerism, extreme inequality, indifference to the poor, the collapse of trust in institutions, and subordination of the local to the national, global and digital. We see sclerotic health systems, the atrophy of local forms of human association. We see the disconnect between the managerial class and the population. We see massive public and private debt. We see the tragedy of displaced people. We see the catastrophic damage done to the natural world. We also see the "malign culture" in the liberalizing of abortion and assisted suicide, in the industrialization of human exploitation—the commercializing of surrogacy, gender medicine, the normalizing of cosmetic surgery, organ harvesting, sexual exploitation, human trafficking.

We see people bravely trying to navigate these storms. We see extraordinary examples of resilience and humanity. But we are also seeing a steep rise in symptoms of human distress—growing loneliness (higher among the young than the old[8]), increases in addiction, self-harm, depression, nihilism, indifference, feelings of meaninglessness. We see the tyranny of a social media culture incentivizing a false idea of freedom.[9]

---

[7] Francis, *Message of His Holiness Pope Francis for the 2023 World Day of the Poor*, Vatican website, 19 November 2023; <https://www.vatican.va/content/francesco/en/messages/poveri/documents/20230613-messaggio-vii-giornatamondiale-poveri-2023.html>, accessed 5 February 2025.

[8] J. Blagden, W. Tanner, F. Krasniqi, "The Age of Alienation: loneliness among young people", *Onward* (8 July 2021); <https://www.ukonward.com/reports/age-of-alienation-loneliness-young-people/>, accessed 5 February 2025.

[9] J. Haidt, *The Anxious Generation: How the Great Rewiring of Childhood is Causing an Epidemic of Mental Illness* (London: Penguin, 2024).

Political economy

The CST tradition helps us to see what is going on in terms of political economy. From *Rerum Novarum* (1891) to *Laborem Excercens* (1981), *Centesimus Annus* (1991) to *Caritas in Veritate* (2009), *Laudato Si* (2015) and *Fratelli Tutti* (2020) (to name just a few), the great papal encyclicals of this tradition train our instincts to the effects of the economy on human beings and nature.

Looking through this lens, we see a system that has undermined the dignity of work, requiring units of labour to be cheap and mobile; that has offshored our manufacturing jobs to low-wage economies; that encourages the importing of workers, away from their own families, to take up low-paid jobs that prop up Western business models. This is a system described as "frictionless" by investors, but in human terms, it has become a recipe for social unrest.

Four decades ago, the idea of moving to find work was regarded as right wing. This is now rebranded as "freedom". This transactional freedom is what led to deindustrialization. It broke parts of our country.

The loss of jobs and investment—with no meaningful replacement—led to civic degradation on a vast scale. Not only in "urban" settings in cities and outer estates, but especially in our coastal towns and former industrial heartlands. It led to the discarding of whole communities, who, to add insult to injury, were then framed as deficient and backward. On top of this, the knowledge economy and the service economies shamed manual labour, further exacerbating the class divide.[10]

What we have witnessed is effectively a politics of abandonment. There is a political and economic bias against the poor. In human terms, the impact of the new, post-industrial economy has been catastrophic, devastating to the common good.

---

[10] D. Goodhart, *Head Hand Heart: The Struggle for Dignity and Status in the 21st Century* (London: Allen Lane, 2020).

Liberalism

In 2015, Pope Francis asserted that "we are not living in an epoch of change so much as an epochal change".[11] He was among those able to identify that the old era was breaking down. This is a time between eras, which can be described as an interregnum.

Every era is shaped by a particular philosophy. The animating idea of the era that is in the process of breaking down comes from the philosophy of liberalism.[12] Liberal ideas have done much good, but today's dominant form of liberalism, the ideology of neoliberalism, turns Enlightenment ideals of freedom into a tawdry and narrow economic logic, in which the free pursuit of profit maximization becomes the highest good.

Constraints on finance capital have been removed, and transactional individualism has been promoted. The result is globalization; a global financial system which largely serves the interests of supranational corporations. The optimal neoliberal arrangement has low wages, big governments that serve businesses, and large welfare states to keep away revolutionary discontent.[13] In the neoliberal economic vision, there is

---

[11] Francis, *Address of Pope Francis, Pastoral Visit to Prato and Florence*, Vatican website, 10 November 2015; https://www.vatican.va/content/francesco/en/speeches/2015/november/documents/papa-francesco_20151110_firenze-convegno-chiesa-italiana.html, accessed 31 December 2024. A similar statement can be found in paragraph 44 of the *Concluding Document of the 2007 General Conference of the Bishops of Latin America and the Caribbean*, colloquially known as the *Aparecida Document*, authored by Pope Francis, then Cardinal Bergoglio; <https://www.scribd.com/document/257681153/General-Conference-of-the-Bishops-of-Latin-America-and-the-Caribbean-concluding-document>, accessed 5 February 2025.

[12] A. Pabst, "How Christian is Post-liberalism?", <https://togetherforthecommongood.co.uk/leading-thinkers/how-christian-is-postliberalism>, accessed 5 February 2025.

[13] W. Streeck, "Globalism Against Democracy", *Compact Magazine* (2024); <https://www.compactmag.com/article/globalism-against-democracy/#>, accessed 5 February 2025.

nothing wrong with relying on increasingly precarious and meaningless jobs that pay wages too low to live on.

This model of political economy also reshaped our conception of welfare. With over 5.93 million people in the UK currently in receipt of Universal Credit,[14] we have shifted from a culture of community interdependence to the impersonal support of money transfers and the government provision of services.

The impacts of this system are not just economic. The reshaping of our conception of work has affected our personal relationships. A labour market dominated by low-skill, low-security jobs, on top of an inflated property market, has undermined family formation and weakened the confidence of the young in their adult prospects. The philosophy underpinning the neoliberal model has led to profound social and moral consequences too.

The Catholic economist Luigino Bruni says that this system "gives birth to and fosters its own sense of being human"; that "it engenders the promise of interpersonal relationships without the wound of the other".[15]

Its amoral incentives to fragmentation eat away at shared values and erode our sense of citizenship; it dissolves the particularity of place; its commodification is undoing what it means to be human. Its individualism ferments multiple pathologies: relationship breakdown, loneliness, mental health disorders, crime, the breakdown of social trust, spiritual, cultural and moral confusion. It results in a de-moralization.

This is why we see the emergence, on both the progressive left and the extreme right, of identitarian politics, distorted forms of victimhood, authoritarian tendencies, the battle of rights and the culture wars.

In this paradigm we are pitted against each other on the basis of identity and opinion, a polarization that alienates us from each other. The result is a distraction from the fundamental problem, which is a

---

[14] House of Commons Library, *Managed migration: Completing Universal Credit rollout* (December 2024); <https://commonslibrary.parliament.uk/research-briefings/cbp-9984/>, accessed 5 February 2025.

[15] L. Bruni, *The Genesis and Ethos of the Market* (London: Palgrave Macmillan, 2012).

dysfunctional political economy generating poverty in all its forms—economic, relational and spiritual. It is very important to understand this distraction.

Within this system there is a denial of the transcendent and a dominance of the material. This denial subverts natural law and generates an anti-human system that some call "the machine".[16] Our eyes may be trained to the so-called "cost-of-living crisis", but this is just one symptom of a deeper dysfunction.

Anthropology

The type of operating system that this philosophy generates is inherently unstable because it is founded upon a false anthropology—a desiccated, soulless conception of the human being which generates a false idea of freedom. At the core of this is freedom from constraint—including from country, from history, from religion, from God, and now even from human nature itself.

In its extreme form, this cult of freedom sees family as a constraint, and tradition and accountability as obstacles to "progress"; even relationship to place is reframed as old-fashioned. Ultimately, its relativism "liberates" society from truth and from mutual responsibility.[17]

Its view of the human being incorporates the idea of "the unencumbered self", emphasizing rights over responsibilities, corroding our sense of mutual obligation. It is effectively an assault on relationship.

This philosophy denies the primacy of God and creates a cult of self. This is quite different from a Christian anthropology where human

---

[16] P. Kingsnorth, "Being Church in the Age of the Machine" (2024); <https://leavingegyptpodcast.substack.com/p/ep26-being-church-in-the-age-of-the>, accessed 5 February 2025.

[17] Francis, *Fratelli Tutti*, encyclical letter, Vatican website, 3 October 2020 (#206, #273); <https://www.vatican.va/content/francesco/en/encyclicals/documents/papa-francesco_20201003_enciclica-fratelli-tutti.html>, accessed 5 February 2025.

beings are understood to be transcendent, relational beings, made in the image of God.

This individualism drives a political economy where we outsource more and more of the things we used to do as communities to the state or to the market: childcare, care for our civic environment, entertainment, care of the elderly. The results include family breakdown, isolation, the fragmentation of communities, corruption and spiritual confusion.

The motivation of this spirit is anti-human, which is why the system is now unravelling. Every country that follows this system is seeing the same effects. Beneath its shiny veneer, we are faced with a disintegration. With a relativistic and materialist logic—no truth and no beauty—its worldview ultimately brings about its own destruction, and in the meantime, "as the old is dying, and the new cannot yet be born … a great variety of morbid symptoms appear".[18]

Our modern pharaohs

CST has long warned about the centralization of power, whether of capital or the state, because it undermines human relationships, weakens social bonds and undermines local agency and democracy. The principalities and powers of our time can be conceptualized as our modern pharaohs.

Whenever finance capital dominates, it has the tendency to dehumanize and exploit. It presents with a friendly face, but its business is the commodification of creation and the financialization of everything: land, water, homes, human beings.

We see, for example, venture capital offering to pay huge sums to farming families for their land.[19] At the same time, we see the state making increasing financial demands on family farms and family businesses.

---

[18] A. Gramsci, *Selections from the Prison Notebooks of Antonio Gramsci* (London: Lawrence & Wishart, 1971).

[19] T. Wray, "An Economy of Land Rooted in the Local" (2023); <https://leavingegyptpodcast.substack.com/p/ep11-an-economy-of-land-rooted-in>, accessed 5 February 2025.

Governments are becoming more authoritarian, with more decisions taken outside of the democratic process. Around the world post-Covid, we have seen government overreach, with increasing surveillance, censorship and the cultivation of self-censorship, and growing interest in digital social credit systems to control behaviour. The results are sure to be disastrous. As John Paul II said, "collectivism does not do away with alienation but rather increases it".[20]

While some find it hard to believe that totalitarianism—even the soft "dictatorship of relativism" that the then-Cardinal Ratzinger warned about—is a real threat in our time,[21] these developments, together with artificial intelligence, foreshadow a dreadful future. Pope Francis too has repeatedly warned about the rise of "the technocratic paradigm"[22] in which "human nature" is seen as a problem to be managed and corrected. He insists that: "We would condemn humanity to a future without hope if we took away people's ability to make decisions about themselves and their lives."[23]

And now we see a collusion between our modern pharaohs, where governments act in the interests of big corporations, insulating them from democratic accountability. This modern Egypt, a corrupt merger of corporate and state power, operates a different kind of slavery, hidden behind a list of pseudo-freedoms. The malign spirit says, "you can have

---

[20] John Paul II, *Centesimus Annus*, encyclical letter, Vatican website, 1 May 1991 (#41); <https://www.vatican.va/content/john-paul-ii/en/encyclicals/documents/hf_jp-ii_enc_01051991_centesimus-annus.html>, accessed 5 February 2025.

[21] Cardinal Joseph Ratzinger, *Homily at the Missa Pro Eligendo Romano Pontifice at Vatican City*, 18 April 2005; <https://www.benedictusxvi.com/homilies/the-dictatorship-of-relativism-and-the-measure-of-true-humanism>, accessed 5 February 2025.

[22] Francis, *Address of Pope Francis to the G7 Session on Artificial Intelligence*, Vatican website, 14 June 2024; <https://www.vatican.va/content/francesco/en/speeches/2024/june/documents/20240614-g7-intelligenza-artificiale.html>, accessed 5 February 2025.

[23] Francis, *G7 Session*, 2024.

mobility, consumer choice, rights and self-determination! You only have to obey a few sensible rules, and not dream about higher things."

Discontent

The liberal consensus is supported across almost the entire British political class. The founding values of both major parties were abandoned as the ideology of neoliberalism became dominant.[24] Over 40 years, the Conservatives forgot their calling to conserve, and Labour lost touch with those who actually labour. Their expressions were different, but both parties were colonized by the same hyper-liberal dogma, in effect becoming a "uni-party",[25] disconnected from reality on the ground.

This philosophy shows up on the right as neoliberal economics, and on the left as hyper-liberal social norms. Both versions are driven by the same logic; they regard limits and borders as unjust and regressive. Each has a blind spot: the right attributes moral unravelling to excessive liberalism, but somehow the neoliberal economic system gets a free pass; the left attributes poverty to neoliberal economics, but accepts unlimited self-actualization, which is seen as progressive.

This misadventure, whether intentional or through naivety or neglect, can be regarded as a liberal hegemony. It led to gross mismanagement by successive governments and has been provoking increasing discontent.

The so-called "left behind" have had enough. After four decades of devastation, they had nothing left to lose. In previous eras their actions might have been understood as a peasants' revolt.[26]

---

[24] M. Glasman, "Why only Socialism can redeem Conservatism", *Oakeshott Lecture Series 2024*; <https://togetherforthecommongood.co.uk/leading-thinkers/blue-labour-why-only-socialism-can-redeem-conservatism>, accessed 5 February 2025.

[25] A. Bastani, "Labour and the Tories are Becoming a Uniparty"; <https://unherd.com/newsroom/labour-and-the-tories-are-becoming-a-uniparty/>, accessed 5 February 2025.

[26] D. Goodhart, *The Road to Somewhere: The Populist Revolt and the Future of Politics* (London: C. Hurst & Co. Publishers Ltd, 2017).

Opposition has extended to the truckers in Canada; Dutch, German and British farmers; the Gilets jaunes in France; the multi-country disquiet around mass immigration, net zero policies, and the gender industry, to poor employment conditions, wage stagnation and high inflation. Although labelled "populist", and despite bad actors harming their credibility, these movements have broad support. This is the resistance of the excluded majority. The hyper-liberal project is being rejected.[27]

While the "legacy" (mainstream) media have ignored or downplayed these developments, a courageous field of independent journalists and commentators has served an audience hungry for authenticity. Growing dissent has fuelled disarray among many established parties, as in the UK and most of Europe, and a political realignment in the United States.

Objections have been framed as extremist in the most derogatory terms by an elite, liberal, managerial "overclass"[28] in an attempt to retain control of the narrative. They could not accept—or even understand— that what they termed "populism" was actually "political blowback against the social disruption that their policies have created".[29]

In the UK, the mainstream political class has become almost entirely disconnected from the basic things that most people—not just the most left-behind—care about. It is as if politicians are saying, "we don't have any ideas, any viable policies to give you dignified and meaningful work, to sort out your housing issues; we don't know how to get the younger generation on the housing ladder". This is how Anna Rowlands puts it. She adds, "this is the disgrace and the dishonesty of the politics that we live with".[30]

---

[27] J. Rutherford, "The New Class War" (interview with Michael Lind, 7 January 2023), *The New Statesman*; <https://www.newstatesman.com/ideas/2023/01/us-political-analyst-michael-lind-interview-new-class-war>, accessed 5 February 2025.

[28] Rutherford, "The New Class War".

[29] J. Gray, "On The Dusk Of Western Liberalism" (interview, 3 March 2023), *Andrew Sullivan, The Weekly Dish*; <https://andrewsullivan.substack.com/p/transcript-john-gray-on-the-dusk>, accessed 5 February 2025.

[30] A. Rowlands, "Catholics and the General Election", webinar, 18 April 2024, *The Tablet and Pastoral Review*; <https://www.youtube.com/watch?v=

The 2024 American presidential election produced a decisive rejection of globalization and progressivism. It is yet to become clear how this will play out in practice. The new political divide is now[31] between the transhumanist oligarchs and the interests of a broad, multi-racial, multi-faith working class. What matters to most people is family, place, decent work, stability, security, economic justice, truth and common sense.

The question now is who can deliver a common good political economy that can underpin a social peace,[32] defend our liberties, meet the needs of families and develop a new orthodoxy capable of taking our society into the future. Populist parties may be asking some of the right questions, but they do not have the answers. In this change of era, volatility will continue until a new settlement is reached. Meanwhile, we can be sure, even if globalization is over, that neoliberal interests will use whatever means and disguises they can to ensure that their economic model continues uninterrupted.

Christian justice

It is imperative that the way we think about justice is consistent with our faith. Christianity is not libertarian, neither is it welfarist or utilitarian. Rather, rooted in the ancient rabbinical tradition, the Christian model of justice is concerned with right relationship, with God and with each other.

For example, the Torah's laws on helping someone in debt[33] involve detailed relational elements. The lender is obliged to accompany the

---

WfWwYHQ63hc>, accessed 5 February 2025.

[31] B. Ungar-Sargon, "MAGA Must Defeat DOGE", *Compact Magazine* (20 January 2025); <https://www.compactmag.com/article/maga-must-defeat-doge/>, accessed 5 February 2025.

[32] Sr H. Alford OP, "Just Peace: On Social Peace and the Causes of Division"; <https://t4cg.substack.com/p/lincoln-lecture-series-ep09-just>, accessed 5 February 2025.

[33] Gmaj Center, "The Mitzvah of Lending", *Gmaj Center*; <https://gmajcenter.org/in/mitzva.php>, accessed 5 February 2025.

borrower, providing support and advice, and must "not exact interest from them" (Exodus 22:25).

This points us in a radically different direction from the way poverty is addressed by our current welfare state arrangements, where help is likely to mean the digital transfer of cash, leaving the person alone in their flat. This utilitarian, welfarist method, following the individualistic paradigm, aims for efficiency and cost effectiveness. But its systems are neither efficient nor cost effective. They are hugely expensive, and, minimizing human connection, they generate unnecessary suffering.

Campaigns that simply call for more benefits perpetuate this utilitarian, rights-based model of justice. The relational imperative ought to be at the heart of Christian campaigns.

Failure to understand the neoliberal political economy has allowed identitarian politics to dominate our conception of justice. For example, treating issues of inequality predominantly in terms of cultural, rights-based intersectionality categories undermines social solidarity and displaces economic justice. This divisive model suits our modern pharaohs, because it splinters opposition and keeps wages low.

A model of justice based on Christian anthropology does not pit low-paid or poor people against each other according to identity. Rather, Christian justice starts with the assumption that human beings thrive in relationship, not on their own. It takes the form of listening to the concerns of all workers[34] and then building relationships between them. From this solidarity alliances are forged, as with the best trade unions, capable of negotiating with the powers.

In God's economy, if you're having a hard time, I'm to walk in relationship with you and accompany you until you get back on your feet, for as long as it takes. It may involve some money or helping you get a job, but primarily it is about accompaniment. Not just give you cash and leave you alone. The Christian justice tradition is anchored in God's economy of mutual obligation and right relationship.

Every year Pope Francis publishes a letter for the World Day of the Poor. He insists that our response is personal, that we are to stop

---

[34] J. Cruddas, *The Dignity of Labour* (Cambridge: Polity, 2021).

outsourcing, that solutions are not to be found in activism or welfarism.³⁵ We are not to use the welfare system or charitable agencies as a way of keeping poor people at arm's length. This is consistent with the Personalism tradition favoured by John Paul II, Dorothy Day, and the Catholic Worker Movement.³⁶

Our primary relationships as human beings should be with each other rather than with state agencies, the market and impersonal institutions. At a time of increasing global instability, these right relationships with our neighbours—local, embedded, embodied, grounded, across ethnicity, sex, age, background and opinion—will become more and more important.

Whose side is the Church on?

Reflecting on the last 40 years, we can see that in the mid-1980s the neoliberal system was just beginning. Its impact since then has been immense. If *Faith in the City* had appreciated the true nature of that era, its recommendations might have been different.

Since then, many communities with proud civic histories have been abandoned and even demonized. Some churches have offered sympathy, but very few leaders have so far demonstrated an understanding of the political economy underlying this civic degradation. These communities have been as let down by the Church as they have by the political class.

To discern our way forward, we should begin by exploring what we can learn from Jesus in His time. There are parallels between our modern

---

[35] Francis, *Message of His Holiness Pope Francis for the Sixth World Day of the Poor*, Vatican website, 13 November 2022, (#7); <https://www.vatican.va/content/francesco/en/messages/poveri/documents/20220613-messaggio-vi-giornatamondiale-poveri-2022.html>, accessed 5 February 2025.

[36] C. Miller, "A Personal Church for the Common Good"; <https://togetherforthecommongood.co.uk/stories/a-personal-church-for-the-common-good>, accessed 5 February 2025.

Egypt and the Roman economy in Galilee,[37] where Jesus was the son of a carpenter. The Roman system privileged the elites who controlled the storehouses and kept down the wages of the workers.

Jesus resisted the excesses of this political economy by promoting the Kingdom of Heaven. His centre of gravity was with the poor, the meek and the lowly: people who had been humiliated, those who suffered, were despised, who had been abandoned. Like the prophets before him, he judged harshly those who were indifferent to the poor.

His instinct was not to start a factional campaign group, but to bring people together in solidarity, across class, ethnicity and educational background, to build a common life. Jesus promoted a non-violent sacrificial resistance characterized by love and just relationship.

From the Gospels, CST derives a framework for good judgement. Among its key principles are solidarity, subsidiarity, the dignity of work, participation, stewardship and the preferential option for the poor. This integrated framework, underpinned by discernment of the Holy Spirit, centres around upholding the integrity and dignity of the human being and the natural world.

These principles call us, just as our Lord called the people he met in Galilee, to be the embodiment of love in a desecrated world. To build the common good with God and neighbour in the places where we live. To accompany each other in solidarity, to offer some resistance to the domination of the principalities and powers. To hold a sacred space in which human beings can be together to encounter the transcendent. To create places to be loved and heard, to share and build bonds, a sense of family.

Much of the work of the Church Urban Fund, the Together Network, and the numerous other networks that have developed over the last 40 years, embodies this relational spirit. There is much to be proud of.

However, serious questions hang over the Christian social action landscape. Volunteer burnout is widespread, many churches are vulnerable, funding is under huge pressure, need is greater, social problems are more complex, and poverty is getting worse. Perhaps

---

[37] D. E. Oakman, *The Radical Jesus, The Bible and the Great Transformation* (Eugene, OR: Cascade Books, 2021).

most concerning is the increasingly estranged dynamic between many Christians and poor communities.

How the Church responds in this period of unprecedented change is of great importance. To discern this response, we can start by looking honestly at some of the problems around this estrangement.

The question of language

The language world that has developed in Christian social action circles is revealing. Terms like "client", "outreach" and "service delivery"—even "social action" itself—do not reflect a culture of friendship and mutual respect. Likewise, professional class terminology like "community development", "projects" and "facilitators" betrays a mindset common to government and NGO culture. One way to explore this is to check which words can be said in front of someone who is poor.

This is challenging for those used to thinking of themselves as activists or service providers. Clearly there are distinctions between charitable organizations and individual Christians. But such managerial approaches can risk engineering out the possibility of hearing the Holy Spirit and make vital, smaller, more informal activity look trivial.

By contrast, a covenantal or synodal[38] spirituality of listening and dwelling with our neighbours[39] is more suitable for our time. Such a posture involves a shift from "host" to "neighbour". This demands some unlearning, patience and availability. Funding is secondary.

The term "marginalized" may sound appropriate from a church activist position, but it depends where you stand. In God's worldview, poor people are not marginal. The number of people classified as poor in

---

[38] "Synodal" here refers to the Roman Catholic practice of synodality, "journeying together with the Holy Spirit"; <https://www.schoolforsynodality.org.uk/our-resources/conversations-in-the-spirit-a-how-to-guide>, accessed 5 February 2025.

[39] A. J. Roxburgh, *Joining God in the Great Unraveling: Where We Are & What I've Learned* (Eugene, OR: Cascade Books, 2021).

the UK alone is currently around 14 million.[40] That includes those who are working, unemployed and destitute. That is a lot of people. It doesn't feel "marginal" to me, even by worldly political standards. We are now post-Christendom and the dynamics have changed: it is now the Church which is marginalized.

The foodbank paradox

The foodbank paradox[41] is well-known: while they are vital, we wish they didn't exist. But there is a bigger problem. The more efficient emergency food aid becomes, the less urgent economic reform appears. This helps to mask the need for the prophetic. Tragically, the foodbank network is now baked into a toxic political economy that props up big corporations.

From the perspective of the CST tradition, any activity around food poverty must be situated within well-articulated demands for economic reform, for decent jobs, retraining, for place-based investment—"to restore the places long devastated" (Isaiah 61:4). CST is also insistent that the dignity of decent, fulfilling work should be central to a politics of the common good. We must not capitulate to a combination of low-wage precarious jobs, worklessness and welfare.

Foodbanks and associated support services, along with other forms of social action, are often sources of pride among churches wanting to serve the community and to demonstrate their usefulness, especially in an increasingly secularized culture. There is of course a vital role for charity, but the Church is not called to be a handmaid to the state: it has a sacred vocation to be transformational, not to be useful.

---

[40] Joseph Rowntree Foundation, "UK Poverty 2024: The essential guide to understanding poverty in the UK" (2024), *Joseph Rowntree Foundation*; <https://www.jrf.org.uk/uk-poverty-2024-the-essential-guide-to-understanding-poverty-in-the-uk>, accessed 5 February 2025.

[41] J. Bartholomew, "The Food Bank Paradox" (2020), *Prospect*; <https://www.prospectmagazine.co.uk/politics/40841/the-food-bank-paradox>, accessed 5 February 2025.

Churches may be providing vital services, but the service–client dynamic can inadvertently alienate the very people it aims to help, and can lead to burnout among those who volunteer. The more visionary leaders have responded by integrating relational elements into their work, such as cafes and conversation.

But Pope Francis goes much further: he says that Christians must stop seeing charity in a service provider mindset and instead look to living a shared life. He says we "must commit to a mutual sharing of life that does not allow proxies".[42]

Church-based food activity has this potential, to be a place of communion at the heart of congregational life, where people in need are no longer peripheral, passive recipients but active companions. This can look like a place to meet and talk, to be known and to be blessed—a place of nourishment in the broadest sense. And more: to be a place of mutuality and reciprocity, with opportunities to help, to create and produce.

Churches must learn to receive as well as give: to become communities of place, where being relational is less of a project and more of a disposition. In this way, charity acquires a constructive, restorative role that addresses the breakdown of trust, loneliness, the loss of agency, the atrophy of local institutions, and other consequences of neoliberalism.

(Dis)empowerment

In writing about *Faith in the City*, Greg Smith[43] observed the need to move on from the Temple tradition and the condescending "effortless superiority" of the established Church. These power dynamics are not restricted to the Anglican Church: they have roots in the wider culture. It can be helpful to unpack certain elements.

---

[42] Francis, *Homily of His Holiness Pope Francis for the World Day of the Poor*, Vatican website, 14 November 2021, #7; <https://www.vatican.va/content/francesco/en/homilies/2021/documents/20211114-omelia-giornatamondiale-poveri.html>, accessed 5 February 2025.

[43] G. Smith, "Is there still faith in the city?"; <https://williamtemplefoundation.org.uk/is-there-still-faith-in-the-city/>, accessed 5 February 2025.

Many Christian charities and volunteering models, just as in mainstream society, have been infected by the culture of individualism, falling into patterns of transactional exchange between the active deliverer or rescuer and the passive recipient, of whom nothing is asked.

It is also true that many Christians say they feel safer in a service-provider posture, or in fundraising for charity, than in getting to know their neighbours. Often there is fear of getting too involved with troubled families. There are issues of confidence and tensions around class.

The scale of class estrangement must not be underestimated. Questions of class and the churches go beyond the wellbeing and recruitment of clergy and barriers to belonging, as important as these issues are. There is a wider problem that needs to be understood. Much of the Church over the last 40 years—just like the Labour Party[44] and many of our other institutions—has been captured by a middle-class culture and has lost connection with poor communities.

An army veteran I know (who goes to church) said, "The church has become a woke foodbank. Handouts are soul destroying. People need dignified work so they can maintain some self-respect."

There are many examples that challenge this perception, and the Church has been truly heroic in the quiet determination of thousands of volunteers in meeting overwhelming need. But it must be said that the inability to comprehend the underlying cultural trends has been a significant factor in class estrangement. If *Faith in the City* had had a more robust theology of political economy, it might have sown the seeds of a better story.

Just as then, many Christians now also fail to recognize the philosophy that lies behind the neoliberal system. Rather than addressing the root causes, there is a tendency to see issues of hunger and poverty in the context of welfare solutions.

Advocacy campaigns to "end poverty" and calls for adjustments to benefits reduce the causes of poverty to government austerity measures. Supposed solutions are then found in monetary redistribution through the tax system. The fundamental problems of the malign culture are ignored.

---

[44] M. Glasman, "Why only Socialism can redeem Conservatism", 2024.

This kind of piecemeal approach, often claiming to be "prophetic", barely addresses the causes, and gives the principalities and powers a free pass. Despite all the good work taking place, the Church is then perceived to be an enabler of the system. More insidious still, this posture feeds a politics of low expectations.

The service–client dynamic can deprive a person of their agency, and over time de-skill and entrench dependency and entitlement. By contrast, a relational approach, as Jon Kuhrt has said,[45] can be more effective in terms of building up a person's confidence. Quoting a formerly homeless woman who said, "It's alright all these agencies giving people things, but you have to want to help yourself . . . ", Jon emphasizes the importance of enabling personal responsibility and "the balance between grace and truth".

The issues around this dynamic reflect the creative tension in CST between solidarity—standing alongside those affected by poverty and advocating for economic justice—and subsidiarity, the principle encouraging responsibility to be taken at the appropriate level, empowering people to help themselves according to their ability.

As Pope Benedict XVI said: "Subsidiarity is first and foremost a form of assistance to the human person [which] respects personal dignity by recognizing in the person a subject who is always capable of giving something to others."[46] This is not only significant for people finding themselves in debt, destitution or unemployment, or with chronic health conditions. It is particularly important in relation to struggling families. Parents desperately need help to withstand the effects of the malign culture on family life. Helping a family in difficulty to reach a place of strength and independence is a gift of inestimable value.

---

[45] J. Kuhrt, "Grace, Truth and the Common Good: The Future of Christian Social Action" (2024); <https://t4cg.substack.com/p/the-2024-series-ep02-grace-truth>, accessed 5 February 2025.

[46] Benedict XVI, *Caritas in Veritate*, encyclical letter, Vatican website, 29 June 2009, #57; <https://www.vatican.va/content/benedict-xvi/en/encyclicals/documents/hf_ben-xvi_enc_20090629_caritas-in-veritate.html>, accessed 5 February 2025.

Christian activists have consistently asserted their role as "a voice for the voiceless". There is much vital advocacy going on, from raising awareness of modern slavery to housing problems. However, sometimes the issues can be limited to the perspective of the advocate (and their funders), rather than reflecting the actual concerns of poor communities. Despite platforms in charity campaign videos and poverty truth commissions, a middle-class presumption persists that the poor don't truly understand their own interests.

Democratic events since 2016 have shown that people from poor communities do have a voice. Their interpretation of the times, however, was different from the views held by most Christian leaders and activists whose position aligned with the establishment and big corporates.[47] It should not then be a surprise that so many poor and working-class communities have become estranged from the Church.

A new story: Communion

The coming years in the UK may be hard. These times may call for a kind of tragic realism,[48] but they also demand a new language deeper and more resonant than that of the urban church era. We are invited into a story of civic *and spiritual* renewal, of truth, beauty and goodness.

The language of CST can not only help us to read the signs of the times and call out structures of sin. It can also inspire us to build structures of grace.

Without being prescriptive or theocratic, the tradition helps us discern a holistic, constructive response that bridges the false dichotomy between evangelization and social concerns. Pope John Paul II puts it in these

---

[47] J. Sinclair, "Rebuilding the Broken Body" (2017), *The Tablet*; <https://togetherforthecommongood.co.uk/stories/rebuilding-the-broken-body>, accessed 6 February 2025.

[48] J. Gray, "Welcome to the Era of Tragic Realism" (Interview, 2022); <https://unherd.com/newsroom/john-gray-welcome-to-the-era-of-tragic-realism/>, accessed 6 February 2025.

terms: "God is entrusting to you the task, at once difficult and uplifting, of working with Him in the building of the civilization of love."[49]

This is humble but hugely ambitious. Our response to the culture of individualism and the threat of a technocratic future begins, in humility, with listening, to God and to our fellow citizens. But given that so many churches have become disconnected from their local communities, the place to start is not so much with projects, programmes and funding applications, but by spending time with our neighbours.

Congregations can develop a practice of listening in the neighbourhood, through the art of the one-to-one conversation.[50] Always anchored in practices of prayer, such as *lectio divina*,[51] the aim is not to recruit for a project or a campaign, but simply to have the honour of hearing a person's story. From this listening, relationships will develop, and what matters to people will become clear. Then, all manner of meaningful things will happen.

These times require speaking truth. Intimidation by political correctness has been a scourge and the Church should refuse it. Without open deliberation, the common good is impossible. Indeed, "truth speech connects us. It is the truth that restores the ties between people."[52] To be truly countercultural, churches ought to be convening social spaces where people are free to speak, where there is respect for diversity of opinion and disagreement is possible without fear.

People need company and are yearning for meaning. The loneliness, isolation and spiritual hunger of our times derive from the individualistic

---

[49] John Paul II, *Address by the Holy Father John Paul II for the 17th World Youth Day*, Vatican website, 27 July 2002; <https://www.vatican.va/content/john-paul-ii/en/speeches/2002/july/documents/hf_jp-ii_spe_20020727_wyd-vigil-address.html>, accessed 6 February 2025.

[50] Together for the Common Good, "One-to-One Conversations"; <https://togetherforthecommongood.co.uk/resources/one-to-one-conversations>, accessed 6 February 2025.

[51] *Lectio divina* is the Ignatian practice of dwelling and discernment with scripture. It is part of my daily routine.

[52] M. Desmet, *The Psychology of Totalitarianism*, tr. Els Vanbrabant (White River Junction, VT: Chelsea Green Publishing, 2022).

and nihilistic philosophy underpinning our culture. To assist people in the unveiling of the sacred, there is a distinctive role for churches in this work of repair, using liturgy both inside and outside church in communal acts of celebration, pilgrimage and solidarity. Our spiritual practices, across the Christian traditions, are rich in both depth and diversity. From fasting to the Eucharist, a new confidence is called for.

Each of us can enable a better story, by living out what it means to love and to care, to suffer with and to trust, to forgive, to be sacrificial and to show what it means to be a companion, a friend, a good neighbour. These things are fast becoming elusive, especially among the young. It is necessary to be intentional.

Pope Francis warns that young people are the most vulnerable to the effects of the malign culture, which, he says, "makes them feel like losers, introduces illusions about the meaning of life, promotes a transactional paradigm, and the idolatry of physical perfection".[53]

The Church can tell a better story through accompaniment—unmediated by digital platforms—in the ups and downs of life, the natural experiences of birth and death; where people can share what it means to be human and what it means to be a person with a soul.

Pope Francis has urged world leaders to recognize the imminent threat to humanity from artificial intelligence and the new transhumanist industries. He stresses the importance of "politics", of strengthening democratic processes, to uphold human agency.[54] The new industrial revolution is not all negative, but it opens the way to the exploitation of the human being on an unprecedented scale, and it has the potential to shame the physical, eclipsing reality.

---

[53] Francis, *World Day of the Poor letter*, 2023.
[54] Francis, *Address to the G7 Session*, 2024.

In this context, the theology of place[55] and local relationships become especially significant. The writings of John Inge,[56] Andrew Rumsey,[57] Alison Milbank[58] and Martin Robinson[59] are helpful here. They can help develop what is most needed: a covenantal model of church and parish, committed to the local, which lives and breathes, celebrates and grieves with the people of the neighbourhood.

These times also call for a better literacy about what a common good political economy involves. The fundamental cultural change required cannot be achieved only by government. A common good story of renewal requires both solidarity—commitment to the good of all—and subsidiarity—where responsibility is taken, whenever possible, by the smallest, lowest or least centralized competent authority rather than by a higher and more distant one. We can begin to imagine a new vision in which everyone is called to play their part.

In this new settlement at the national level, governments will balance different interests, for example, across class and educational background, between business and unions, young and old, urban and rural, migrants and host communities,[60] capital and labour. Governments support the conditions that prioritize communities and families; they deconcentrate

---

[55] I. Geary, "Place: personal, prophetic and political" <https://togetherforthecommongood.co.uk/stories/place-personal-prophetic-and-political>, accessed 6 February 2025.

[56] J. Inge, *A Christian Theology of Place (Explorations in Practical, Pastoral and Empirical Theology)* (Aldershot: Ashgate, 2003).

[57] A. Rumsey, "Modernity's Mistake" (2022); <https://togetherforthecommongood.co.uk/stories/learning-from-modernitys-mistake>, accessed 6 February 2025.

[58] A. Milbank, "Home for Good" (2021); <https://togetherforthecommongood.co.uk/leading-thinkers/home-for-good>, accessed 6 February 2025.

[59] M. Robinson, *The Place of the Parish: Imagining Mission in our Neighbourhood* (London: SCM Press, 2020).

[60] J. Sinclair, "Immigration and the Common Good" (2024), *Trinity Forum*; <https://togetherforthecommongood.co.uk/from-jenny-sinclair/immigration-and-the-common-good>, accessed 6 February 2025.

the power of capital by permitting regional banks and energy providers, and by fostering shorter food supply chains.

State power is distributed, where appropriate, by resourcing autonomy at local and regional levels. Welfare is delivered through national mutuals[61] based on the contributory principle. A national industrial strategy centred around the dignity of work, implemented locally, incentivizes place-based investment, job creation and retraining—balancing environmental measures with livelihoods. At the heart of this new settlement is a unifying narrative, and a restoration project to correct the damage done to the most abandoned places.

At the regional level, there is intentional collaboration between businesses, employers, investors, educational bodies, regional associations, religious and other networks working together for the renewal of their region, attracting investment to create a robust economy with decent jobs for local people.

At the local level, local government creates conditions that enable a civil economy and the autonomy of local people to run their own organizations. Relationships grow between local businesses, schools, sports clubs, charities, local associations, churches and other religious bodies; each meeting local needs, working together for the good of the community, enabling local people to find fulfilment.[62] This local ecosystem, centred around the recognition that the family is the fundamental building block of society, is geared to cultivate family life, encouraging families to support each other and their neighbours, and to teach young people civic responsibility and the importance of good local relationships.[63]

---

[61] F. Field, "Contract Welfare: Back to Basics" in *The Future of Welfare* (2014); <https://www.theosthinktank.co.uk/cmsfiles/archive/files/Reports/The%20future%20of%20welfare%20a%20theos%20collection%20combined.pdf>, accessed 6 February 2025.

[62] L. Bruni and S. Zamagni, *Civil Economy: Another Idea of the Market* (Newcastle-upon-Tyne: Agenda Publishing, 2016).

[63] See the Common Good Schools programme by Together for the Common Good at <https://commongoodschools.co.uk>, accessed 6 February 2025.

At the personal level there is a culture of civic friendship,[64] of mutuality, of borrowing and lending, a reciprocal gift economy. There is more interdependence and less reliance on market and state.

Each Christian has a particular vocational responsibility to fulfil. Despite determined attempts to undermine and privatize Christianity, and intense pressure to conform to secular ideologies, the faithful are called not to hide away but to play our part to bring about this common good vision.

Amidst all the brokenness, we must live with the expectation that God is at work. Our calling is to become attuned to the movements of the Spirit in the mundane, in conversations at the bus stop, in the taxi, in the local shop. Moments of mutual acknowledgement, acts of loving kindness, intentional acts of listening, truth telling, making eye contact, putting down the smartphone—all of these can rehumanize, restore and uphold the human space. We need holy, unmediated time together.

When we listen to the Spirit in this way, we invite a new imagination to stir among us. New forms of local association may emerge, forms that make "provision for each person to have a hand in shaping and benefiting from the material and social conditions under which they live and work". This is how Luke Bretherton describes the Catholic philosopher Jacques Maritain's vision of Christian humanism. Maritain saw local democratic forms of association "as a vital means through which humans can realize their true natures as those created in the image of God".[65]

Whether around local mutual aid, sport, entertainment, care of the vulnerable, energy, land or housing, such grassroots collaborations can develop into forms of economy that, embedded in local relationships, have greater resilience.

As Wendell Berry puts it: "An economy genuinely local and neighbourly offers to localities a measure of security that they cannot

---

[64] Francis, *Fratelli Tutti*, 2020.
[65] L. Bretherton, "The Conversion of Public Intellectuals", *Comment Magazine*; <https://comment.org/the-conversion-of-public-intellectuals/>, accessed 6 February 2025.

derive from a national or a global economy controlled by people who, by principle, have no local commitment."[66]

Small and local forms of Christian social action offer possibilities too. Foodbanks, community hubs, pantries and social supermarkets, night shelters, Places of Welcome, credit unions and churches of all shapes and sizes, when connected, hold the promise of an interconnected energy greater than the sum of their parts. But to be truly transformational, models of ownership need to change.

Churches are well placed to help poor and working-class communities forge mutually beneficial relationships between, for example, charitable food provision and farming communities. The challenge is to discover ways that extend beyond charity to local production; to nurture the latent potential of a truly participatory grassroots economy that is owned and run by the people themselves.

This era calls for a relational church,[67] for local Christian communities to be constructive partners, living a shared life with neighbours on low incomes, sharing each other's joys, hopes and tragedies, acting together to build a place where our children can make a life. We *are all missionary disciples now*,[68] called to join in the restorative work of the Holy Spirit in our neighbourhoods. The times call for a new formation and an ancient discipleship: to seek the welfare of the city.

But there is a deeper reason why Christians are called to live in solidarity with people trapped in poverty. Pope Francis says the Church needs to be evangelized *by* the poor.[69] Why does he say this? He says that people who are poor tend to have retained a common sense, a sense of their need for others that the affluent and the busy so easily lose. Without

---

[66] W. Berry, *It All Turns on Affection: The Jefferson Lecture and Other Essays* (Berkeley, CA: Counterpoint, 2012).

[67] J. Sinclair, "The Relational Church"; <https://togetherforthecommongood.co.uk/from-jenny-sinclair/the-relational-church>, accessed 6 February 2025.

[68] Francis, *Evangelii Gaudium*, encyclical letter, Vatican website, 3 October 2020, #120; <https://www.vatican.va/content/francesco/en/apost_exhortations/documents/papa-francesco_esortazione-ap_20131124_evangelii-gaudium.html>, accessed 6 February 2025.

[69] Francis, *Evangelii Gaudium*, 2020, #198.

them, Christians will misread the signs of the times. Recognizing the cost of mission drift, Francis sees that relationships of mutuality and reciprocity with poor communities will keep the Church grounded in truth and close to God.

My conclusion is simple yet challenging. This time of interregnum could be an inflection point for the churches. I want to honour the energy that *Faith in the City* generated, its many fruits and its legacy. But I sense that another such report may not deliver what is hoped for. What is needed now is an examination of conscience, and then a quiet but determined revolution.

1 2

Drawing together the themes

Terry Drummond and Joseph Forde

In this volume, we have seen how *Faith in the City* was an important contribution to thinking on urban and public policy, which was encapsulated in its commitment to social and economic transformation. It was an example of the Church of England speaking truth to power, by challenging the government of the day to rethink its approach in policy areas it believed were adversely affecting urban communities in cities and towns up and down the country. Though it had only a limited impact on altering the direction Mrs Thatcher's government had taken on social and economic policy, its criticisms resonated with many members of English society, and it was a report that was generally well received by members of its own congregation. Further, we have seen how, during the 20 years following its publication, it was foundational for shaping the Church of England's approach to urban mission and ministry, as well as for the priority that it placed on that work.

However, in the period since, we have seen how there has been a change of emphasis, with more money being invested in what are perceived to be new and innovative forms of outreach and evangelism, as a response to tackling the steady decline in affiliation and observance that the Church of England has witnessed since the early 1960s. While this has been, and remains, an important strategy for ensuring that the message of the gospel is shared with as many people as possible, it has resulted in less focus being placed on urban mission and ministry, and the support it provides to those who are economically and socially deprived. The contribution from Sophie Valentine Cowan on estate churches, and the vital contribution that they make to supporting some of the most socially and economically deprived people living in England today, is a powerful argument for why more resources should be allocated to supporting this work.

The offering from Alan Billings reveals how the strategy adopted by the *Faith in the City* commissioners added credibility to the conclusions that it reached. The time they spent meeting with representatives of residents in urban parishes, alongside taking evidence in person and in written submissions from organizations working in urban communities, meant that they built up an accurate picture of the impact that government economic and social policy was having on their lives, and particularly the lives of the poorest members of these communities. Local parish ministry places the parish community at the centre of mission and addresses both the individual and the corporate needs of the community. Yet we have seen evidence in the essay from Terry Drummond of how the historical and intellectual foundations that underpin contextual urban mission and ministry are not as embedded in the Church as they once were. The loss of historical perspective is described in the introduction to *The Hope of Things to Come* (2010), in which Mark D. Chapman addresses the issue of a church that places the emphasis on refreshing mission and identifying new ways of developing ministry. He writes:

> There is, however, an inevitable danger with freshness and newness. It can perhaps dampen the enthusiasm for history which can appear rather stale and old. As a historical faith however, Christianity is always an amalgam of the old and the new: the two live off one another...[1]

The critical issue in the discussion of urban mission and ministry is that, while some urban congregations may be small, they are often at the centre of local social action initiatives, diligently serving their communities. In addition, they reflect a tradition of social ministry that has much to commend it, so it would be a mistake if the Church of England were to pay insufficient attention to it. Yet, we have also seen in the essay from Ian

---

[1] M. Chapman (ed.), *The Hope of Things to Come: Anglicanism and the Future* (London: Mowbray, 2010), p. xii.

K. Duffield how there is a danger of becoming too binary in our thinking, by adopting narratives that can sometimes be crude and simplistic, "where everything is seen in binary terms and suspicion lurks at every corner". In defending the parish system, therefore, it is important that we do not allow ourselves to become resistant to new ways of developing ministry, where they can be seen to have merit, and where they do not pose a threat to the parish model.

Finally, we have seen in these essays how there is much evidence of there still being "faith in the city", both spiritual and practical, despite the trend that we have witnessed towards greater secularization in English society in the 40 years since *Faith in the City* was published. Hence, we are of the view that this anniversary year should be a time to celebrate all that is good about urban mission and ministry in the Church today.

Suggestions for further reading

Atherton, J., C. Baker and J. Reader, *Christianity and the New Social Order: A Manifesto for a Fairer Future* (London: SPCK, 2011).

Barrett, A. (ed.), *Finding the Treasure: Good News from the Estates* (London: SPCK, 2023).

Billings, A., *God and Community Cohesion: Help or Hindrance?* (London: SPCK, 2009).

Bradstock, A., *David Sheppard: Batting for the Poor* (London: SPCK, 2019).

Brown, M. (ed.), *Anglican Social Theology: Renewing the Vision Today* (London: Church House Publishing, 2014).

Bunch, D. and A. Ritchie, *Prayer and Prophecy: A Ken Leech Reader* (London: Darton, Longman & Todd, 2009).

Church of England, Social Policy Committee of the Board of Social Responsibility, *Not Just for the Poor: Christian Perspectives on the Welfare State* (London: Church House Publishing, 1986).

Cottam, H., *Radical Help: How We Can Remake the Relationships Between Us and Revolutionise the Welfare State* (Stevenage: Virago, 2019).

Drummond, T., "Poverty and Theology: Towards a Renewed Understanding", in K. Leech and R. Williams (eds), *Essays Catholic and Radical* (London: The Bowerdean Press, 1983).

Duffield, Ian K. (ed.), *Urban Christ* (Sheffield: UTU, 1997).

Faith in the City: A Call for Action by Church and Nation: The Report of the Archbishop of Canterbury's Commission on Urban Priority Areas (London: Church House Publishing, 1985).

Forde, J., *Before and Beyond the 'Big Society': John Milbank and the Church of England's Approach to Welfare* (Cambridge: James Clarke & Co., 2022).

Forde, J., "The NHS and the Covid-19 Pandemic: A Vindication of Christian Realism?", *ABC Religion & Ethics*, August 2022.

Forde, J., "R. H. Tawney, Equality and the NHS at 75", *Crucible: The Journal of Christian Social Ethics* (January 2024), pp. 51-60.

Forde, J., "Blue Labour, welfare and Catholic social teaching", *Theology* 128:3 (2025).

Green, L., *Blessed are the Poor? Urban Poverty and the Church* (London: SCM Press, 2015).

Gutiérrez, G., *A Theology of Liberation: History, Politics and Salvation* (Maryknoll, NY: Orbis, 1973).

Hanley, L., *Estates: An Intimate History* (London: Granta Publications, 2023).

Jacobovits, I., *From Doom to Hope: A Jewish View of Faith in the City* (London: Office of the Chief Rabbi, 1986).

Kinston, W., *Working with Values for Results: Beyond Quality to Total Ethical Management* (London: Sigma Centre, 1992).

Kinston, W., *Working with Values: Software of the Mind: A Systematic and Practical Account of Purpose, Value and Obligation in Organisations and Society* (London: Sigma Centre, 1995).

Living in Faith in the City: A Progress Report by the Archbishop of Canterbury's Advisory Group on Urban Priority Areas (London: Church House Publishing, 1990).

Lowe, R., *The Welfare State in Britain since 1945*, 2nd edn (London: Macmillan Press, 1999).

Lucas, S. (ed.), *God's Church in the World: The Gift of Catholic Mission* (Norwich: Canterbury Press, 2020).

McKenzie, L., *Getting By: Estates, Class and Culture in Austerity Britain* (Bristol: Policy Press, 2015).

Milbank, A., *The Once and Future Parish* (London: SCM Press, 2023).

Milbank, J., "The Big Society Depends on the Big Parish", *ABC Religion & Ethics*, November 2010.

Preston, R., "Middle Axioms in Christian Social Ethics", *Crucible: The Christian Journal of Social Ethics* (January/February 1971), pp. 9-15.

Sedgwick, P. (ed.), *God in the City: Essays and Reflections from the Archbishop of Canterbury's Urban Theology Group* (London: Mowbray, 1995).

Sheppard, D., *Bias to the Poor* (London: Hodder & Stoughton, 1983).

Spencer, N., *'Doing God?': A Future for Faith in the Public Square* (London: Theos, 2006).

Spencer, N., *Doing Good: A Future for Christianity in the 21st Century* (London: Theos, 2016).

Spencer, S., *William Temple: A Calling to Prophecy* (London: SPCK, 2001).

Spencer, S. (ed.), *Theology Reforming Society: Revisiting Anglican Social Theology* (London: SCM Press, 2017).

Staying in the City: Faith in the City Ten Years On: A Report by the Bishops' Advisory Group on Urban Priority Areas (London: Church House Publishing, 1995).

Tawney, R. H., *Equality* (1931) (London: Unwin Books, 1964).

Temple, W., *Christianity and Social Order* (London: Penguin, 1942).

Truss, R., *The Pattern of God: David Jenkins' Theology in Church and Public Space* (Durham: Sacristy Press, forthcoming, 2026).

Wells, S., R. Rook and D. Barclay, *For Good: The Church and the Future of Welfare* (Norwich: Canterbury Press, 2017).

EU GPSR Authorized Representative:

LOGOS EUROPE, 9 rue Nicolas Poussin, 17000 La Rochelle, France

contact@logoseurope.eu

www.ingramcontent.com/pod-product-compliance
Lightning Source LLC
Chambersburg PA
CBHW070756230426
43665CB00017B/2382